Making Love
Last Forever

Making Love Last Forever

GARY SMALLEY

W Publishing Group

www.wpublishinggroup.com

A Division of Thomas Nelson, Inc.
www.ThomasNelson.com

Library of Congress Cataloging-in-Publication Data
  Smalley, Gary.
    Making love last forever / Gary Smalley.
    p. cm.
    Includes bibliographical references and index.
    ISBN 0-8499-1194-X
    1. Marriage. 2. Intimacy (Psychology) 3. Love.
  4. Man-woman relationships. I. Title.
HQ734.S6863 1996
    306.7—dc20
                                                    96-21566
                                                      CIP

Printed in the United States of America

Dedication

I dedicate this book to several outstanding families, all of whom made this book possible. Without them believing in me and investing so much of their resources in my work, this lifelong project would never have been realized.

Steve and Shannon Scott

Jim and Patty Shaughnessy

Bob and Marjorie Marsh

John and Nima Marsh

Dave and Leslie Marsh

Ed and Laurie Shipley

Jeff and Karen Heft

Ben and Marion Weaver

Frank and Katie Kovacs

The staff at American Telecast

Contents

Acknowledgments

I wish to thank a number of dear people who have made this book possible. First my wife and three children who had to put up with all my trial-and-error methods of building a healthy marriage and family. They were willing to take several different paths with me until we found the ones that worked best for us. We're all still great friends and enjoying our adult lives a lot more because of our journey together.

Most importantly, I wish to thank Larry Weeden for his outstanding ability to capture my thoughts and desires within each chapter. His wordsmanship is greatly appreciated and his loving and gentle attitude made the whole project a very pleasant experience.

Thank you, thank you, thank you doesn't begin to express my deep appreciation to Joey Paul and F. Evelyn Bence for their outstanding editorial help in the final stages.

Mike Hyatt, my literary agent, of Wolgemuth and Hyatt, has not only been a very caring friend over the years, but he has worked diligently with me to prepare this newest manuscript. Our involvement goes all the way back to his University days when my wife Norma introduced him to Gail, his wife to be. Also, his commitment to help in all the promotional developments has been superb.

None of this project could have been started without the inspiration and encouragement of the men and women of American Telecast. They are the ones who produced all three of our TV infomercials, "Hidden Keys to Loving Relationships" with Dick Clark, then, Connie Selecca and John Tesh, and our last one with Kathy Lee and Frank Gifford. Without them the four million plus videos would not be floating around the world. Particularly, I'd like to thank Steve and Shannon Scott, Jim and Patty Shaughnessy, the Marsh family, and all the other employees of their outstanding company.

Another very important group of people on this project were four psychologists who not only teach on the graduate level, but who are warm, personable, and loving men: Dr. Rod Cooper, Dr. Dan Trathen, Dr. Gary Oliver, and Dr. Ken Canfield. I thank them for the many insights they gave me over the last few years. These men all helped me develop my video series for national TV, eighteen sessions in all. They met with me for days at a time and imparted their wisdom and research. Then after I had taken their instruction and developed each session, they would again listen to my sessions and evaluate the accuracy and validity of each session. In short they have not only greatly enriched my life over the past few years, but they have been truly great friends in stretching me to learn so many terrific new things about marriage and life. Dr. Canfield presently has the single largest database of fathering research of any marriage and family center in the world. The other three men all have regular counseling responsibilities, teach in a graduate school of psychology, and help with an organization that hopes to inspire and challenge almost one-half million men to become more loving to their families and to learn how to relate better in their spiritual lives.

Then there's Dr. John Trent who is not only a good friend, but the one who first introduced me to the best personality inventory I have ever studied. He has an unusual grasp of this concept and I'll always be indebted to him for his inspiration, love, and instruction.

I also want to thank Bill Butterworth for his help in the initial stages of our project. He had a great ability to help me retell my own stories with humor. Randy Marshall also gave me excellent assistance with stories and jokes.

Then I wish to thank the many couples who allowed me to review each chapter with them week after week as we were developing it. Terry and Janna Brown, Rick and Trish Tallon, Todd Ellett, Chris and Sonja Meyer, John and Karen Hart, Chris Zervas, Jack and Sherry Herschend, John and Lisa Clifford, Amy Davis, Smith and Gail Brookhart. Then, following this unique group's help, I had another large focus group of men and women critique each chapter after the book had been finished. Terri Felton and Terri Norris headed this delightful group. They were great. They met for an entire day and rated each chapter and gave suggestions on how to improve each one.

Thanks to my publisher, Word, (all of them, who also read and helped in the final stages of editing and marketing).

All in all, this has been the most involved project I have ever under-taken. It has taken almost two years of writing and over twenty years of gathering the information. But, I'm very aware that this project could not have happened without hundreds of precious individuals helping in the process. Thank you for your valuable help!!

Getting the Most from This Book

If you keep your eyes open to three specific things while reading this book, I believe you will get far more from the suggestions offered here.

First, stretch your mind to at least entertain the idea that you are fully responsible for your own quality of life, no matter what your circumstances have been, are, or may become.

Second, be open to the idea that falling in love with life is the best way to equip yourself to stay in love with your spouse—forever. To help you do this, I've divided this book into two parts offering separate sets of principles. The first half of the book is based on this critical truth: You will never know the deep satisfaction of a life-long love with your spouse if you are not first in love with life. In this half of the book I'll give you five ways to enrich your own life. Then, in part 2, I'll present eight practical helps for understanding and, yes, loving your mate. These principles hold and can bring about positive change in a relationship whether or not your spouse is willing to make personal changes in his or her lifestyle or attitude. Having said that, of course, the ideal is for the two of you to work together at improving your relationship.

Third, read through the entire book while marking sections that strike you as: *Yes, this describes me or a dynamic in my marriage. I need to hear this out.* Then go back to the marked pages that apply to you; reread them and work through those issues. Look for deeper insight as you go for a love that lasts forever.

As you work through the book I'll give you pointers for tapping resources at hand—family, friends, and coworkers—to help you follow through on many of the ideas shared within these pages. And the books referenced in the endnotes are additional invaluable resources. You don't have to live with the gnawing feeling that the happiness you discover will never last. Love and contentment can!

You'll see that everything I teach or write about has a basic theme. I'm always trying to expose the age-old struggle between the life-giving principle of honor and the destructive emotion of anger that too often creeps in when we don't get what we expected. I see honor and anger as being opposites, at two ends of a pole. Each of us can make daily choices about which emotions we will experience. When we choose anger over honor, we unknowingly (or knowingly) welcome the stress-producing, life-draining, divorce-creating thoughts that lead us down a path of personal and relational destruction. But choose honor, and you choose life.

Over the past five years, I've had a learning-curve explosion. It's as if I'm back in graduate school. I don't know what hit me; maybe it's the vitamins, or could it be that wonderful Ozark Mountain air, but my hunger to learn has rocketed. This newfound knowledge has greatly expanded my understanding of many principles I've written about in the past. You'll see the exciting new aspects I've discovered lately and have shared in seminars across the country and on videotape. Thousands of couples can tell you these principles have worked wonders. And with every passing year, as I learn more about myself, my family, and the human race, I understand the truths at a deeper level. This book reflects that growth, that comes as we choose to face new challenges placed before us.

I urge you to join me on this journey to forever-love.

Making Love
Last Forever

Part I

The Love-for-Life Factor: How to Fall in Love with Life

The first step toward achieving the deep satisfaction of a lifelong love with your spouse is learning to love life itself—every part of it, good and bad, harsh and rewarding. But just how do you nurture this attitude, this exuberant *joie de vivre?*

Here in part 1 of *Making Love Last Forever* I present five key choices that are placed before you. Your decisions in these areas can mean the difference between (1) Your full celebration of life's journey and love, or (2) A disastrous collision that can sink your love into the depths of despair.

To help get you off to a quick start, in chapter 1 I'll share love's best-kept secret. Then I'll describe five "icebergs" that have the potential to sink your marriage—and the choices you can make to navigate around those icebergs and ensure a safe and rewarding marriage journey for you and your mate.

In chapter 2 I'll show you how to detect your own level of anger, one of the most dangerous icebergs. The average person has little or no idea how damaging forgotten or ignored anger can be—alienating loved ones, sabotaging relationships. Worse yet, most people don't even know how much destructive anger they're carrying around—and from past experiences, everyone has some degree of buried anger. Like a ball and chain, it weighs one down. But we can choose to break free of that destructive anger; I'll show you how. Then in chapter 3 I'll describe seven ways to release anger's control over you and your relationships.

In chapter 4 I'll show you a second choice. You can choose a disastrous route—ignoring the value of any trials that come your way, or you can choose to see that every painful encounter contains a "pearl of love" you can add to your life to build a priceless collection. When we face hardship, we don't have to get bitter. We can choose to use the hardship to make love grow bigger and better.

In chapter 5 we discuss the perils of "putting all your eggs in one basket." I'll show you how you can choose to diversify your life interests and increase your chances for remaining satisfied with life and for staying in love.

Chapter 6 shows two great truths that have transformed my and my wife's attitudes and increased the safety we feel with each other because we've learned to avoid our past patterns of sabotaging our love. I'll share how we've chosen to not allow people and circumstances to "take away" our love for life because we've seen how this can lead to a relational disaster.

Finally, in chapter 7 I'll discuss the choice of establishing your own personal spiritual journey. Being disconnected from a living and loving God is like untying and pushing away a life jacket, thinking we're better off without it. God's love is the fuel we need to move into warmer water, away from damaging icebergs.

After discussing these five choices to help you avoid the icebergs and choose to fall in love with life, in part 2 I'll give you the best ways I've found to celebrate your love and enrich your relationship with your mate. Most of these principles will also improve your relationships with children and friends.

When you assume full responsibility for your present and future, you come to a place where you—like thousands of others—can make a deep commitment to your spouse and your kids: "I don't want to be bound to the past anymore. I want a 'new generation,' a fresh start."

When you do, you'll be taking the first step on the journey to forever-love.

1

Love's Best-Kept Secret

If I were to ask the question: "What is human life's chief concern?" one of the answers we should receive would be: "It is happiness." How to gain, how to keep, how to recover happiness, is in fact for most . . . at all times the secret motive of all they do, and of all they are willing to endure.

—William James

Will our love last forever? It's the hope of every starry-eyed bride and groom who clasp hands and say, "I do."

If your marriage is anything like mine, a few years after the wedding, you or your spouse—or both of you—were wondering why you had ever chosen this person to live with. "Till death do us part"? Impossible! "To love and to cherish"? You've got to be kidding!

I take much of the blame for the first disastrous years of my marriage. I was a wounded young man who had learned wounding tactics from my wounded, angry father. I knew how to lash out, clam up, lecture, and get my own way. In response to my tirades, my wife, Norma, learned how to cope.

But for Norma and me . . . something happened on the way to "forever." We discovered the principles I present in this book. We set a new course that has renewed our love and deepened our relationship. Today after thirty-one years of marrage, we are in love—with life and with each other.

Is it really possible to marry and then see that starry-eyed love actually get better? Yes.

Restoring a Wrecked Relationship

Whenever I see love win out in a marriage that looked hopeless, my confidence is increased, and I've found ways to help almost anyone stay in love despite impossible odds. Take this seemingly "shipwrecked" relationship:

Who would have thought that John and Sharon would reconcile and eventually enjoy a good marriage? It was eleven o'clock one night when the phone rang. Norma and I were already in bed. At the other end of the line was John, a popular, local business executive. He was locked in a major argument with his wife, Sharon, and the dispute was so fierce that he was glaring and saying things like, "I'm sick of trying. I want to get on an airplane and fly to another state. I just don't have any energy left to stay with this woman." Before he took such a drastic step, however, he was making this one last attempt to reach out for help. "Is there anything you can do for us?" he asked. "Can we come over tonight and talk with you?" Norma and I had a quick discussion, and we invited them to come over.

John and Sharon made their way to our home, and the argument continued in front of us. The issue they were facing was serious: John was addicted and out of control sexually, and to add insult to injury, he had given Sharon a sexually transmitted disease. She was nauseated by his behavior and disgusted with him.

Despite the gravity of the situation, a couple of things happened that night that are comical in hindsight—especially if you like seeing Murphy's law lived out. For instance, at one point in their arguing, Sharon kicked our coffee table, driving it toward me and causing it to cut my leg. At another point, Sharon was nearly breaking my fingers in an effort to get out of my grasp so she could run outside and attack John. (Norma had taken him into the front yard in the hope of cooling things down a bit.)

By 12:30 or 1:00 A.M. I had been beaten up, yelled at, and deprived of sleep, so I felt I had earned the right to say something to this couple. (They hadn't allowed us to give them any advice yet.) I began, "Well, as I've listened to both of you, I think there's something you can start working on even tonight."

But John looked at his watch and said, "I am so tired. I am so discouraged. I don't have any more energy. I've got to leave."

And with that they both left. I fell asleep that night thinking, *This will never work out.*

I share this extreme case because unfortunately more than 50 percent of the marriages in this country end in divorce—and it doesn't have to be that way. In time John and Sharon acted on most of the principles I've shared in these pages—and their relationship turned around. When things had cooled down, we met several more times, and we helped them connect with a counselor who specializes in their particular conflict. Finally John accepted the need to address the issues head-on with their counselor and with the help of a small support group. He came to understand that he had used illicit sex as medication for the pain of being hatefully rejected by his dad and of knowing his marriage relationship was weak. For her part, Sharon came to understand how her anger had blocked her ability to establish any type of meaningful relationship with John. She didn't understand how conflict can be the doorway to deeper intimacy.

Now, several years later, this couple whose relationship was so critically fractured is together and, believe it or not, they are in love. What's more, John and Sharon are helping other couples discover the joy they found as they made the midcourse adjustments that renewed their love.

I trust your marriage is far from being on the rocks. Maybe you're reading this book simply because you want to do everything you can to make a new marriage last a lifetime—or because you want to revive a love that seems a little off course. You can avert the loss of your love by heeding certain warnings and choosing to make small changes to get yourself back on course. Later I'll show you five important choices that can make the difference between disaster and a satisfying voyage.

Not long ago I was bowled over as I was reminded of how every aspect of my life is influenced by the choices I make. This particular wake-up call had to do with my physical condition, but the lesson I learned opened my eyes to these five choices.

The Lesson of the *Titanic*

When it comes to my blood-pumping heart, I know I'm a high-risk patient. My dad died of a heart attack in his fifties. One brother died of heart failure at fifty-one. My oldest brother had a massive heart attack at fifty-one and has since had another. Now that I'm fifty-five, my own medical exams have prompted the doctor to shake his head with concern.

For years, although I knew our family history, I chose to believe that I didn't need to pay much attention to the doctor's preventive (I called it drastic) advice, though at Norma's insistence I did occasionally get myself to the Cooper Clinic in Dallas, which specializes in heart-related matters. Recently I was in Texas for another exam. After all the tests had been completed, I sat in the doctor's office, listening and laughing, trying to make light of some of the results. Then I noticed that the doctor had a painting of a ship hanging on the wall. In a joking way, I pointed to it and said, "That's the *Titanic*, isn't it?"

The doctor didn't miss a beat. Playing along with my jovial mood, he nodded and said, "It's interesting that you'd bring that up. Do you know why I have it there?"

"No," I responded.

"Do you know much about the *Titanic*, Mr. Smalley?"

"No, I don't," I admitted, walking into his trap. I know it's at the bottom of the ocean; that's about it."

"Well," he explained, "the experienced captain of the *Titanic* was warned six separate times to slow down, change course, and take the southern route because icebergs had been sighted. But he ignored all six specific warnings because he was the captain, and he thought, *This ship is unsinkable . . .*"

"I had no idea the ship received that many warnings," I said, still not seeing where he was leading me.

". . . then *rip*—the ship hit the iceberg. It went down quickly and disastrously," he said. Then he leaned across his desk and looked me straight in the eye. "And how many times have you been warned about your heart?" he demanded.

"Lots of times," I replied weakly as his point struck home.

"And when will you take it seriously and change course?" he asked.

As a result of that conversation, I've made some basic lifestyle changes that have great potential for improving my health and prolonging my life. Almost anyone can make small adjustments if he or she believes it will make a lasting positive difference.

If you change course when warned, you can avoid disaster—and then celebrate the voyage. It's the strongest principle anyone can learn from the *Titanic*. And it's also the best-kept secret of making love last forever. If we tune our ears and eyes to the warnings, we can change much more than our life expectancy. Here in part 1 of this book, I give you my sighting of five icebergs that can sink your love forever. Only you can make the choice to heed those warnings and change the course of your voyage. In part 2, I'll share eight thick "steel" linings that will make it nearly impossible for your love boat to sink.

I've designed this book to help you *stay* in love with your mate but also to *fall in love with life*. What does loving life have to do with loving your spouse? Much of what you read in the first half of this book is based on this truth: *For your love to last forever, you must be in love with life*. Think in terms of the oxygen-mask instructions given by airline flight attendants. They say that passengers flying with children or others who need assistance should fasten their own masks first before trying to help someone else. If you don't make the choice to reach for oxygen for yourself, there's no point in your trying to help anyone else. You won't have the strength or ability to do it. That's how it is with love: Learn to love your own life first, and then you have the resources to give and receive love.

Your life or your marriage doesn't have to hit the rocks—the icebergs or immovable objects that can sink your love. Your discontent can be a warning you can heed. *Change course. Avoid disaster. And celebrate your life and love together—a long and gratifying voyage.*

Note what I didn't say. Love's best-kept secret is not *change (or exchange) your spouse* or *change your job* or *change your address*. It's *change your own course*. Even small changes in your behavior can lead to major changes in your life—no matter what your past, no matter how much pain you've plowed through. In the same way, even small personal changes can have enormous positive effects on your marriage, according to research on the crucial factors that keep a couple happily married.[1] (Personally, this gives me great hope, because, though I'm calling for change, no one's talking about sainthood!)

You Can Choose to Get on Course

Do you want to know the deep satisfaction that comes from being in love? It's simple. It's your choice.

My choice? you're thinking. *But you don't know what I've been through. You don't know what I have to live with. You don't know my mate!*

I agree this may be a hard truth to swallow, because it also means you no longer have any excuse to be miserable! I hated the idea at first. For more than half my life, I would find all kinds of reasons why I wasn't fulfilled and in love. I could place blame with the best of them. Then, little by little after age thirty-five, I started seeing what so many had already said about our enjoyment of life and our love being in our own hands.[2]

Someone who continually blames problems on others or on his or her circumstances becomes what author Stephen Covey calls "the reactive person." Reactive persons allow others to rob them of their quality of life.

Covey sees another group of people as *proactive*. They're ones who believe "as human beings we are responsible for our own lives. Our behavior is a function of our decisions—our choices—not our conditions. We can subordinate feelings to values. We have the initiative and the responsibility to make things happen."[3]

One of my favorite writers in this area is Dr. Harriet Goldhor Lerner. A chapter in her book *The Dance of Anger* could convince anyone that one's marital happiness is mostly in one's own hands.[4] She also says that putting our energy into changing another person to enhance our own enjoyment of him or her is a solution that "never never works."[5] If we focus our attention on adjusting someone else's life so we can find happiness, we fail to exercise the only power we have for enriching our own lives: the power to choose for ourselves. In short, here is the formula: (1) We can't change other people. (2) We can choose to make changes in ourselves. (3) As changes occur in ourselves, people around us usually adjust their responses and choices according to our new behavior.

If this seems too hard for you to take right now, please withhold judgment until you've finished the next few pages. Then see if it doesn't make more sense.

To flesh out this truth, let's look at someone who chose to take responsibility for his own emotional well-being. When Richard first came to see me, he was not a happy man. Picking up the phone to call a counselor was a first step in acknowledging that his dissatisfaction with life was a warning that something was wrong. He was frustrated, disappointed, and fearful things were never going to change. And yet a wee bit of hope for something better prompted some changes in his life.

Richard was in his fifties, a husband and dad, a classy dresser, and the president of his own large company. After more than thirty years of marriage to Gail, he'd grown tired of her nagging and hatefulness. But he had also grown tired of expecting Gail to change and meet his relational needs, as she had in the early days of their marriage. And even though he hated the thought, he was contemplating divorce. But before he took that drastic step, he sought out and acted on my advice.

After the usual counselor-client preliminaries, I asked what had brought him to me. He answered, "I'm aware of my part in messing up with my wife and kids. I've spent so much time building this company. Now I recognize that even though it's late, I want to have a better relationship with them. I'm very successful financially, but I'm not very happy, and neither are my family members. I don't know how to go about changing things, especially after being the way I've been for so many years."

Then he added something highly significant. "I didn't have much of a relationship with my own dad," he said. "In fact, he was always too busy for me, just the way I've been with my family."

Right there was a key factor in Richard's past failure as a husband and father. His own dad had never built a close relationship with him, and that pattern probably had gone back for several generations. So Richard's model as a parent was weak, and Richard didn't get the opportunity to see a man loving his wife. His grandfather's example as parent and husband got passed from generation to generation. As a result, Richard didn't know any other approach.

If Richard had been hooked on the blame game (where you "win" by finding someone else to blame for everything wrong in your life), he could have stopped his growth at this point. With a little bit of new insight, he could have said, "Okay, it's mostly my father's fault!" Or he could have said, as so many workaholic people do, "But I was providing for my family! I did it all for them so they could have a better standard of living. If they can't understand my good motives, it's their problem. Hang this 'relationship' bit."

If Richard had chosen to blame his father for his own problems, he might have had some justification. Research has shown that people raised under strong, controlling, and rejecting parents may, in turn, reject and control their own families.[6] But Richard was no longer looking for a scapegoat. He took responsibility for his response to the way he had been parented. At this point Richard learned two powerful truths:

1. What I am today is because of the choices I've made in the past.

2. I am 100 percent responsible for all the choices I've made.

Richard began to distance himself from the age-old rationalization: *The devil made me do it.* Richard no longer was going to empower his father to ruin his relationships. He took responsibility for himself. He said things like, "No more, Dad; I'm not going to follow your example any longer. I'm going to discover what I need to do for myself and for my wife and children and finally find satisfaction in these vital areas of my life." All he needed was some guidance to start avoiding the icebergs and sail toward warmer seas.

Richard was also willing to start the process of adjusting his own life before his oh-so-irritating wife changed. As a counselor, I love situations like that where I can jump right in the middle of a gigantic mess and try to help turn it around. So I said, "Let's start with your kids. I'll go with you, and we'll go to see one child at a time. We'll just talk to your children. Let's face the truth about what has happened between you and them. Let's find out what we can do."

(Incidentally, most wives love it when they see husbands rebuilding their relationships with their children. It can offer hope to the wife that the husband is serious about changing his relationships, especially the one with her.) When Richard told Gail his plans, she was doubtful but indeed encouraged.

The first call went to their twenty-seven-year-old son, a graduate student. Robert agreed to meet with us, so we flew to the city where he lived and met him in a hotel room.

We sat and made a lot of small talk, and then as moderator I said, "Robert, your dad has asked me to help both of you restart your friendship. Could I ask you to begin by rating where your relationship with your dad is today? Rate it from zero to ten—zero meaning 'rotten relationship' and ten meaning 'great relationship.' Your father really wants to know how you see your relationship with him."

Robert stammered uncomfortably as if he felt unsafe. He fidgeted for a while before he said, "Well, about a two or three."

As low as that number was, I knew his totally honest rating would have been a zero or one.

Richard responded, "Son, I'm not surprised with that at all. I know I never spent the time I needed to spend with you, and I really feel bad about that." And then this dad said, "Son, I've come to tell you sincerely that I want to be your friend. I've missed a lot of years, and I feel terrible about that. I've never known how to be a good father and friend. As you know, with my dad, I just never learned how. But I want you to understand that I'm here today because I want to find out from you what it will take to be your good friend."

Big tears welled up in Robert's eyes, and an awkward silence instantly filled the room. No one wanted to talk. We all just sat there hoping someone would break the ice. Then, without coaching, Richard stood up and walked over to his son. Robert also stood. As they faced each other, Richard said softly, "Son, for years I've wanted to say that I love you, but every time I tried, something always seemed to block me. But today, in front of a friend, I want to say to you . . . I love you with all my heart. I've always been proud of you, and I hate myself for not saying it. Why have I been so mute? I do want to be your good friend, and I just hope it isn't too late."

Robert threw his arms around his dad, and they just held each other, melting in each other's arms. (Of course, I was bawling.) After a few minutes, they sat down, and Robert stared at his dad for a while. Then he said, "All my life I've longed for you to say what you've said today, but, to be honest, I never thought it would happen. And here you are, sitting in this room, saying the things I've wished for. Dad, thanks for coming."

Before we left, Richard asked for and received his son's forgiveness. Then Richard asked, "How can we start to get to know each other and build a real friendship?"

"Why don't we play golf today and talk about it?" Robert suggested. "Let's begin with that." And that's what they did.

In the months that followed, Richard and Robert spent more time together. And although I didn't go with him again, Richard also went on to meet with each of his other children. I later heard from them about how excited they were that "my dad still thinks enough of me to want to become my friend." Dads, it's amazing how powerful our words are. Never take them lightly!

Richard changed course to avoid the first destructive iceberg. In the next chapter you'll see what Richard, along with John and Sharon, began to avoid and how their love and marriages moved into warmer water. Richard and his children and wife are still working at their relationships. They've made progress—because of one person's initiative to go for something better.

The Future Is Yours!

Richard did two key things—the same two things I had to do in pursuing satisfaction in life and love in spite of a painful past—the same things we all need to do. He took responsibility for his own future choices, and he accepted the reality of the past while choosing to live beyond it.

Taking Responsibility for One's Own Future Choices

To change the course of his marriage and his relationships with his children, Richard first owned his own problems and took full responsibility for his future with a clear plan of action. In other words, he had to accept the fact that we're responsible for our present and future. Our future is a reflection of our past and present choices. How we handle unhealthy things from the past, the current state of our marriage, our children, our friendships, our job, and so on is up to us. Wherever we find ourselves, the buck stops with us! Whatever it takes, we need to be willing to grab the reins of the future and say, "Somehow, some way, I'll find what I need to have a good life for myself and my family!"

In one sense I see humans as being like cars. When young, we had "warranties"—reasonable expectations—that our parents and others could fix most of our problems for us. But as adults, our warranties are up. We've gone the years and covered the miles. We have to say, "If this thing called 'my life' breaks down, I'm the one who has to get it fixed."

That's what Richard did. He assumed the responsibility to make things right. He didn't blame his father for being a poor role model. Nor did he blame his career for keeping him away from home so much. That approach would have been the surest route to continuing failure. He did need to understand the lasting effect of his heritage, as I had to do when faced with my own heritage, discussed below. But then he needed to ask, "What do I do to overcome my past?"

Accepting the Reality of the Past and Choosing to Live Beyond It

The second course correction Richard made was to accept the truth of his past. He looked realistically at what his father had done to him, and he decided to take the good and discard any of the bad as he saw it. He didn't want his past to control his present and future.

I know what it feels like to grow up with an angry father. I know that my dad's behavior affected me, along with my brothers and sisters. At times, I used to wish things would have been different. But they weren't. So now I have to take what was given to me and do the best I can with the available resources. This has truly been a releasing and joyful experience as I've come to realize I'm free to take the counsel of others—friends, family, books—and decide to do what I believe is best for me and my family. I don't have to waste time wishing things had been different. I'm free to **choose how I will respond** to everything that happens or doesn't happen to me.

While we can't succeed by blaming the past for our current unhappiness, we do need to understand and interpret our inherited tendencies so we can consciously grow beyond them. If we don't, I've found that we usually remain "frozen" at a lower maturity level.

A personal illustration: On one of our first family trips to Hawaii, Norma, the kids, and I were all excited about hitting the sand and being together. As we prepared to go down to the beach for the first time, however, I was delayed for some reason. Everyone else wanted to get going. But I explained, "I'm just not ready."

"Okay," they said, "we'll go on ahead. Come find us when you're ready. We'll be right down here." They pointed up the beach.

"Sounds fine," I told them. About half an hour later, I left the hotel room and went looking for my family. I walked up and down the beach as far as I could go in both directions, but I couldn't find them. As time went on, I started feeling irritated and hurt. *Wait a minute,* I thought. *We're here in Hawaii as a family to be together, and they've deserted me! I've been rejected!*

Basically, I was pouting and showing my immaturity. I never did find them, so I went back to the hotel and waited impatiently. Eventually they came in, and I was sulking. "What's wrong with you?" they asked.

"You left me," I said glumly.

"We told you where we were going," they responded.

"Yeah, well, I went there, and you weren't there," I accused them.

"We meant that other beach just a little farther down," they said.

"Well, that wasn't very clear!" I insisted, unwilling to be appeased. After that, I wasn't speaking to anybody. Thank God for our son Greg, who has always had the capacity to confront his father.

"Dad," he said cautiously and respectfully, "I thought you wanted a 'new generation' with our family—to be a better father than your own dad was in a lot of ways."

"I do," I insisted, glaring at him.

"Well, Dad," he said, "is this really the kind of example you want to pass on to me?"

"No," I had to admit grudgingly. "And I realize I've asked you guys to help me when I'm not responding well."

Now, here's the really interesting thing. My wife said, "You know, this is exactly how your father acted when he was upset. He would be angry, sulk, be silent, and close everyone out." And she had said to me in the past, "The worst thing you do to me is when you become silent, because then I feel we're not connected." That was my way of punishing the family when I wasn't happy with them, and that was also some of my dad coming out in me.

Greg was in high school when this conflict occurred, and as it escalated, he intervened. "Okay," he said, "let's get this solved. Let me hear your side, Mom . . . Now let me hear your side, Dad . . . Dad, don't you understand what you did here? . . . Okay, Mom, do you understand? Good. That fixes it." He actually helped us solve that minor skirmish. No wonder he's now working on his doctorate in counseling!

By handling the situation so directly and drawing the comparison to my father, my family made me see the level of immaturity at which I was stuck. It's important to take such a look at our level of maturity from time to time. And when we find ourselves thinking only of ourselves, a lot of that can be traced right back to our past. One expert says the worst thing a husband can do if he wants his love in marriage to last is to close out the family with the "silent treatment."[7] That was me. But I don't have to let this type of behavior continue. I understand my past, but I'll be hanged before I will allow it to determine my future!

The Challenge

What about you? Have you come to the place where you're agreeing and willing to take full responsibility for the quality of your own life? Can you—like John and Sharon and Richard and Gary Smalley—turn away from the blame game, no matter how difficult your past has been, and embrace the great, freeing truth that *you will be as content as you choose to be?* I trust you will, and I know that if you do, the rest of this book is going to be like a trip to a buried treasure chest for you. You'll find insights all along the way that will help you to make your life the best it can be.

If you're a victim of abuse, you're probably going to need help to deal with your situation and to rediscover love for life and love for your spouse. And if others react negatively to the changes you try to make, the going won't be easy. But even then you still choose your own response to each situation, and you, too, can decide to be persistent and hopeful. If you do, I can almost guarantee your future will be better than your past.

The next two chapters discuss the critical choice of draining unresolved anger from your life. This anger causes more pain, drowns more marriages, sinks more children than any other power I know. It's the mother of all "icebergs." You'll not only see the damage it does, but you'll see how you can keep it far removed from you and your loved ones.

Forever-Love Principles

1. Forever-love does not work to change or exchange a spouse. Instead, it realizes, "If something's wrong, it's up to me to change my response and my mind-set."

2. Forever-love believes that even small behavior changes can lead to major improvements in relationships.

3. Forever-love is possible, no matter what your circumstances.

4. Forever-love calls for courage to move beyond the status quo.

5. Forever-love says the future = hope.

6. Forever-love says, "I'll take responsibility for my own choices—past, present, and future."

7. Forever-love accepts the reality of the past but lives beyond the blame game.

8. Forever-love *can't* change the weather. It *can* choose how to respond to the weather.

9. Forever-love is willing to move beyond inherited, intergenerational negative patterns.

2

The Number One Enemy
of Love: Unresolved Anger

*Individuals or whole peoples can gnaw on old grievances, remembering them
again and again, renewing them obsessively until the shape of memory and desire
is permanently warped along the lines of anger.*

—William Stafford[1]

There's a major destroyer of love on the loose; I've found it to be the leading cause of divorce and the single greatest thief of one's love for life. It may already be at work in your life and marriage.

This destroyer is *forgotten, unresolved anger*—not just the kind that gnaws at one's stomach night after night but also the type that quietly disappears. At least I used to think it disappeared. But when we bury anger inside us . . . *it's always buried alive!* Then, when we aren't even aware of its presence, it does its damage, destroying like rust on a car, like moths in a dark closet.

But it doesn't have to remain buried; it doesn't have to wreak its havoc in our lives and relationships. There is hope—when we choose to rout it out.

Anger—Buried Alive

Let me tell you how anger worked its damage in the life of a friend, Larry, who for nine years was angry at me. He tried to say the anger would go away, but it didn't.

17

At one time we were great friends. Then I sensed there was a wall between us. We were still casual friends, and I attributed any distance between us to the fact that we no longer lived in the same city; we now lived halfway across the country from each other. And anyway, I figured that if there were anything between us, he would talk about it.

Well, not long ago, I was staying in a hotel in the town where Larry lives. While I was there, I got a call from him. "We've got to talk," he said.

"All right," I answered, "about what?"

"I've been upset with you for about nine years now," he answered, amazing me. As he went on, I was even more appalled. "I've been really angry with you all that time, and I can't shake it," he said, his voice quivering. "I've tried to tell myself I would get over it in time, but it won't go away. I think about it a lot. Now it's affecting what I do in my job and my other relationships too. I don't want to live like this anymore. I have to get this thing resolved. Can we meet?"

Words like that from a friend make you sick to your stomach. As Larry spoke I asked myself over and over, *What did I do? What does this involve?* Of course I agreed to meet with him.

We got together in a restaurant, and there the story came out, though it took about five hours. Larry cried, I cried, and at one point it got so emotional that his nose started bleeding. One messy scene! But he finally got out this deep anger he had been carrying for all those years.

The problem had grown out of a decision we had made nine years before: Together we were going to confront a guy with whom we both had major disagreements. This was a very serious situation, and we were both equally upset. We went to see the man, and when we got there, the guy said to me, "I'll discuss the problems you and I have with each other, but I'd rather not have both of you ganging up on me."

So I talked it over with Larry, who agreed to leave the conversation—and the scene. I remember, as we parted, telling Larry I was sorry and that we would talk later. But as things turned out, Larry thought I had sided with the other guy and deserted him as my friend. I had actually doubled Larry's anger. I left him with his anger toward the other person unresolved and unintentionally I also added hurt to his anger.

So Larry walked away thinking, *How could Gary have done this to me? We were going to talk to the man together, and he just discarded me like I'm not of any value.* Yet I had never understood what I had done or how my friend felt about it until that day in the restaurant.

When I heard his feelings and how the incident had affected him for nine years, I grieved deeply. I had not intended to give more loyalty to our adversary than to my good friend.

Fortunately, our relationship was healed that day. We cried together, hugged each other, and sought each other's forgiveness. The anger was finally drained out of my friend but not before he had suffered depression and other signs of unhappiness for nine years. And since that time, we've gone on to develop a deeper friendship than ever before.

Some might say that Larry was overreacting and in time would have gotten over it. That's what he had thought would happen, but it didn't. There are thousands of people who wish they could shake off the effects of old offenses, but the truth is, many just can't. And because they aren't able to get over it, the damage continues inside them, sometimes for years.

Before you dismiss this chapter as being not for you because you're not an angry person, let me point out that most of us bury our anger so quickly that we don't know what we're doing. Then it does its sneaky damage. It often leads to our lashing out at others. Or it gets turned inward, where it can become depression. Some may pretend it's simply not there, but it is.

This chapter is designed to take a close look at anger, what causes it, and the massive havoc it wreaks. The next two chapters will help you drain away as much destructive anger as you need to.

Anger Springs from Three Separate Emotions

Anger is an emotion. Like all of our emotions, there's nothing wrong with it in and of itself. It's our human response to something that occurs, or at least to our perception of that occurrence. In fact, some anger is good; we *should* get angry when we see an injustice or when someone is trying to violate our personal property lines. In such cases, our anger is what motivates us to take appropriate action. But after anger motivates us to do something good, we can't afford to let it linger inside us. We have to get it out. Anger is a good emotion when it gets us moving, but if we let it take root, we set ourselves up for a great deal of potential harm.

Dr. Howard Markman of Denver University, a leading expert in the prevention of divorce, gives a strong warning about hidden anger. He reminds us that all those little discussions that just don't seem to get resolved and continually provoke an inappropriate outburst—issues that don't necessarily call for heated feelings, such as whether the toilet paper rolls from the top or the bottom or whether the toilet seat is up or down—are usually driven by anger that's just below the surface. No matter how many times a couple tries to resolve those issues or enter into deeper intimacy, the anger can keep them apart and in turmoil.[2] Living with angry people is like living in a minefield. If you say or do the wrong thing, *kaboom!* They explode all over everyone. And you're left thinking, *Oh, I had no idea that one thing I did would cause such a reaction.*

Actually, anger is a secondary emotion, not a primary feeling. It arises out of *fear, frustration, hurt,* or some combination of these three. For example, if someone says something harsh to us we first feel hurt and *then* anger. When we strip the word *anger* down to its deepest level, we see a thread that runs through this entire book—*unfulfilled expectations.* Frustration is not receiving what we had expected from other people or from circumstances.

Hurt is when we don't hear the words or receive the actions we expected from other people or from circumstances. And fear is either dreading that what we expect will not come as we wish it to or expecting that something bad is going to happen. In his book *Banishing Fear from Your Life,* Charles Bass clearly explains, "The process by which fear provokes anger is relatively simple: we use anger to cope with fear." He goes on to tell a wonderful story of counseling a couple "who interacted with a fear/anger reaction." From the husband and wife he heard two completely different stories. Here's the husband's version:

> Every time I come home, Mary is waiting for me with a chip on her shoulder. I hate to go home. As I drive home, I get more and more tense. When I get home and see her waiting for me with her hands on her hips, it just makes me mad, and I tie into her before she can get the jump on me.

The wife's story:

> Joe is always mad at me over something. . . . He always comes home in a bad temper. I really have to stand up to him to defend myself.[3]

For both people a smoldering anger was fueled by fear—of the other's anger.

There's a wonderful line in the classic Christmas carol written by Phillips Brooks. "O Little Town of Bethlehem" refers to "the hopes and fears of all the years." If those hopes aren't realized and those fears *are* realized— anger can settle in. Anger at ourselves. At specific others. At the more generic world. At God. We feel the need to blame our unhappiness on someone or something.

Anger is our choice. We choose to respond in anger when something happens to us that's outside of our control. It's a normal response, even a good response, when it's controlled. But we are the ones who choose to hold on to anger or to let it go. We can choose to see its powerful potential for destruction and take the steps to reduce it within us. Otherwise it's an iceberg sinking our love.

A Dangerous Substance

Anger should not be welcomed as a heart-guest. When we allow anger to linger and settle in, it brings harm not only to ourselves but also to those around us. Just think of all the times you've felt frustrated, hurt, or fearful. Is it your practice to ignore these emotions or to face them and then walk past them?

Think of anger as a sticky, bad-smelling, dangerous substance that can be compressed and stuffed into something like a spray can. Different people have different-sized cans—and different degrees of compression—depending on how much anger they're carrying and for how long.

What happens? Angry people tend to go around spraying their anger on other people. The spray is felt by others as meanness, insensitivity, negativity, and general offensiveness, and the "sprayers" may not even realize how they're behaving or how it affects other people. They just keep spraying in every direction everywhere they go like skunks that constantly feel threatened. And anger spray stings like an acid that burns.

How do we respond when we get sprayed by someone else's anger? Too often, without even thinking about it, we make the unhealthy choice of letting ourselves marinate in the angry person's spray. (Then we also begin to emit the foul odor.) After a while, it starts seeping inside us and filling our anger can. When this happens in families, anger is passed down from generation to generation, wreaking intergenerational havoc.

Sometimes a debilitating anger starts in childhood, perhaps with some sort of abuse. I have to confess that in the past, I had a big anger can that too often exploded on my wife and kids. The anger started to compress when I was a child because, as I already mentioned, my dad sprayed me often from his anger can. Since I was the youngest child, my brothers and sisters actually got sprayed a lot more than I, but I got my share.

My daughter made me aware of what I was doing when she confronted me one day about the way I treated my son Michael, who was in high school at the time. "Dad," she said, "you're so critical of Michael, of little things he says and does. You're really going to hurt him."

That took me by surprise. Frankly, I hoped she was exaggerating the seriousness of the situation. So I went to Michael, told him what his sister had said, and asked, "Is that true?"

"Yeah," he answered.

"Really?" I said, still not wanting to believe it.

"Dad," he said with great feeling, "I've had enough criticism for a lifetime!"

Then I had no choice but to accept the truth of it. And that realization helped me continue to drain my own anger and deal with it so I could stop the generational pull inherited from my dad. Again, our anger may be buried, but it's buried alive, destroying our own happiness and our relationships—unless it's routed out.

Have you ever wondered why there's so much abuse and violence in our country today? A lot of this anger that leads to violence started with parents who didn't know the effects that anger was going to have on their children. I expect that most of these parents were also unaware that their anger level had anything to do with nurturing their children. But consider the implications of this story: A prison volunteer got the idea that the prisoners might like to send Mother's Day cards to their moms. So she wrote to a greeting card company and asked it to donate some cards.

The company responded graciously and generously and, sure enough, those hard-bitten men gobbled them up. The demand was overwhelming! The volunteer ran out of cards before she ran out of sons who wanted to send expressions of love to their mothers.

Well, Father's Day comes just one month after Mother's Day, so the woman figured that was such a success she would do the same thing for Father's Day. She contacted the card company, and once again it honored her request.

The woman let the prisoners know that free Father's Day cards were available, then she waited for the men to rush in and get them. And do you know how many of those felons, many with a history of violence, asked for a card this time? Not one. Not a single prisoner wanted to express love to his dad. And that's when the woman learned that such men usually carry a deep resentment and even hatred toward their fathers—many of whom were absent from their sons.

The Consequences of Unresolved Anger

Even if your anger never turns violent or illegal, it can prove destructive—as it did for my friend Larry, as it has for me, and as you'll see from the consequences of unresolved anger I describe in the next few pages.

Distance from Other People

One of the most common results or symptoms of deep anger is relational distance, an unwillingness and inability to let others get close. It seems to block our ability to give and receive love. You're sincerely trying to develop a satisfying and loving marriage, but the anger spray in either you or your mate can greatly inhibit your efforts. Consider this truly unfortunate story of a couple that had been married about seventeen years:

The husband knew things were not going well; he wanted to do something about it, and he asked me for help. Because he lived in a different state, we had to communicate by phone and letter. He would describe a difficult domestic situation, and I would suggest something he could do to improve the relationship. A few days later, he would call and say, "I tried that, Gary, but it just doesn't seem to work. She didn't respond well at all."

We went back and forth like that several times, and after a while, I started to get a little irritated with him. *What's the matter with you?* I thought. *Can't you get this?* But that's not what I actually said. I'd suggest he try a little different approach.

A week later I would receive a letter stating, "Gary, I really want to love my wife, but I can't seem to do it."

This long-distance counseling continued off and on for about three years. Sometimes I wouldn't hear from him for months. And then one day he called to say, "I really appreciate all your help, but I'm leaving my wife."

I can't stand that kind of call! I dislike divorce, and I dislike losing a couple I've been trying to help. *Failure!* I thought. Again, that's not exactly what I said to him. I asked, "Why are you giving up?"

"Well," he answered, "when I woke up this morning, she was standing by the bed with a knife in her hand."

Whoa, I thought, *that could motivate a person to leave, couldn't it?*

But why didn't this husband's effort work? Why did their relationship get to the point of knife-wielding and eventually divorce? The one time I talked with the wife, I discovered an extreme bitterness toward her mother because of a series of childhood incidents. For years, without even realizing the implications, she had carried this deep-seated anger toward her mom, and it poisoned her relationship with her husband. She had been so hurt by her mother that she had decided unknowingly that she was never going to let anyone get close enough to hurt her again. No matter what advice I gave her husband and no matter how hard he tried to love her, his efforts were doomed. She simply wouldn't let him get near her heart. It's as if angry people can't allow others to get too close! The unhealed hurt holds them at arm's length, sabotaging relationships.

The irony is that *after* the divorce, the woman went to a counselor who specialized in uncovering anger, and he helped her overcome the deep bitterness she felt toward her mother. She learned how to forgive her mom. Through their children, this divorced couple eventually became good friends, but in the meantime she had remarried, so the damage to that first marriage was permanent.

Why hadn't the woman sought counseling earlier? She simply didn't know how much her anger was influencing her attitude and behavior; nor did she realize how much distance anger—very old anger—can create in a relationship.

The process can work like this: We are hurt. That hurt creates anger that's not dealt with; it fills our anger can. Now we grow cautious, unable to trust; our fear might cause us to reject others before others reject us. The pain may linger only in our unconscious minds, but we automatically try to keep others at a safe distance. Whenever people get too close, our anger can starts spraying, usually sabotaging relationships through negative words or actions.

Many people I've counseled or who have attended my seminars have run up against this. A man—like the one whose seventeen-year-long marriage ended in divorce—will get fired up in one of my sessions and decide, *I'm going to go home and love my wife and children better.* But when he gets home and tries to be a better husband, his wife resists and pushes him away emotionally. Why? Often it's because she was hurt in the past, and as a result her anger can is relatively full and she simply doesn't feel comfortable with the idea of her husband getting closer to her.

This distancing mechanism can neutralize the positive perks that someone else tries to give. My good friend Dr. Gary Oliver was counseling with a couple whose divorce was going to be final in a week. He told them he wasn't a miracle worker; looking for a last-minute solution to their problems, they said they were willing to try anything.

So Gary got alone with the husband and said, "I'd like you to give it a shot—admittedly a long shot. For the next seven days, I want you to praise your wife very specifically three times a day. Write down what you say. Then we'll meet again and see what happened."

Seven days later the three met again. Gary asked, "Have things changed much in the last week?"

"Nothing much is different," the wife said.

Gary asked the husband, "What did you do differently?"

"Well, I praised my wife twenty-one times this week," he reported.

"What?" she protested. "How can you say that?"

"I did," he insisted. "I wrote them all down."

"Why don't you read the list to us?" Gary suggested.

The husband pulled out his sheet of paper and read off all twenty-one praises.

Now here's the interesting thing. As the man read, his wife just shook her head in amazement. She had never heard even one of them in the entire week. It was as if he had gone to make a deposit in her bank account and found a sign saying "bank closed." When she realized he had, in fact, praised her all those times, she reached over and touched him tenderly for the first time in months.

Why was she blind to his attempts to show her love? Because people like her who have too much anger deep inside tend to neutralize the positive things that happen to them. They simply can't see or hear them.

In any relationship, this tendency to miss the positive and accentuate the negative is a very destructive force—one fed by chronic anger. Marital experts Drs. Howard Markman, Scott Stanley, and Susan Blumberg highlight the fact that negative beliefs and interpretations can powerfully filter out the positive and leave one seeing only the negative. It's such a destructive force, they call it one of the key danger signs for a marriage.[4]

Are you aware of how your angry moods may be affecting how you see others? Having this automatic distancing mechanism is like living inside a relational box made of thick plate glass. Anyone who tries to become more intimate with a "hidden-anger" person seems to smash into this glass barrier. And then when the offended one tries to move closer to others in relationship, the glass plate seems to magnify the "outsider's" image; this can scare the angry person into moving back to a "safer" distance.

Unfortunately, when you're in relationship with someone who retains old anger that predates your relationship, you can feel as if you've just eaten a restaurant meal and then been handed a bill for ten thousand dollars. You explain to the waiter that there's no way your bill could be so high, maybe even joking about how you couldn't possibly eat that much.

But then the waiter says, "Your bill is ten thousand dollars because we want you to pay for everyone who has eaten here today. Is that okay with you?"

"No, that's not okay!" you insist.

Yet that's exactly what people (perhaps you or your spouse) do when they hold too much anger inside. They make others—often it's their spouses or family members—pay the "bill" for those in the past who have offended them.

When you're around these hidden-anger people, you can just sense that these are folks you can't get close to. In such cases, sadly, everyone the hidden-anger person knows pays. That's why it's so important to get the anger out as soon as possible.

This may be the main reason why people from divorced homes have such a hard time staying married. Their own anger level pushes the mate away and sabotages the marriage. Dr. Scott Stanley told me these children of divorce typically were never able to access their anger, bring it to the surface, and solve it. They kept it bottled up inside.[5]

And if these children said to themselves, *I'll never be like my dad or mom when I get married*, they almost assuredly predicted the failure of their future relationships. Why? Because their harsh determination is frequently fueled by unresolved anger. The cycle can go on generation after generation as angry kids become angry adults who have kids of their own.

We each have to face our past and check the level of our own anger. We can stop this generational pull of ruined relationships by taking responsibility for reducing the level of anger within ourselves. (To assess your own level of hidden anger, see the anger inventory at the end of this chapter.)

Distance from God

A second consequence of unresolved anger can be spiritual blindness or feeling particularly distanced or alienated from God. A recent Gallup poll revealed that over 90 percent of Americans say they believe in God. That's great as a base, a starting point. But in my counseling, I've observed some reverse correlation between anger and faith: It seems the greater a person's unresolved anger, the more difficulty that person has in developing a meaningful spiritual life. The spiritual side of life offers us love and asks us to be loving and sensitive toward others, but anger appears to darken the heart, making it impossible to see the "call" or receive the love offered us from God. Anger can function like an automatic rheostat, turning down the spiritual light that could be shining within and from us.[6]

I experienced this myself when I was deeply angry at one man—at one time a coworker—for more than six years. I had little desire for or interest in spiritual things; I didn't want to be with other people who were worshiping God; I had sparse spiritual insight; I was also discouraged and at times depressed. I didn't recognize the cause at the time, but when I finally started getting my own anger out, I saw how much it had affected me in this area. With the release of the anger, my spiritual interest and satisfaction with life returned.

Distance from Oneself

Another consequence of unresolved anger is a lowered sense of self-worth. In this case the anger and low self-worth are so intertwined and so circular that it's hard to separate causes and effects. Let's say that a child's—or an adult's—personal sense of being or of his or her personal boundaries was drastically, maybe repeatedly, violated. Hurt, frustration with feeling helpless, and fear lead to anger. And that anger can set in and take this form: *I can't be worth much if others—and "life"—treat me like this.* The anger prompted by someone else's actions or attitudes can quickly become blame or guilt—directed at oneself. Such anger turned inward can become depression.

Take another example, this one of children of divorce. The initial question, *How could Mom and Dad tear apart our home?* might be answered, *Maybe I'm to blame. Maybe they don't love me and don't want to be around me.* In her book *Children of Divorce*, Debbie Barr notes, "If a preschooler has fleetingly wished any disaster upon a departing parent, the child's guilt may multiply."[7] As a result the child's self-worth plunges; his or her anger compresses. Again, ultimately these children tend to follow the same path as their parents did. After they marry, they sabotage the relationship and try to keep their spouses from hurting them again.

Dr. Earl D. Wilson makes this observation: "Anger can be a cover-up for guilt." I would add that this can be legitimate or illegitimate (false) guilt. Wilson goes on to tell a brief anecdote of a client named Bob who had quite a temper and who always kept his girlfriend at a distance. Wilson ends the discussion by saying, "After some time in counseling, Bob was able to see that the reason he couldn't accept Janice's compliments about him was that he saw himself as anything but nice. He had to deal with this guilt and his feelings of failure (anger at himself) before he was ready for a close relationship."[8]

The greater the pain we carry inside, the greater the temptation to engage in addictive behaviors to get relief—temporary relief. The addictive behavior can include an unhealthy addiction to another person. According to Dr. Scott Peck, unchecked anger is a critical element in the most common psychiatric disorder: People with a passive-dependent personality disorder come to believe that they cannot live a quality life without being cared for by another person. Passive-dependents set themselves up for emotional bankruptcy, because no one can ever fill them. No amount of positive praise or affirmation is ever enough. They are endlessly angry because people are continually disappointing them.

They're locked into a pattern of living where they must have others, but when they get them, they smother them and usually kill the relationship. They find someone else, and the same thing happens. As they continue to fail, their anger—fueled by hurt (feeling abandoned) and frustration (feeling a failure) and fear (of being alone)—can alienate them from themselves and others, eating away at them just as if they actually turned on themselves and gnawed at their ankles until they reached the bone.[9] Is anger destructive, or what?

The cycle of anger and the sense of low self-value feeding off each other also can produce physical problems. Many people today go to the doctor and complain of backaches, neckaches, or headaches. But when the doctor looks into it, he or she can't find any physical cause of the pain. And some doctors are concluding that this epidemic of aches and pains may be the outworking of buried anger.

This anger alienates us from our own bodies. Consider the results of tests with students in medical school and law school in the 1960s. By using basic personality tests, hostility was measured. Twenty-five years later the students were tracked down. By the age of fifty, only 4 percent of the low-ranked "easygoing" lawyers and 2 percent of the doctors had died. Lawyers who had ranked high on hostility had a 20 percent mortality rate; doctors, 14 percent.[10]

Anger in the form of chronic hostility has also been clearly and strongly linked to heart disease. Those who are more hostile are more susceptible to heart attacks—the leading cause of death in our country.[11] Hostile anger can boost heart rates, raise blood pressure, and lead to increased clogging of the arteries. What's worse, the risk of heart attack seems to be greatly increased during the two hours following a bout with anger.[12]

Keep in mind, these are just some of the physical risks of anger. When you think about all the problems anger and hostility cause in relationships, you really get the full picture of how destructive this emotion can be if it's not handled correctly.

Distance from Maturity

This last distance caused by unresolved anger is connected to all those previously mentioned. Unresolved anger freezes our emotional maturity level near where it was when the hurtful offense occurred. I discussed this briefly in chapter 1. Let's suppose your parents divorced when you were twelve. You were devastated, and your anger can began to fill. In all likelihood, you also got stuck near that emotional level. You may have an adult body, but you've probably got the heart of a wounded twelve-year-old.

Maybe you're not the angry person but you live with one. In that case, you may find yourself asking from time to time, *Why is he so childish?* or *Why does she say those off-the-wall, immature things that hurt us?*

For example, a father says to his six-year-old, "Hey, son, get that quarter out of your mouth. It's been on the floor and has germs all over it!"

But the wife immediately responds, "Oh, Jimmy, that's okay. Don't worry about it. Even germs can't live on what your father earns."

Where might a juvenile, cutting remark like that come from? Most likely from a big can of unresolved anger that started to develop when the woman was young herself. Inside, she's still a hurting, angry child.

Anger Has the Power to Keep Us Miserable

Read that subhead again and allow the truth to sink in: Anger has the power to keep you miserable.

Think back to my friend Larry, whom I offended and who stayed angry with me for nine long years. All that time, he was continually replaying his videotape of my offense. He was seeing my face and hearing my words of betrayal over and over, and the pain was fresh almost every time. That event and my behavior were exerting a tremendous, debilitating influence on his life long after I had forgotten the entire incident. He was actually empowering me to keep him miserable. He allowed my offense—which happened on one particular day—to go right on offending him day after day for nine years. (*Gary really did that to me!*) He unwittingly allowed me to control him.

Fortunately, he finally took the healthy steps of contacting me, getting his anger out in a good way, and restoring the relationship.

Unresolved anger and blame can imprison us and bind us and make us miserable at heart and miserable to live with. Conversely, there is truth to the song that says, "Freedom is a state of mind." You can break free of unresolved anger. You may need further insight and support to break free, but that freedom is available. And it is a key to staying in love with life and for life.

Reason for Concern . . . and Hope

The good news about all this deep, destructive anger is that there's hope for the future. It can be resolved. Whether it's you or a loved one—perhaps your mate—who struggles with this, there are healthy, freeing steps that can be taken. The anger we've kept for so long can be drained away; damaged relationships can be mended. In the next chapter, I'm going to show you just how this can be done.

For now, I hope you can see how unresolved anger is a very serious problem that demands attention. When I stop to consider all the damage caused by buried anger—the countless divorces and other broken relationships, the millions of violent crimes, the uncountable mean-spirited words and actions and the resulting hurt feelings that breed more anger, the physical pains and the billions of tax dollars spent to treat them—I'm amazed and appalled. I trust you are too.

But it's my hope that by this time you share my conviction that we've got to see our anger for what it is and choose to deal with it in a healthy way. We simply can't let anger stay inside us, unresolved, and build up over two, three, or more years. The price is too high. So please take the anger inventory that follows to see just what your current level of anger is. Then move on to the next chapter and see how to get this hidden destroyer of relationships under control.

The Anger Inventory

All of us have some unresolved anger remaining in us at all times, but the key is to reduce it to as low a level as we can. While this is not a scientifically constructed test, you may find it can give you some idea of where you stand in regards to your anger or your potentially anger-producing background. This is not a pass-or-fail evaluation but rather an aid to help you reduce the size of your own anger can. You may wish to discuss your results with your mate, a friend, or a trained counselor.

To take the inventory, simply rate each statement below, on a scale from 0 (very low) to 10 (very high), for how much it applies to you. Then look to the following chapters for help in dealing with your level of anger.

_____ 1. I have frequently recurring minor health problems.

_____ 2. I tend to have difficulty remaining close to people. Others have even said I am "cold."

_____ 3. I continually fail to see the pitfalls in business deals.

_____ 4. I have little interest in religious matters.

_____ 5. I have many doubts about the existence of God.

_____ 6. I tend to see religious people as "a bunch of hypocrites."

_____ 7. I tend to be judgmental or overly critical of people.

_____ 8. I have a general inability to see my own shortcomings.

_____ 9. My image is very important to me. What I wear and drive are big concerns.

_____ 10. I often struggle with feelings of low self-value.

_____ 11. I often fail to see that my words or actions hurt the feelings of others.

_____ 12. My parents divorced before I turned eighteen.

_____ 13. I think one or both of my parents drank too much alcohol.

_____ 14. My parents seemed addicted to drugs or other substances.

_____ 15. My parents abused me.

_____ 16. My parents seemed too distant or neglectful to me.

_____ 17. I felt that my parents were too controlling of me.

_____ 18. I often struggle with feelings of discouragement or depression.

_____ 19. I seem to be at odds with several people for long periods of time.

_____ 20. I tend to be overly controlling of my mate, children, or friends.

_____ 21. I have general feelings of anxiety; I can't put my finger on what it is that I'm uneasy about.

_____ 22. I have sometimes thought about suicide.

_____ 23. I have had a hard time forgiving others when they hurt or frustrate me.

_____ 24. I have a hard time confronting others when they hurt me, and I know that I'm not that good at getting my anger out.

_____ 25. I find myself overly busy most of the time.

_____ 26. I find it easier to blame others than to take responsibility for my mistakes.

_____ 27. I often overreact to what others say or do to me.

_____ 28. I feel I'm motivated far too often by fear of failure.

_____ 29. I often wish people who have hurt me could be punished somehow.

_____ 30. I frequently think that I've been cheated out of important areas of life.

_____ 31. I get into fights with others that sometimes result in physical aggression, such as throwing things, slapping, or hitting.

_____ 32. I don't really trust anyone other than myself.

Now add up the thirty-two numbers—your rating.

My total score: _____

If your total score is more than 100, the next two chapters are especially important for you. If your score is more than 200, you may want to see a counselor who is trained in helping people uncover and deal with anger.

Finally, as an additional help in assessing your level of anger, list below the people toward whom you hold anger, and rate your anger toward each on a scale from 0 (very low) to 10 (very high):

_____

_____

_____

Forever-Love Principles

Our list of forever-love principles continues from the previous chapter:

10. Forever-love does not welcome anger as a heart-guest.

11. Forever-love knows the destructive, alienating power of anger.

12. Forever-love says no to anger's misery and yes to inner freedom.

3

Seven Ways to Unload
Unresolved Anger

Most of us, unfortunately, . . . say things like: "He made me so mad." "You really get to me." "Her remark embarrassed me terribly." "This weather really depresses me." . . . We are content to blame others, circumstances, and bad luck. . . . [But] we can rise above the dust of daily battle that chokes and blinds so many of us; and this is precisely what is asked of us in the process of growth as a person.

—John Powell[1]

As we saw in the preceding chapter, unresolved anger is that videotape of past offenses that keeps playing over and over in our minds, doing incredible damage to us and to everyone around us. We simply must deal with it—eject the tape, if you will. It may not be easy, but it's possible. There is a way to do it. If Linda could make it work, I believe anyone can.

Linda, a college student, came to me for help. She was discouraged, depressed, and visibly losing stamina. "I can't go on like this," she said. "I'm so miserable!"

"What's troubling you so much?" I asked.

"This is really embarrassing," she replied. "I've never told anyone because I just know that somehow it's going to come back and hurt me even more in the future."

"I'm here to help," I assured her. "I want to listen and do whatever I can."

She paused a moment, deciding whether she could trust me. Then, through tears, she told her secret: Her father had sexually abused her over a period of years. "I can't get over it," she said. "It has wiped me out and destroyed so much of my life that I don't know what to do about it. Is there anything you can do to help?"

As we talked, her negative emotion came pouring out from an understandably deep cistern of anger toward her dad. By coming to me and facing the deep pain within, she was finally able to take responsibility for her response to her father. What had happened to her was not her fault. But she was now responsible for how she would handle the memories and negative emotions resulting from the abuse that was beyond her control. She was choosing to confront the past.

The deep anger in her ran a continual "replay of tapes" of past offenses. It was in her power to eject the tapes, quit the damaging reruns, and go on to a new level of emotional maturity where she could fall in love with life and with someone special.

Remember what we discussed in chapter 2: Anger is a secondary emotion that arises out of fear, frustration, hurt, or some combination of these three. If someone disrespects us, for example, we first feel hurt and then we choose anger over other options, such as denial, forgiveness, or using the circumstance to lead us to personal growth.

That means that those three underlying emotions—fear, frustration, and hurt—can be seen as warning lights as bright as the "check engine" sign on a car's dashboard. Or they can serve as warning signals as clear as those received—and ignored—by the captain of the *Titanic*. When we see a warning light, we have a choice. After a hurtful, fearful, or frustrating experience, we can move in one of two directions: toward getting better or toward getting bitter.

Some of us, like Linda, have ignored the warnings for so long that a deep-rooted anger has started to destroy any happiness we ever had. But for Linda—and anyone reading this book—it isn't too late. By going to a counselor for help, Linda was acting responsibly, wisely, and humbly—unlike the cocksure captain of the ill-fated *Titanic*.

Well, all of us have warning signals in our lives. Ignore them at your own peril! Keep steering and pushing on your course without stopping, and you'll burn out your engine, hit a relational iceberg, or both.

I explained these things to Linda and asked, "What do you want from life? Do you want to be better? Or do you want to hold on to the negative and grow increasingly bitter?"

"I want to get the negative stuff out of my life. I want a better life. I want someday to have some joy in my life."

"Okay then," I said. "Let me take you through the steps that helped me deal with my own anger."

Switch word pictures with me once again and think of anger in terms of that dangerous substance that's compressed into a spray can. Some of these steps, or tools, will drain a little anger at a time while others may let out half of it all at once. Some bring immediate results while others give help over a longer period. Even though some may cause you to think, *I don't know if I can do that*, let me assure you that none of them is impossible. I've seen all of them work for me and thousands of others. Try them. After several weeks you'll find yourself saying, *You know, I don't have that same sick and empty feeling I had before*. Why? Because your pressurized anger is going, going, nearly gone.

You may contemplate the most obvious way to get the pressure out of the can: letting it explode in one violent rip. But let me caution that you are the "can" that may well be hurt in the blast! I hope instead you'll consider the healthier steps I suggest here.

Linda was willing and even eager to learn practical ways to live a life free from bitter anger. I gave her the seven steps that follow.

1. Define the Offense

Think about it. Aren't most of your actions motivated by the desire for gain or the fear of loss (or a combination of the two)?

Those hopes and fears—expectations and losses—can trigger anger. We get angry because someone (maybe even our own mortal, inadequate self) is taking something away from us that we don't want to lose, or else we're being denied something we want to gain. We blame something or someone for a loss—maybe even the loss of an unfulfilled dream or the loss of our peace of mind. The first step is to analyze and define exactly what happened, what you've actually lost or were denied.

As we analyzed Linda's anger in this light, I asked her, "What did you lose that led to your anger? If you can write it down—name it and try to look at it objectively—that alone can begin to drain out some anger."

I use the word *objectively*, but I acknowledge that here we're naming the offense in somewhat *subjective* terms. Naming a perceived loss can bring clarity and lead to healing. What did Linda perceive her loss to be?

Linda recognized a number of losses, but the two biggest ones really stood out. For one thing, she felt that her father had taken her childhood away from her—had stolen it from her, in fact. But the worst pain came from the feeling that he had taken her future, especially her future husband.

"What do you mean by that?" I asked.

"Well, I can't date anybody," she said, looking at the floor. She paused for a minute, unable to continue.

"Take your time," I offered gently.

She nodded silently, and tears filled her eyes. Finally she took a deep breath and said, "I feel so unworthy; I feel that if I meet the right guy, someone I really like, as soon as he finds out what happened to me, he'll think I'm trash."

Again she paused. I could see her body start to shake. At last she sobbed, "Nobody is going to want me or stay with me, because I'm not worthy of anyone!"

Those agonizing feelings of despair and shame growing out of her deep sense of loss produced many of the symptoms of anger: making her keep her distance in relationships, feeling alienated from God and from herself. She first needed to name her pain, to try to look at it from outside herself, much as I once had to do . . .

In the last chapter, I referred to a man toward whom I was very angry for six years. When I looked at that situation and tried to name my loss, I realized I felt he had stolen some of my dignity. Maybe deeper than that, because we were coworkers and our conflict made me feel I couldn't stay in the same organization, I also felt he had taken my future. I had enjoyed that job—had thought I was finally where I wanted to be in life—and then, because the place "wasn't big enough for both of us," I felt deeply resentful.

Another personal story leads into my second point. When my brother Ronnie, four years older than I, died at the age of fifty-one, I was angry with him for months. He had been an angry person himself; he was generally distrustful of people and somewhat explosive at times. He didn't like doctors, so he refused to get checkups the way he should have.

I would tell him, "Ronnie, heart trouble runs in our family. We've inherited this. You've got to get your cholesterol and your heart checked."

But he would respond, "I don't like doctors. They rip you off." And he would refuse to go.

Finally he had a heart attack and had to go to the doctor. But even then, he wouldn't follow the doctor's instructions for how to take better care of himself. He figured, *I'm strong. I'll be all right.*

We were just getting to be closer friends when he died, and I got angry. Getting past that anger took time, and it meant I had to face the reality of my loss: I had lost a brother and a friend. Just admitting what I had lost and allowing myself to feel it (see step 2, described below) helped a lot to get rid of my frustration and anger.

What about your own anger? Think of the things others have done that are still playing on that videotape in your mind. What did they take away from you or deny you?

2. Allow Yourself to Grieve

The second step in unloading anger is to allow yourself to grieve your loss. You've identified and written down what happened in the offense. Now accept that your pain—your sense of loss—is real; this person—your mate, boss, friend, parent, or maybe even yourself—did take something from you or deny you something. Don't minimize it! He or she didn't treat you with respect. Say the words: "You hurt me!"

You are angry, so look at it realistically. It's not only okay to grieve your loss, whatever it is, for a period of time, but grieving is also essential for your healing.

Elisabeth Kubler-Ross found that people go through stages of grief whenever they learn of their impending death: denial, anger, bargaining, depression, and acceptance. M. Scott Peck adds that we go through these same stages of grief every time we're about to grow in psychological or spiritual maturity.[2] If the conscious, grieving process feels painful, think of it in terms of final results: You're about to have an important "growth spurt" in your life. At the final stage of acceptance you will be able to say, "Yes, I can live with the loss; I can see beyond the loss."

Many people refuse to grieve their losses. They stay stuck in denial, the first grief stage. They try to be happy and say, "I'm strong. I'll get over it in a hurry." It's much healthier to allow yourself to hurt for a while. As they say, De-nial is not a river in Egypt! It's more like quicksand. Some serious offenses or losses need to be grieved—the pain acknowledged and released little by little, like slowly letting the air out of a balloon. Depending on the magnitude of loss, it can take months. That's a vital part of releasing your anger, something a woman named Wendy was unaware of.

Wendy was a stay-at-home mom until her youngest child went to school. Then she took a little nest egg she had set aside and used it to realize a dream: She opened a small coffee shop. She knew the risks going in, but she wanted to give it a try.

After fully investing her time and energy for four hard months, Wendy was forced to close the shop. The money ran out. She was so disappointed. Through her sadness, she experienced serious mood swings. Her kids noticed how quickly she snapped at them for the least little thing.

But the brunt of her anger was saved for her husband, Ron. Through no fault of his, Wendy became increasingly hostile and cold to him. She tried her best to avoid being with him—for a reason she couldn't put her finger on. It became an extremely trying time in their marriage.

Wendy's eyes opened only after she recognized her denial. She needed to allow herself the freedom to grieve the loss of her business venture. And then her family relationships, which had grown distant, slowly returned to their former closeness. We're mistaken when we believe the only grieving to be done is after the death of a loved one. We must grieve the loss of relationships, projects, personal goals, work-related issues—just about any loss. It's essential for emotional health.

Now let's return to Linda's story. Week after week in our counseling sessions, I simply allowed her to express her deep anguish. There were times when she would ask me, "Will the pain ever end?" Her "grief therapy" certainly could not be described as "brief" therapy! She needed several months to start the healing because her loss was so great.

The most dramatic change in her grief came the day I asked her to relive her childhood feelings as she remembered them. We focused on one particular time when she lay on her bed feeling deep shame and hatred for her dad. During a three-hour session with a great many tears and much anguish I listened to her pain—a young girl whose body had been violated and whose heart had been crushed by the man whose duty it was to protect, cherish, and nurture her. I had to fight back my own desire to go after him with a baseball bat. To put it mildly, I was getting angry myself!

Linda even found that grieving—continuing to acknowledge the pain and loss—was needed after things started to get better for her. Her experience was something like that of a woman who called me one day and said, "Mr. Smalley, I have a very serious problem, and I need to talk to someone. I'm in danger!"

Frankly, I didn't know if I wanted to get involved if there was physical danger, but I finally agreed to meet with her.

"I appreciate your meeting with me," she said when we got together.

"My husband, who is well known in this community, is doing something illegal. I can't live this way anymore. I'm extremely angry about what he's doing and the way he treats me. I've got to expose this so I can get help myself. But I don't know what he's going to do to me—or to you—if he finds out I've told you."

I sat there thinking, *Thanks a lot, lady. This is great! Is he part of the underworld or something?*

She went on to describe what her husband was doing. I knew who he was, and although it was a scary prospect, I decided that the best approach was for his wife and me to confront him. "Maybe he'll respond well and do the right thing," I told her hopefully.

The two of us did confront him, and although he resisted initially, I'm happy to say that he surprised me by eventually responding well and straightening things out. But the reason I tell this story is that the wife— and this is perfectly normal—still had her anger even after her husband had turned around. I could help her realize what she had lost and go through a grieving process, but she had to express the pain. Only then did her anger start to drain away. This was also true for Linda, whose pain would reappear now and then even after she started to heal.

In dealing with your own anger, it's best to face it. And don't cut short your need to grieve.

3. Try to Understand Your Offender

The third step in resolving anger—trying to understand your offender— may seem impossible and the benefits of it incomprehensible. It may take awhile, but as soon as you can do it, I assure you, it can speed your release. Some of the healing power of this step is just in trying it. As you attempt to understand the person and why he or she might have committed the offense, you set a process in motion: You may well see how your offender could have acted out of his or her own hurt.

This step has meant a lot to me personally. When I took it, it was like draining half of my anger can at once. Let me explain. Remember the man I was angry with for six years? I was so tied up inside that I would wake up early in the morning thinking things like, *I'm going to get revenge* and *I hope something bad happens to him today.* I was grinding away, playing the old tape in my head. Then one day, a person I was counseling came in with an article clipped from a magazine. The client said, "This article really describes me and tries to help people like me understand how they can get better. Would you read it? Maybe it will give you a better understanding of me, and you can use some of the ideas to help me."

"Sure," I said. I took the article home that night, though frankly I wasn't thrilled with the idea. But as I started to read it, I was amazed. I thought it described my own offender to a T! It was the first time I had any understanding of him and why he might have acted as he did. *So that's why he was such a jerk to me,* I thought. *That's why he did all those things. It makes all the sense in the world. No wonder!*

As I gained some understanding of the potential pain in his life, I actually felt twinges of compassion for him. I hadn't planned it or expected it at all. But realizing his hurtful actions toward me could be caused by his own hurtful experiences helped me see everything in a whole new light. He was an anger-filled, sabotaging man.

Stephen Covey calls what happened to me a "paradigm shift"—an entirely new perspective on a particular subject. He gives a personal example to illustrate a complete change in attitude. He was on a train when a man boarded with his children. The kids were irritating all the other passengers, including Covey. But when Covey found out that the man's wife had just died and the family was coming from the hospital, Covey's attitude changed instantly and utterly.[3]

That's somewhat like my experience. As soon as I understood for the first time just how wounded my offender might be, my attitude changed; a great pressure behind my anger was released.

Let's say your father offended you. Then at some point you find out about his own history—how his father and mother and maybe his grandfather treated him. That new information gives new insight into why he acted the way he did toward you. And as you make that discovery, you will practically feel some of the resentful emotions draining from you.

My son Greg saw this happen in a dramatic way. As a counselor, he specializes in child therapy. One time he was helping a nine-year-old girl who was feeling rejected by her father. Greg recognized that the problem went beyond the little girl; it was a family system problem. So he asked the dad, "Will you come in and meet with us?"

"Fine," the man said, not knowing what Greg had in mind.

The father joined them for a session, and during the conversation, Greg asked the girl, "What would you really like from your dad?"

Her teary eyes gazed downward, and she said softly, "I would love for my daddy, just once, to tell me that he loves me."

The man immediately replied, "Honey, you know I love you."

Big tears rolled down her cheeks as she looked up at him and said, "Yeah, Daddy, but I would just like to hear it."

Her dad's heart broke. Through his own misty eyes, he told her, "Honey, for some reason I can't say that. I never heard it when I was growing up. I never heard my mom or dad tell me they loved me, so I don't even know how to say it. I'm sorry, Honey, but I just can't say it."

The little girl was sobbing now as she said, "Daddy, I really wish you would!"

At that point Greg suggested, "Why don't we practice right here? Why don't you say it to her right now?"

The man felt awkward and uncomfortable, like being asked to propose marriage in front of an audience. But seeing how important it was to his daughter, he said, "All right, I'll try."

Then with great tenderness, he reached over and took his child's hand. "Honey," he said with difficulty, barely able to look at her, "I just want to say that I love you." With that, he started sobbing. The girl was still crying too. And then Greg started in, so that all three of them were crying tears of love and joy and understanding for both of the hurting children in that room.

When the daughter realized that her father had never heard words of love from his own parents, she could understand, and it amazed both men when she said, "So that's why you couldn't say you love me! That makes sense. Daddy, you lived in a home like the one I live in." That insight instantly drained some anger from her life. And fortunately in this case, the offender—her dad—was willing and able to move beyond his own hurt and say the things he needed to say to heal his child.

What that father learned—that you can choose to move beyond the limitations of your childhood—is something I had to learn as well. As an adult, I was in a meeting once when we were supposed to write out the first time we heard our fathers praise us. As I sat there, I thought, *Okay. Let's see. Uh-huh.* I couldn't think of a single time I had heard words of praise from my dad! Then I thought, *This must be something that has affected me for sure.* And I realized that I had always had a hard time praising other people.

Had that stopped me from ever praising others? No. It had been difficult, but I had learned to do it. And the more we practice the positive, in spite of the way we were raised, the easier it gets. But as in the case of that girl's father, we might need a counselor or a support group to provide a safe environment for our first attempts.

This step was another major turning point for Linda. When I found out that her father had come from an alcoholic family, I felt sure that an understanding of what that meant to her father could help her own recovery.

Linda's grandfather was an alcoholic. And addictive people usually don't know how to and usually can't develop close-knit, meaningful relationships. They generally ruin most of their relationships and send their children into the world with major empty holes in their hearts. It's as if children of alcoholics are missing part of their relational ability. The resulting pain these children feel can cause them to seek out a medication in the form of addictions of their own.

Linda's father was sexually addicted, from a pornography habit to the incest he inflicted on her. She was, in some ways, like a drug to him—as alcohol had been to his father. I tried to help her see his pain and understand why he acted the way he did. That insight wasn't all she needed for her own healing, but it did allow her to release a big chunk of her anger. She saw that he was as wounded by his dad as she was by hers, but in a different way. He wasn't just setting out purposefully to "steal her childhood." His actions reflected his own deep pain and emptiness.

For myself, I gained yet more understanding of the power of trying to understand an offender when I went to speak at a major university. I was supposed to address several groups of faculty, administration, and students, and we gathered in an austere, formal room for the first meeting. They were a serious-looking group, and as I got up and started to speak, I could see that things weren't going well. I was trying to be funny, and they weren't laughing. As far as I was concerned, the session couldn't end soon enough.

About halfway through, things got even worse. A woman stood up with a real hostile look on her face, and she said, "This upsets me. I can't hear any more of this!" And she stormed out of the room.

I was instantly hurt. *Is that offensive, or what?* I thought. Her behavior ruined the rest of the session for me. I had no desire to continue. I only wanted to disappear through a trapdoor, run to my rental car, and get out of there. I figured maybe everyone else in the room felt the same as that woman, and she had been the only one brave enough to stand up and say what they all were thinking. That's what her outburst did to me. But I managed to stumble through the rest of my presentation.

Afterward, I was really feeling low, drained of energy. There was a big gap between what I had expected and what I had actually experienced. My frustration and hurt warned me that anger was close at hand. But I decided to face this head-on. *I'm going to find out why she would be so rude and offensive to me. There has to be some reason.* I knew there must have been some hostility in her life because she had clearly sprayed me with her "anger can."

I asked someone about the woman and learned she was director of a university department and a leading spokesperson for the women's movement. As I made my way to her office, I thought, *Whoa! Should I really do this?* But I kept walking, right up to the receptionist. I respectfully asked, "May I see your boss for a couple of minutes? I'd just like to talk with her."

The receptionist checked for me, then came back and said, "No, she's not able to see you now. She's real busy."

"Could you ask her one more time?" I pleaded. "Tell her I won't take more than five minutes. I just want to ask her an important question."

The receptionist checked again, and this time she told me, "Okay, she can give you five minutes. That's it."

I walked into the office, and the woman glared at me as if to say, *What are you doing here? Didn't you get enough abuse already? Do you want more?*

"I want to thank you for what you did," I started.

Yeah, right, her look said.

"You got my attention, as you can well imagine," I explained, "and I would love to know what you heard in my talk that you reacted to so strongly. You see, I speak all over the world, and maybe what bothered you bothers other people, too, and they're just not telling me. So I'd really like to know what disturbed you."

"Oh," she said. "Well, you . . ." She talked about this and that and so on. But then, within three or four minutes, she started to cry and tell me how angry she was with one of her colleagues. "I hate this person," she told me, continuing with a litany of his offenses.

As I sat there listening, I thought, *Wow! This is one angry person.* All her emotion seemed to be wrapping around my neck and choking me, it was so strong. But I just let her vent, listening carefully and saying things like "Bless your heart" and "Oh, you have to put up with that?"

Next came an even bigger surprise. After a few more minutes she asked me, "How many more times are you speaking on campus?"

"Two more," I said, wondering what she had in mind.

"I'd like to go with you and introduce you," she said.

"Really?" I replied, shocked.

"Yeah," she said with a smile.

Just a short while before, she couldn't stand me. Now she was my buddy, and all because I had listened, shown some compassion, and helped her to see some things she could do to resolve her anger! What's more, *understanding what had made her so angry released the anger starting to churn in me because of her outburst.* My time on campus had started with the making of a new enemy, but it ended with the making of a new friend.

Remember, when someone has offended you, it's often (not always) spray from his or her own anger can. When that's the case, you're dealing with a person who has probably unknowingly placed himself or herself at a distance from others, God, self, and maturity. And you can choose not to allow that person to exercise control over your life.

Try this step: Make the effort to understand the individual's background and motivation. Let your new understanding of that person's pain and life-difficulty drain some of your anger.

4. Release Your Offender

This step in dealing with anger involves giving up your desire for revenge, releasing your offender from your wish to get even. This step sometimes comes "naturally" once you have understood some of the causes of the offensive behavior toward you.

Releasing your offender can drain several ounces of resentment at once, and it usually involves learning how to forgive. The original definition of *forgiveness* actually means that you untie or release someone. As long as you remain bitter and unforgiving, you're tied to that person with emotional knots. So being untied involves a conscious and deliberate release of the offender through an act of forgiveness.

It's a good idea to say the words out loud, preferably with someone else present, because then the impact is more powerful. In my forgiveness of the coworker who had so offended me, I said the words aloud but alone. I took several hours, and I relived those situations in which I had felt such deep hurt. In my mind's eye I was with him again in those painful incidents, but I was also observing "from a corner of the room." In this private scenario, as we came to a place where he had given offense, I would stop him and say, "I forgive you. I'm untying you from the emotional ropes that have held me to you. I release you. I'm not responsible to you anymore, and you're not responsible to me. It's over for us. I'm going to turn my life in a different direction. I'm not going to run that video in my mind anymore; I'm pushing the eject button. I won't wish harm on you any longer. You're a wounded person; I may not know the source of all your own anger or wounds, but I hope someday you find your own healing. In the meantime, your woundedness is no longer my fault. You blamed me, but I receive your offensive behavior toward me as your sick way of showing your woundedness."

I experienced many emotions during those hours, but I felt that I got a lot of anger out. And about a week later, I realized I was enjoying a new sense of release and freedom because of what I had done. My own anger can had shrunk, and I wasn't feeling so miserable anymore; nor was I spraying others so much. That reminded me that we either release those who have hurt us or else our anger can consume us, and that's too high a price to pay for hanging on to bitterness. Wanting revenge—something bad to happen to the other person—will only heap more anger on ourselves, and we'll potentially get more anger-spray in return.

An important though difficult part of releasing someone is giving up the expectation that the person will eventually see the error of his or her ways and take the initiative to make things right with you. This was a big hang-up for Linda. Her father had emotionally and physically abused her, and she kept expecting that someday he would turn around, recognize his error, and do something wonderful for her.

"Someday my dad is going to tell me he loves me," she insisted. "He's going to hug me and admit he was wrong. I know it's going to work out—like in a fairy tale."

I knew that wasn't likely to happen. From what she had told me about him, I was sure her father had his own enlarged anger can. You can't expect nice things from people with big cans of anger compressed by their own deep wounds, so you've got to release them from that expectation. It's as if they live in darkness and can't see what they've done. For quite some time, Linda couldn't understand that her expectations were unrealistic. Finally I got through to her when I said, "Linda, please walk over to that lamp, put your arms around it, and give it a big hug."

She gave me a funny look, but she got out of her chair and followed my instructions.

I asked her to sit down again, and then I asked, "How long will it take for that lamp to come over to you and return your hug?"

"A long time," she answered with a grin. "It never will."

"And why won't it?" I asked.

"It's unable to," she said.

"That's right, Linda," I told her. "And your father isn't able to do what you want, either, because of his own conflicts. You've got to give up waiting for that wish to come true and turn your own life around. He's a little wounded kid in adult skin. He has a huge hole in his heart. That hole makes him unable to see your wounds."

I also told her a story of the battleship out cruising on a very foggy night. A lookout reported that he saw the light of another ship directly ahead. The captain ordered, "Radio that ship and tell it to turn twenty degrees to port."

The call went out, but a message came back, "No, YOU turn twenty degrees to port."

The captain was a little irritated by that, so he commanded, "Listen here. I'm the captain of a battleship, and if you don't veer off right now, I'll see that you're through in the navy."

This time the message came back, "Sir, you may be a captain of a battleship, but I'm a seaman first class in charge of this lighthouse, and I'd suggest you veer off in a hurry, or you're all history! Sir."

Most people who have hurt us are like that lighthouse. They're not going to change course and become more loving. They're stuck in place like a rock! Either we turn away from them by releasing them from our anger, or we head for disaster.

The next step has so much potential for draining anger that I've devoted a whole chapter to it. But I'll give you an overview here.

5. Look for Pearls in the Offense

This tool in overcoming anger is to search for "hidden pearls" in the offense committed against you. The idea here is that some good can come out of any bad situation—if you'll just look for it. Find the good, and you can be grateful for it. And . . . gratitude and anger can't coexist. This is yet another step that can drain a lot of anger all at once. It's an alternate choice you can make in how you respond to hurt, fear, or frustration.

As I looked back on my journey to releasing anger toward my coworker, I realized that a lot of good had come from a "bad" situation. For example, because I was hurt by what happened, I developed a greater sensitivity and compassion as a counselor. The way things worked out, my leaving that job (what I'd perceived as the "loss of my future") opened gigantic new doors for me to write, speak, and counsel.

Would I want to go through that same kind of pain again? No way! But it's in the past, and I can now be grateful for the good that came from it.

There's a lot more to be said about pearl-hunting in the next chapter. Keep reading.

6. Put Your Feelings in Writing

Another helpful step in working through anger is to put your feelings in writing in the form of a letter to the person who offended you. I'm not saying you have to mail the letter. But when you spell out your hurts, frustrations, and fears, researchers say it's almost as if your anger is released through the ink of the pen. You may not feel the effect immediately, but you can in time.

What do you write? Clarify what you lost or were denied—what it is that caused you pain and has led to your anger. Talk about your resultant feelings. Express your desire to set aside—and live beyond—your anger and know the freedom that comes with forgiveness. And one of the best things is to state how you would like your offender to respond.

Normally, I don't encourage people to send such letters to—or confront—their offenders; the offender usually reacts badly and increases the offense. It can make the problem worse for everyone involved.

As an old proverb says: Do not reprove a fool, or he will hate you and spread all sorts of lies about you.[4] Foolish people (often angry, emotionally blind people) can't see most of their own faults and shortcomings. Being confronted with their hurtful actions and words can threaten them with so much pain that they may respond by lashing out—hating you for forcing them to look at what they cannot face; they may subsequently do whatever they can to discredit you.

But Linda, the young woman who was abused by her father, wrote such a letter, and she went ahead and mailed it to him. She knew it was risky; he could have hurt her doubly by denying he had ever abused her. Or the letter could have been read by someone else; that always complicates things. But we both thought the risk was worth taking in this case in the hope that she could be further healed.

I'm happy to say that her dad responded better than either of us had hoped. When he got her letter, he called her immediately. His first words were something like, "Honey, I've waited all these years to talk about this, but I never could. I couldn't admit what I had done because it was too painful. I have suffered for years. When you told me in your letter that you had forgiven me and released me, I was so grateful!"

A short time later, they had a tearful reunion full of hugs and healing. I had told Linda at one point that I didn't think her father would ever be capable of responding in such a way, and I'm happy to say that this time I was wrong.

As Linda continued to heal, she met a fine young man and eventually married. (I was honored to be a part of her wedding.) She's now a very caring and loving wife and mother. A negative intergenerational cycle has been broken.

Again, as I said before, I generally advise against mailing a letter written to an offender. But just writing the letter can help unload some of your resentment whether or not you mail it.

7. "Reach Out" to Your Offender

This last step in resolving anger may well be the hardest. It doesn't come naturally, and it requires a huge act of the will, not to mention a high degree of maturity and love. But when you're able to do it, it can release a lot of anger.

What does this involve? Finding some way to help in the healing of the person who offended you. Again, I suspect this sounds impossible, but I've seen its benefits to those who can get to this point.

Recently, I talked with a young woman about helping someone who had offended her. She had been deeply hurt in a dating situation while in college, and she admitted, "There's no way I can ever take part in trying to heal the man who wounded me."

"I understand that," I said. "I know you may never be able to do this. I'm not saying you should do it. But I'm saying that if you can come to the place where you can have some compassion for the man because of the pain he's also been through, it can provide a great healing for you. Guaranteed: He is a wounded man, sick and in need of healing. I've tried to do this myself for people who have offended me; it has been very emotional, but I could feel my anger releasing. But I know it won't be easy for anyone."

It's never easy to reach out in a loving way to those who have hurt us. A man named Earl realized this when he took steps to reconcile with his father. Already in his late thirties, Earl realized that some of his own coldness to his wife was due to his upbringing by an alcoholic father. He realized he needed to work through his anger toward his dad, whom he felt had "cheated" him out of a portion of his youth.

Earl talked the situation over with his wife and decided, *My dad's an out-of-control alcoholic, but maybe I can do something as the son. I don't want to keep passing on the same unhealthy behavior to my wife and kids, so I'm going to start the ball rolling.* This involved a conscious change in his demeanor toward his family. And it prompted him to call his dad, thinking, *I've never in my whole life told him the things I want to say now, but I'm going to call and tell him I love him, and all is well with me toward him.* Just think how much courage that call would require! But Earl was learning how to forgive his dad and wanted to get the relationship on a new footing.

Earl's father, who lived across the country, wasn't a real talker, but Earl placed the call. They made small talk for a while, and then Earl said, "Dad, incidentally, I've been thinking a lot about us lately, and even though I've never said this before, I wanted to tell you that I love you."

Click. His dad had hung up on him!

Earl couldn't believe it. So he called him right back and said, "Dad, I was trying to tell you that I love you."

Click.

Earl turned to his wife and said, "I don't understand this! My dad is hanging up on me."

"You just have to keep trying," she encouraged.

So he waited a few days, called his dad again, made small talk for a couple of minutes, and then said, "Dad, don't hang up on me. I want to tell you something. I really love you."

Click. He hung up on Earl again. He just couldn't handle Earl's words, maybe because he had never heard them from his own father. And who knows how many generations of that family had gone without hearing the words "I love you"?

A few weeks went by. Then one day Earl's mom called. "Son, I don't know how to tell you this, but your dad's disappeared. He's gone. No note. He's run away. We've looked everywhere and tried everything. I hate to tell you this, because I know you wanted to do something with him." Earl was crushed.

Everyone in the family was thinking the worst, but a month later, his dad came home. Where had he been? He had checked himself into an alcoholic rehab center. His explanation? "I want to love my son, and I want to be able to talk to my son about loving him and him loving me, and I couldn't do it with what alcohol was doing to me. I've been so messed up all my life, and this is the first time I've really wanted to get help."

Once home, he called Earl, who flew across the country; the father and son determined to learn how to love each other with the help of a counselor. Then they drove to see the other brothers and sisters. They didn't call ahead to say they were coming, and when they arrived at the first brother's house he screamed at the father, "Never come in my home again! I never want to see you as long as I live!" He then ran out of the house, got in his BMW, and left.

Though tragic, I'm not surprised by the second son's reaction. There was a deep, deep anger inside that son toward his dad. His father was trying to clear things up with him, but he wasn't interested. The story is still unfolding; I haven't heard the final chapter, but I know the dad is continuing to try to get through to all his kids and heal their family. Already, he and Earl have a better relationship than they ever had before. And Earl and his wife have drawn closer, their relationship reaping the benefits of Earl's courageous move to try to reach out to his offender.

To return to Linda's story, in time she was able to ask her dad what he was doing to overcome the grandfather's abuse toward him. For both the father and the daughter, their continued conversations went a long way toward healing the intergenerational wounds.

When you're ready to reach out to someone who has hurt you, perhaps a good starting place is to pray for the offender to be released from the anger in his or her own life. As we've seen, any healing actions we take can, in time, drain away some of our own personal anger.

Using These Seven Steps to Drain Your Own Guilt

If you are the offender—if you've "provoked" someone to choose anger because of your hurtful, frustrating actions or words—or if the pain of your own guilt has turned into anger toward yourself, consider this statement as a step that reaches out to heal both the offended one and you, the offender: Each of the seven steps to get rid of your own anger can also be used in reverse to release anger in someone you have offended (as well as anger-produced guilt in you, the offender).

You remember the story of my friend Larry, who was angry with me for nine years? Let's just imagine a different scenario from what actually happened. Suppose right from the beginning I had been aware I had wounded him. Suppose I had called him that very week, met him for coffee, and ana-lyzed or named my offense, apologized and made some explanation for my actions, then sought his forgiveness. I could have helped loosen the lid on his anger—and the guilt that would have been eating at me.

Let's review: Analyzing the offense that gave rise to your anger. Grieving your loss. Understanding your offender. Releasing the offender and turning away from bitterness. Looking for pearls in the offense. Writing a letter. Reaching out to heal. These are all steps that add up to forgiveness and will release you from the anger that can otherwise eat away at your insides.

A Story of Release

Let me close with a story that illustrates many of these elements. I have a friend who once played professional baseball. At one point in his life, he came to a startling realization: *I really didn't enjoy playing baseball as much as my father did. He forced me to play from the time I was a little guy. He was my coach and inspiration. In fact, I didn't even see him a lot except for baseball. And the bottom line is that I'm very angry at him for the way he raised me.*

He came to that understanding in a movie theater. He was in his late forties by that time (his father was in his early eighties), and he and his wife were watching the film *Field of Dreams*. As he sat there watching the movie, he started crying, then sobbing. *What in the world is going on?* he wondered. And his wife was giving him a *What's wrong with you?* look. But he just sat there crying, even after the credits had run.

"Honey, the movie is over," his wife said as the lights came up.

"I don't know what's going on with me," he said, "but this movie brought out all kinds of feelings about my dad. Honey, I don't know if you'll understand this, but I'd like to go see him right away. I really feel I need to. What do you think?"

"That's fine," she said.

My friend called his mother that night and said, "Mom, I'm going to fly up and see Dad. Make sure he's home tomorrow night, because I'm coming up to do something with him."

So he got up there and told his dad what he wanted to do, and the father replied, "What! You flew all the way up here for us to go to a movie?"

"That's right, Dad, I want to watch this movie with you." That's all he told him.

They went to the theater together, and this time they both sobbed all the way through. At the end of the movie, they drove to an all-night restaurant, where they talked over what had happened and how they felt. By early morning, this son had forgiven his father, and they were reconciled in a way that neither had ever before experienced.

I understand *Field of Dreams* has had a similar healing effect for many fathers and sons. In this case, although the whole process took place rather quickly, my friend used many of the steps described in this chapter. He clarified and grieved his loss—as a young man he hadn't realized his own goals and dreams. Then he forgave his father and reached out to heal both him and their relationship.

I trust that these steps of forgiveness can help you or someone you love to drain away all kinds of anger. To the extent that you can experience inner healing, you'll be better equipped to love the people around you. For the sake of our society as well, we need to see families healed and brought back into harmony. We need to say "Enough is enough!" and start learning how to forgive each other. When that spreads, just watch what happens in our world! I pray that you'll be right at the heart of that movement.

The next chapter gives much more insight to help you forgive or reduce your anger level. Just imagine: Whether you've been hurt by life in the past or you're being hurt now or you get hurt in the future, you can use the concept in the next chapter to turn it all into something good for you.

Forever-Love Principles

Our list of forever-love principles continues from the previous chapter:

13. Forever-love listens to the heart's warnings—fear, frustration, and hurt—and makes the choice to get better, not bitter.

14. Forever-love seeks to identify an offense. Name a fear or a loss, and anger begins to lose its debilitating power.

15. Forever-love does not deny a grievance but grieves the harm's loss.

16. Forever-love tries to understand any "why" behind another's hurtful actions.

17. Forever-love chooses to forgive—to untie the knot of anger and release the bitter blame.

4

You Can Turn Your "Sand Storms" into Pearls

Precious memories may remain even of a bad home, if only the heart knows how to find what is precious.

—Fyodor Dostoyevsky

I could be happy; I could be in love with life, if only . . . Most not-yet-happy people have one or more "great" ways to finish that sentence. *If only my spouse would drop dead. If only I had a spouse. If only I lived in a better neighborhood. If only I were to win the lottery.* These people believe they could love life if only they could somehow reduce the number of their troubles, leave behind the frustrating, anger-producing negatives—as a snake slithers out of its skin and leaves it behind.

But just the opposite is true! Without some painful encounters, our quality of life is diminished. Scott Peck begins his classic book *The Road Less Traveled* with a now-famous line: "Life is difficult." He continues: "This is a great truth, one of the greatest truths."[1]

On these two counts I agree, and I also say that contained in every difficulty are good and great things that we can learn to appreciate—that we can use for our benefit and enrichment.

All our trials, great and small, can bring more of the two best things in life: love for life and love for others. But only those who take full responsibility for their responses to trials find these loves in their lasting form.

No one can escape his or her share of life's problems. One might try to, like old Charlie, who thought he could find true happiness by escaping the pressures of life. With this hope, he entered a monastery where silence was the rule—the only exception being chapel prayers. Every five years, however, you could speak two words to the abbot. At the end of his first five years there, Charlie chose his words carefully: "Bad food," he said. After five more years Charlie said, "Hard bed." Finally, after fifteen years, Charlie declared, "I quit!"

Disappointed, the abbot responded, "I'm not surprised. Ever since you came, all you've done is complain."

Trials, hardships, hurts, and all the other painful experiences we encounter are like personal "sand storms." They might blind us, sting us, irritate us, anger us. But as we respond to them, we have a choice I introduced in the previous chapter: *After a trial we can get better or bitter.*

We can find the road to a love that lasts forever as we get to the place where we regularly use our "sand storms" to our advantage. I call the process of transforming hurts into benefits *pearl-counting.* I use that word picture— that image—because the pearl found within an oyster started with an irritating piece of sand.

Those precious jewels are there for us—ours for the taking. In fact, every trial contains several pearls. Once I caught on to this principle, I got excited about seeing how many I could find in each crisis. Some provide a whole "necklace" suitable for prominent display. The more pearls, the greater your riches.

But you might ask, "What good comes out of my business going under . . . or having been abused as a child . . . or my mate's serious illness . . . or . . . ?" Although those situations are initially devastating, they each eventually can produce a set of beautiful, valuable pearls. Usually this process doesn't happen too quickly. It usually takes several months for an oyster to add layer after layer of secretions to make the larger, valuable pearls.

As you dig into your tribulations and discover the gems buried within them, your self-worth will soar, and so will your ability to give and receive love. One of the greatest life-giving principles I've found is that all trials, big or small, can add to our "love chest" if we search for it.

How One Couple Turned Their Trauma into a Pearl

At age thirty-eight Terry Brown had finally found his dream bride, Janna. But one week before their wedding, Terry received a midnight call from his brother: Their mother had been diagnosed with acute cancer; doctors gave her only twenty-four hours to live. Terry flew to Florida the next day to be by her side, where he and his brothers stayed until she slipped into a coma. Meanwhile, Janna came to me in tears, wondering what she could do to support Terry and asking if they should postpone their ceremony.

As Terry's mother lingered on life support, other family members urged Terry to go forward with his wedding plans; no one knew for sure how long she would last.

As it turned out, the mother lived until her son's wedding, which took place as originally planned. That evening, following the ceremony, Terry heard that his mother, without regaining consciousness, had slipped away earlier in the day.

At this point, Terry and Janna's plans did change. The next morning, when they were supposed to be starting their honeymoon, they flew to Florida for what would be the first of three memorial services. Then, still on their "honeymoon," they flew to Chicago for the funeral.

We can all sympathize with Terry's loss and the unfortunate timing. But follow with me and see what they did in response to their tragedy.

Several months after the wedding, I listened as they explained their response to the terrible events. Terry confessed that even though he was losing the mother he had loved for thirty-eight years—and though he knew his mother wanted more than anything to be with him for his long-awaited wedding—he was gaining the closest friend he had ever known. He said it was a strange, conflicting set of emotions: On the one hand, he was losing a most important loved one. On the other hand, he was feeling so encouraged by and such a tender tug toward Janna, who was demonstrating such unconditional love for him. She was far more concerned for him and his feelings than she was for her own honeymoon. Through this terrible situation, he could see her friendship in action—unbelievably supportive, caring, and relaxed.

This traumatic beginning of their life together convinced them that they would be able to go through almost anything. The crisis was so bonding for them Terry later admitted that the whole week was the most encouraging time of his life. His bride's love for him far exceeded anything he had imagined possible.

Because Terry had previously learned the secrets of pearl-counting, he was somewhat aware of these positive possibilities while still in the midst of the funeral (honeymoon) week. He just started looking for—expecting—

something good to come out of that mess. And it did! Terry found pearls: a deeper bond with Janna, the assurance that he has a friend committed to him even in hard times.

Before we get into the specific steps of pearl-counting, let's look at what enables someone to find treasure within pain. Several key foundational issues have been covered in the previous chapter. As you work through the steps to releasing unresolved anger—as you quit blaming others and yourself for your troubles—you're better able to find pearls. Here's another key foundational mind-set: Don't overreact to problems.

Avoid Extreme Thoughts

When we hit hard times, we often overreact and panic, thinking, "This is the absolute worst thing that could happen!" "Nobody has ever gone through anything as devastating as this circumstance!" But the truth is that neither of those statements is true.

Try to refocus some of your energy away from all that's bad and instead search for anything that could possibly be good in the trial you're facing. Try to think of what new opportunities this situation may bring. *What can I learn? What future happiness lies in store as a direct result of this incident?*

As hard as it seems, relax. Again, most trials are not as bad as they seem at the time. As Mark Twain once said, "I am an old man and have known a great many troubles, but most of them never happened."

One extreme but subtle thought we can try to avoid might be boiled down to this: *I am the center of the universe.* A recent *Newsweek* cover featured a big, bold word: "Exhausted." The inside story, titled "Breaking Point," paints a picture of a frazzled America—stressed as never before. Why? Because "we have cell phones in the car and beepers in our pockets, and we carry them to Disneyland, to the beach, to the bathroom."[2] We think the world will fall apart if we don't respond *right now.* When everything becomes an emergency that only we can fix, life quickly lurches out of control.

Facing an emergency, the human body revs up, ready for the challenge: increased heart rate, constricted muscles and arteries, pumped adrenaline. That ready-to-fight stance may serve us well to ward off physical attack, but "it's horribly suited to the unremitting pressures of modern life."[3] Extreme thoughts hurt us physically and psychologically; we too often turn daily challenges into "dog attacks."

Even the threat of a real dog attack can prompt unnecessarily wild thoughts, such as *This is it. I'm dead.* I know. I've been there. Years ago I was at a speaking engagement in Florida and scheduled to stay in a private home. On my very first evening there, well after dark, I was dropped off at my host's home, and my ride drove away. Then I discovered I was locked out of the house. No key. No one at home. I knew I was at the right house. I knew I was expected. What to do?

I walked over to the front window to see if it would open. No. It was locked. I thought I'd try a back door. As I fumbled my way to the back, I saw that the yard was surrounded by a substantial iron fence. I tried to open the gate. Yes. Success.

I entered, closed the gate, made my way up the back walk, and met my worst nightmare—a *huge* dog. Our eyes met, and he immediately saw the fear in mine. Sensing his victory, he bolted toward me with what seemed to be incredible speed. I knew I was a dead man. The adrenaline kicked in. I was ready to fight him off with nothing but my bare hands and maybe my teeth—though I knew his would win.

He sped over to me, put on his brakes, and slid down the walk until he was right on top of my shoes. Then he instinctively did what he was trained to do: He started licking my feet!

I leaned over, petted him, and said, "Nice doggy . . . that's a good doggy!" Meanwhile, my heart was beating so hard, it felt as if my whole body were that one pumping organ!

Anyone would have extreme thoughts with a huge dog racing toward him. I tell the story to illustrate a larger point: that in real life, most of our trials are something like that "dog attack"; the perceived threat or even the perceived damage doesn't match the reality of the actual damage.

Even when the damage is real (even if I had been mauled by the dog), that trial still leads to the creation of one or more pearls—there for the finding.

Several years ago, a guy named Tom went through the most agonizing trial of his lifetime. With no recognized warning, one day his wife left him. She meant business; the separation quickly led to a divorce.

In Tom's own words, it wasn't like a "sand storm," it was more like a "sand *hurricane*." He had always wanted a happy marriage, and he had no clue as to why his wife had aborted their relationship. The accompanying tailspin is not uncommon in such situations. Tom was hopelessly depressed. He questioned why he should even go on living.

But Tom gradually regained a proper focus on life; his extreme thinking at the time his wife left him proved faulty. He realized that his life was not utterly destroyed, and he felt a growing desire to help others facing a trauma similar to his.

So Tom went back to school, eventually completing his Ph.D. He gained extensive counseling experience. In time he started a national organization, Fresh Start, which specializes in helping people through the trauma of an unwanted marital breakup.[4] He told me, "As I look back, my divorce has turned out to be the greatest and most rewarding experience of my life."

During his crisis Tom thought nothing could ever match the pain he felt. But that pain was redeemed. Tom's life-career opened up as a result of his own pain. Tom has remarried, and the relationship he has with his new wife and children is better than he had imagined possible.

As I've grown older I've conditioned myself to avoid extreme "panic" thinking. If we can slowly reverse our thinking from "all that we're losing" in any trial to "all that we will eventually gain," we'll become much more positive and not so easily shaken by negative circumstances. Just think how much easier you'll be to live with once you grasp this principle. Your mate or friends might throw a party in celebration! You might throw your own love-for-life party.

Reminder: Allow Yourself to Grieve the Pain

Even though I urge people to keep an optimistic outlook when confronted by a negative experience, it's still important to allow yourself to figure out what took place, analyze how it makes you feel, and feel the pain associated with the event. If you don't use this last key, you can stuff the feelings so deep within yourself that you think you've solved the problem—when actually you're simply denying the problem.

Remember that "counting pearls" is the fifth step in releasing unresolved anger, one step in a larger process that involves working through grief and accepting the reality of one's trial and one's loss. There are exceptions, but generally we are able to find pearls not before but during and especially following our grief.

How to Find Priceless Pearls in Every Trial

Now we get to the specifics of how to find those pearls in the "sand storms" of our lives. Remember, these steps are not something we use just for a short time after a trial; we continue doing them until our thinking actually changes and we realize the positive results—until we find the pearls that exist in every trial. You will have victory over your pain only when you feel and see the benefits to you. What do I mean by benefits? More connection with others, yourself, your God, and an underlying heart-happiness. New opportunities. Keep reading to identify more pearly gems.

Counting pearls is transforming bitter into better. When you're bitter, you're angry and feel low self-worth. When you're better, you feel grateful and enjoy an elevated sense of self-value and happiness.

Five Practical Steps in Pearl-Counting

To get a handle on the basics of the pearl-counting process, take out a sheet of paper and pencil and get ready to draw yourself a "pearl chart." This entire chart is positive. It may not seem like it at first because the chart will include a list of trials, or crises. But when you've finished filling out the chart, you'll see how your crises have brought you numerous benefits. The benefits aren't simply vague character traits; you'll find specific pearls that fit into every area of life.

With the long edges of the paper as the top and bottom, divide the page into five columns from top to bottom. Each step in pearl-counting will have its own column. Or you might use five separate sheets of paper, one sheet for each column described below. Give a title to each of the five columns:

Column 1: My Lifelong Strengths

Column 2: My Most Painful Trials

Column 3: My Support People

Column 4: My Pearls from Each Trial

Column 5: My Loving Action Because of Each Trial

Now let's discuss what each column is about.

1. My Lifelong Strengths

In the first column, list your strengths—what you're grateful for in yourself and in life in general. To think of things to include in this column, it might help if you finish this sentence: I'm glad I'm alive because . . .

Naming your strengths might be an easy assignment for you, but it's a hard challenge for some people. Self-appreciation is not an unhealthy, narcissistic indulgence but a healthy exercise in personal value. It's a realistic look at yourself.

What do you like about yourself? This is not the time to be overly humble. What we're looking for is an accurate view of the positive things about you and what you truly appreciate about who you are. What types of activities do you do well? How are your people skills? Hobbies? What do you bring to relationships that others appreciate? If you can't think of several strengths about yourself, ask your mate or friends—and read on. It gets better!

2. My Most Painful Trials

Write down the most painful trials you've been through. Think back over your whole life history, and list your personal "sand storms." Include ones that have lowered your sense of self-value or caused you shame or guilt.

It may be too hurtful to list some, but I encourage you to list any—and all—in the future as you're able. If the listing process does become unbearable, focus in on two or three trials and deal with the others at another time.

I have searched for every pearl in each major "storm" of my entire life. Because of that, I can honestly say there is nothing that remains negative about me in my mind. Don't misunderstand me; I don't see myself as even close to perfect, and others may still see negative things about me, but I've done my best to turn everything around to a positive inside my own heart. I get to spend every day bathing in a pool of value about what has happened to me. It's like soaking in "pearl water."

The negatives in my life started early. Let me name one particular negative I've come to see as a positive—a poor academic record and a resulting poor self-image. My parents didn't place a high premium on academics. Neither one of them had gone far in school. And their lack of interest had a discouraging effect on my life. Besides that, we moved often. I'd change schools every year, sometimes twice a year. In first and second grade I was in California, where they were experimenting with some new educational philosophy that didn't last long. It was one of those "the-child-will-learn-when-he's-ready" approaches that didn't suit me well. Apparently I wasn't ready to learn, because by third grade I was far behind my peers.

Further complicating the issue was a move to Washington State. By the time I got to the end of third grade, my parents were told things like, "We'd really like to see Gary be a leader in school," and, "We want to see Gary mature around the others." The translation was clear: *I had flunked third grade.*

To this day, my kids tease me mercilessly over this issue. "Dad, how could you flunk third grade?" they'll ask. Then we all laugh together.

Truthfully, I was deeply embarrassed for many years about having failed a grade. It was a secret I tried to keep as private as possible. Once I completed this pearl-counting exercise, however, I was able to turn it all around. You'll see how this occurs as you read on.

Before you leave this category, you may want to number your trials in the order of their severity. Give the worst pain you endured a number one, the next-worst a number two, and so on.

3. My Support People

In this column, list the people you can turn to for support in helping you pearl-hunt, people who have helped you through some of your more serious trials. I would imagine your spouse would be on top of the list if it's a recent trial. Others would be folks like your parents, a professional counselor, a minister, a friend, or your extended family. In the midst of a trial, it's also possible to pray for God's wisdom and understanding. Maybe God is on your list.

Tremendous support may be nearby, and that support can help you as you move to column 4.

4. My Pearls from Each Trial

Next list all the benefits you can identify from each trial. Here is the very heart and life of finding your own pearls. These pearls are more valuable than the earthly pearls one strings for a necklace; they are so treasured you can encase them on your heart's trophy shelf.

In column 4, start listing the positive aspects of each painful encounter in your life. Besides your own answers, it would be valuable to ask for the input of those who know you and love you—the support team you identified in column 3. They can often add a perspective to your suffering that you may have overlooked.

Also refer back to column 1 and the personal strengths you identified. Have any of those strengths come as a result of particular trials? That column identifies strengths you've gathered—from where? Often from what you've learned by trial and error—in every sense of the phrase.

The next few true stories will give you more specific examples of how a trial can be turned into precious pearls.

Pearls from Flunking. For years I saw nothing positive about my poor academic record. Flunking third grade and being a poor reader and speller were completely negative for me. But I now see positives in my entire educational development. One such benefit is this very book you're reading. Can you imagine how amazed all my elementary-school teachers would be if they knew I've written twelve books? And for reasons beyond my understanding, some of the books have actually won awards! How can this be?

Most of the reason goes back to my being a poor reader. In those years learning disability tests weren't given. But if they had been, I wouldn't be surprised if I had been placed in that category. Since I know the struggle of a poor reader, I realize a book must possess a certain excitement about it that will keep the reader's attention, and I strive to add enthusiasm and excitement to everything I do. My goal is also to make a book as understandable as possible. And I appreciate the concept of "salt," that special "thirst creator" in a book that makes me want to keep on reading.

I work hard at achieving these things in my books. It's not uncommon for me to go through twenty or more rewrites of each chapter to reach that ideal blend of content, excitement, and salt. I'm still not the greatest reader. So if a chapter doesn't interest me or force me on, I redo it until it does. I'm very grateful today that I had that weak childhood training—not that this is license for anyone to do poorly in school, but if life deals you a painful "piece of sand," turn it into a pearl and use it in a way that can benefit you and others.

Throughout this whole chapter I've talked about turning sand into pearls. Consider this equally interesting fact: "The silicon in a computer chip comes from ordinary sand. Yes, sand. What makes the chip so fantastically complex is the amount of human engineering and design that goes into it."[5] When your life is a desert, think again! Consider the possibilities!

Pearls from a Heart Attack. Remember it is always possible to find treasure in physical trauma. One person who learned that lesson was George, a typical hard-driving executive. He looked ten years younger than his age, forty-five. Great job, great family life. It was a classic case of "George is the last guy I thought would have a heart attack!"

But that's exactly what happened.

On a Tuesday afternoon, in the middle of an upper-management strategy session, George complained of chest pains and then collapsed onto the boardroom table. As he was rushed to the hospital by the paramedics, George just kept repeating his wife's name: "Barb, Barb, Barb." And Barb was at the hospital waiting when George arrived.

He was wheeled directly into the operating room from the emergency vehicle. After hours that seemed like days, the surgeon appeared at the waiting-room door to assure Barb that George was going to be all right. "But he must take it slow," the doctor warned.

Barb took it upon herself to ensure that George experienced a full recovery. She helped him with his slow and steady climb back to a normal life. George can barely get through recounting this time in his life without choking up. "Barb was the most amazing helper I had ever seen," he says. "For all the years we were married, I had prided myself on a healthy physique—so much so that I secretly doubted if Barb would even be interested in me if I let myself go—or worse yet, got sick."

George continues, "But it was through this horrible trial that I saw a side of Barb that had been hidden in the twenty-one years we had been married. I was treated to a glimpse of a woman who loved me unconditionally. Her love wasn't dependent on my good looks, firm physique, or good health. She just loves me . . . no matter what. I wouldn't wish a heart attack on anybody, but I do have to say it has been the greatest aid in strengthening our marriage. I now see life so differently. I've slowed down; I smell the roses. I can honestly say I'm glad it happened to me." That's a glimpse of finding very precious pearls as a result of a life-threatening sickness.

Pearls from Depression. Fran is another good example of searching for her own treasures to turn bitter into better. Here is her story in her own words:

"After being married for a while, my husband and I experienced three years of marital upheaval. During this time I stuffed issues down inside, becoming rageful. I cried often. I was sick for a solid ten months, until I 'crashed' emotionally and physically. My word for it was I 'died.' I remember how my body parts felt disconnected from me, and I felt like I was removed from my body. My voice didn't even sound like it was coming from me. I felt like I had been stripped down to the core of me—like a straw house falling down to its tiny foundation."

When Fran was struggling in the depths of this "disconnected" misery, she attended one of my seminars and became acquainted with pearl-counting. As she thought about her bouts with deep depression, she began to see things in a different light.

"Depression is a gift," Fran concluded. "I didn't see it at the time, but depression is your body's way of saying, 'Slow down—no more stuffing anger. Be reflective; take a look at how you take care of yourself.'"

Fran excitedly searched for her pearls. Through this process, she started to see for the first time that every area of her life could bring her something good.

In her family, Fran's depression became like smelling salts, waking her husband to her needs. He hadn't noticed that his busy schedule didn't allow any time for her and the kids. Now Fran can't believe how good their relationship is: a pearl from a problem.

Counting Your Pearls. If any of these stories inspires you, take your time listing the benefits that have come as a result of your trials. We usually don't see them all at once; you may have a trainload of pearls waiting to be discovered one carful at a time. The following is a partial list of great qualities of love or benefits to you in general that have been created, enriched, or increased as a result of your painful trials.

You are:

- Patient
- Kind
- Tender
- Forgiving
- Appreciative; praising others more
- Empathetic—feeling the pain of others and caring about them more
- Enjoying the simpler things in life
- Persevering
- Hopeful
- Calm about life in general; relaxed
- Aware that you can live through most trials
- Interested in enriching the lives of others before yourself
- Thoughtful
- Serious about life
- Developing a deeper spiritual life
- In touch with your feelings and the feelings of others
- Careful about what you say because it might hurt another
- Responsible at work

You are much less:

- Fearful
- Jealous or envious
- Arrogant
- Humorous at the expense of others

Let me recommend another resource—a wealth of immediate encouragement whenever you go through "valleys." A hilarious comedian, Andy Andrews, has put together two volumes of letters from famous people telling how trials have bolstered them toward success and happiness.[6] Check it out.

5. My Loving Action Because of Each Trial

In the last column, list ways you can turn pearls into loving action. When major disasters strike, priorities have a way of realigning; in the midst of crises, most people first search for their family members, not their belongings. Suffering has a way of bringing people together; the most important things on earth come into sharper focus. This increased interest in being with and helping others during a crisis is a demonstration of love.

The key to this final column in your chart is understanding how love works. It's as simple as this: We use love or we lose it. We take hold of a new appreciation for "connections," reorganized priorities, and new sensitivities we've gained in hard times, and we share with others the new joy that results from that connectedness—or we lose the joy.

One couple, David and Linda, were attending one of my seminars and realized how they needed to find any value they could in a devastating loss. Five years earlier, their precious daughter, Sara, had died just two hours after birth. David and Linda both lived the following years carrying anger, resentment, and frustration.

After allowing themselves time to feel the pain of their grief—their loss—they gained enough strength to start their own hunt for any good that could come from this tragedy. And what did they discover? David and Linda now realize how they appreciate the little things in life that they once had taken for granted. But Linda found a more specific way to use her search for pearls to help someone else.

She writes, "A friend of mine lost her brother and sister-in-law in a tragic auto accident. As a result, three young girls were left as orphans. But over the last three and a half months, I've been able to talk to this friend. When she expresses hurt, frustration, and agony, I can say, 'I know what you're feeling,' and really mean it!"

Linda goes on to say, "I actually thank God that I had Sara for the short time I did, because I learned so much from her death. I'm so much more alert to the suffering of others. I can be an understanding companion to my friend and her family, and I look forward to helping more because of my experience. When I'm with those three girls, they know that I not only love them but also that I deeply understand their loss as well. I can tell they know I understand and care. Through searching for treasure, I feel my daughter's death has finally given me a purpose. I still miss her a great deal, but I can now help others like I never dreamed I would. And helping them has been so rewarding."

In the previous chapter I told the story of another Linda, a young woman whose father had abused her. Linda's journey was long, but eventually she was able to identify and claim several pearls as a result of her childhood trauma. Again, what the father did was reprehensible, massively unloving. And what happened was beyond Linda's control; it was not her fault. But now, years later, Linda has chosen to walk toward forgiveness and to search for some good that might have been given her by her father.

And she has succeeded. She has seen how extremely sensitive she has become to the hurts and pain of others. She is a very caring, kind person. I helped her see that the greatest gift in life is genuine love. At twenty years of age, she could see that she had been given several key ingredients to genuine love: sensitivity, compassion, empathy, a deep desire to care for others who suffer, and a keen ability to pick up on signs of abuse in other young women. These are all characteristics that make for an effective counselor—and they are priceless pearls gathered from a situation that could have ruined her life had she chosen to let it. Instead she chose to respond by finding pearls and then turning them into loving action and reaching out to others, including her own husband and young child. Her faith in God has greatly increased, and she sees finding the very special man she married as a precious pearl.

Perhaps you are one who has endured the most horrible trial imaginable. You've been put through so much, you feel there can't possibly be any kind of treasure in your circumstances. Pain has been a way of life for you.

But pearl-counting can help! I urge you to give it a try. Imagine yourself as a caterpillar. Your cocoon of pain totally envelops you. You want to be free, but you're afraid. Do you know the secret of a butterfly's breaking free of its cocoon? The very struggle of working to get free from the cocoon is what strengthens the wings to allow it to fly. Imagine the beautiful butterfly that emerges as a butterfly of love. You can emerge as a new person—and the process starts as you take one knock at the enclosing wall, as you take one step toward working through your anger and searching for the positive.[7]

I know of nothing more helpful to those who suffer than to at least begin the slow process of breaking through the cocoon of anger and the feeling of being cheated in life. The crisis of breaking out is the opportunity of a lifetime!

Now Return to Column 1

After you've filled out all five columns of your pearl chart, go back and look again at column 1. Can you now identify new "personal strengths" that you see as a result of your tragedies-turned-to-triumphs? Yes? Then go back and add another pearl to your list: *Increased sense of my own capabilities.*

Actually, with every trial, you can walk up one full flight of a staircase that has five clearly marked "landings," as shown in the illustration below.

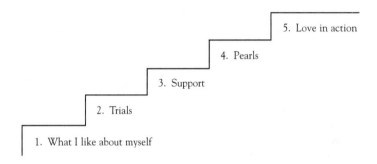

At each landing, you've increased your capacity for loving life and others.

I've never found an exception to this principle for myself or for anyone I've tried to help. There are pearls in every trial. The bigger the trial, the greater the potential for making your love last forever! And for anyone who truly desires to keep his or her love alive, the next chapter exposes another "iceberg" that can sink your love if you're not careful.

Forever-Love Principles

Our list of forever-love principles continues from the previous chapter:

18. Every painful trial is like an oyster, and there is a precious pearl— a personal benefit—in every one. Every single one.

19. Forever-love digs up the pearl buried within every trial.

20. Forever-love avoids extreme thoughts.

21. Forever-love assumes that things will get better, not worse.

22. Forever-love gives a wound time to heal.

23. Forever-love reaches out to share the joy of life.

24. Forever-love: Use it or lose it.

5

How to Balance Expectations and Reality

If we could first know where we were and whither we were tending, we could better judge what to do and how to do it.

—Abraham Lincoln

Taking responsibility for how you respond to circumstances and keeping your anger levels low—these are major leaps toward a life of love. And choosing to find pearls in all your past failures and difficulties helps you keep your head above water. Now I want to show you how you can prevent the loss of valuable, vital strength you'll need for loving life and for loving your spouse.

The insights in this chapter are based on this foundational insight: *The wider the gap between what we expect and the reality of what we experience, the greater the potential for discouragement and fatigue.* The gap between expectations and reality is like a drain through which we lose the *joie de vivre*—the joy or love of life.[1]

When you hit a crisis situation—when reality opens a trapdoor—don't let your energy drain away. Here's how you can minimize the trauma of any future crisis you face—and crises are inevitable. Some are predictable; they're called life-cycle crises. Some are beneficial. All can be redeemable. But . . . there are specific ways you can protect yourself. As you run with me through the next story, you'll see a truth about life in general, and you may begin to see there is something you can do to prevent energy loss. (Special thanks to Dr. Dan Trathen for his insights and help in this chapter.)

Creeping Sun and Slithering Snakes

When I was about twelve years old, I got the scare of my life. It was the worst thing that ever happened to me. In fact, I'm amazed that I'm alive today to tell this story.

My family was living in the state of Washington, out in the country. One fall day I was outside playing with my best friend. Having great fun, we weren't paying much attention to the clock. As the sun crept toward the horizon, we suddenly realized it was time to be heading home. So, like the two adventurous boys we were, we decided to take a shortcut through a wooded area.

We had no path to follow, but that didn't bother us. We were just running along, the wind whistling past our ears. And then, all of a sudden, we heard this deafening and horrifying rattling sound very close by. We stopped, froze, and listened. The sound was all around us, and it seemed to be coming from everywhere at once.

We looked at the ground. It was moving. We were in the middle of a field of rattlesnakes! Hundreds of them, in all sizes. And they were striking out blindly in all directions.

My friend and I knew we didn't have long to live.

Fortunately, we had the presence of mind to jump up on a snake-free log that was well above the ground. We yelled for help at the top of our lungs, but we were too deep into the woods for anyone to hear.

"What are we going to do?" my friend shouted.

"I don't know," I answered, "but we've got to do something soon because it's getting dark!" *Will the snakes crawl up onto our log?* I wondered.

Then one of us got the idea of breaking long branches off the log and using them as extended arms or "swords" to flip the writhing, rattling creatures out of our way as we cleared a path to make our escape. And that's what we did. One snake at a time—what seemed like one inch at a time—crying all the way, we made a path to the edge of that sea of snakes. The slightest slip or fall would have landed us on top of a half-dozen of them, but we kept moving.

We only had about thirty feet to cover to get into the clear, but it seemed to take forever. When we finally left the last snake behind, we were trembling and exhausted. But we gathered our remaining strength and ran home as fast as we could to report our own near-death experience.

I'd like to use this childhood crisis to symbolize all of life's crises and how we can reduce the energy loss and shorten the duration of the trauma they cause.

Disaster Protection

Whenever a crisis strikes, we can be just like two boys running along near the safety of home and suddenly finding themselves in the middle of a field of deadly snakes—smack in the midst of a seriously unpleasant, potentially disastrous, situation.

As you can imagine, my friend and I weren't prepared to deal with rattlesnakes that day so many years ago. We were just wearing sneakers, jeans, and T-shirts—easy for a snake to bite through—and we had no weapons except our sticks. But suppose things had been a little different. Suppose that instead of wearing low-cut sneakers, we had been prepared for the reality we faced; suppose we had been wearing hip-high boots made of multiple layers of strong, thick leather—so strong that a snake's fangs would break off before they could penetrate to the skin underneath.

If I had been wearing such a pair of boots and knew they would protect me, my whole attitude toward the scene would have been different. Instead of being terrified, thinking I would die at any moment, I would have walked right into that mass of snakes with confidence! I would have simply kicked them out of my path as I made my way to the other side of the field. "Go ahead, take your best bite, make my day!" I would have challenged them boldly. And the protective boots would have kept me safe.

What kind of "hip boots" can we wear to protect us in all of life's crises? What can shield us from the harmful effects of such situations? *We "put on a thick pair of hip boots" by maintaining balance in our life.* To switch metaphors and use a common cliché: If we've put all our eggs in one basket and that basket falls to the ground, our life expectations are dashed. But if we carry several baskets, each holding a different life interest, and then drop one, causing disappointment in one area of life, we are able to maintain strength, hope, and joy because we're still holding several baskets. Let me explain.

When the "Big One" Hits You

Here's an illustration of what can happen when the "hip boots of balance" aren't worn: Two years ago Gene's life fell apart. His small business went bankrupt. The business was most of his identity. He'd given it so much time and attention that his wife and children were "distant" housemates, providing little support in his despair. Gene's friends—business-related contacts—also scattered like frightened birds when he filed his court papers. Nonwork friends? He had none. And where was God? It had been a long time since Gene had paid any attention to faith.

With no intimate friends, distance at home, no spiritual center, and then the loss of his career, Gene felt overwhelmed. Nowhere. Hopeless. At age forty-two, Gene took his own life. A two-word note was found by his body. His message to the world: I failed. Maybe Gene's basic failure was that he had neglected to develop any "life support" outside his business.

Let me contrast that with another story. Granted, this is not as drastic as a foreclosure and a suicide; nevertheless it was a severe career crisis for a young man—my son Greg.

As each of our children formed a career path, we began to share a dream that someday we could all work together, maybe speaking on the same platform.

Not long ago Greg felt he was finally ready to make part of our dream come true. He was prepared to stand in front of a large audience and teach some of the principles I regularly present in seminars. As you can imagine, I was thrilled.

I invited Greg to join me and speak at an upcoming seminar. As I said, Greg was ready—but nervous and apprehensive. He spent hours getting ready for his talk. As the day approached he was losing sleep and feeling nauseous because of performance anxiety.

The big moment soon came for Greg to get up and address the audience. For me—proud papa—it was a magical experience, one I'll never forget. My years of fatherly dreaming were about to be rewarded. As I introduced him to the group, I had to stop for just a second to wipe my misty eyes.

Greg stood, approached the podium to warm applause, and turned to address the audience. He started off very relaxed, saying what a delight it was to share the platform with his dad. Then he added, "It's always good to be with him at times like these when he's sober." After the laughter died down, he added quickly, "Just kidding. He's a teetotaler." Now the crowd was with him. Sitting down in the front row, I thought, *With a start like this, it's going to be awesome!*

Then, halfway through his presentation, Greg experienced a major crisis. He went blank. Right there, standing all alone in front of two thousand people, with every eye in the room on him, he forgot what he was supposed to say next. His dilemma was instantly and painfully obvious to everyone.

Greg did the only thing he could, referring back to his podium notes. But since he had memorized his talk and hadn't been following along in the printed outline, he couldn't find his place. His notes were useless.

To make matters worse, I could see he was starting to lose his saliva as he tried to stumble ahead—an understandable case of extreme nervousness. But a dry mouth is death to a speaker. I saw him deflate and lose steam as all the energy seemed to drain from his body and spirit. I'm sure he was thinking, *I'm bombing! I'm going down in flames!*

Watching any speaker struggle that way is hard. As a speaker myself, I would naturally empathize. But this was my son. I was rooting for him, praying for him, and a part of me wished I could run up and rescue him somehow. I knew I couldn't, though. He had to learn to get through the crisis on his own.

Mercifully, Greg's memory finally kicked in, and he resumed his talk. All seemed well . . .

Until he went blank again . . .

And again a third time just a few minutes later.

Fortunately, the audience was behind him 100 percent. The people stayed with him, listened attentively, and pulled for him every time he went blank. He managed to finish his talk, and everyone was happy and relieved—except Greg, of course.

He came up to me afterward as I was chatting with some friends and apologized profusely. Then he pulled me aside and whispered, "Dad, can you give me any helpful advice?"

I looked into his eyes and told him soberly, "Son, remember this: It's always the darkest . . . just before it goes totally black!"

As we laughed together, Greg shot back, "Thanks a lot for your encouragement, Dad!"

I tell that story because it illustrates so well the core message I want to get across in this chapter. For just as Greg found himself in a crisis that drained away much of his energy, so any of us can experience a crisis at any time. If the crisis occurs in one of the most important areas of our life, such as our job, marriage, children, friends, or our spiritual side, we can suffer massive loss of emotional and mental energy. But Greg was already doing something that allowed him to recover quickly from his crisis and regain his strength and the ability to move forward.

Fortunately, there's a way to overcome a crisis and regain equilibrium quickly. It worked for Greg, and it can work for you. Let me explain. Greg experienced a crisis in the career area of his life. For the moment, the failure drained him, frustrated him, caused him pain, and dragged him down. But in four other major areas of his life, he was doing well. As a husband, his marriage was solid and fulfilling. As a father, he had a great relationship with his child. Spiritually, he felt he was on good terms with God. As a friend, he had several buddies who would stand by him no matter what.

Because these other important areas of his life were doing well, they balanced out this crisis in his career. In other words, in the other four "baskets" of life, reality was relatively close to expectations. Remember, the narrower the gap between what we expect and what is actually happening, the more strength we maintain. For Greg, four life areas buoyed his spirits and provided an added reserve of energy that helped him get through his crisis. Not long after suffering probably the greatest embarrassment of his life, he was optimistic again and looking forward to his next chance to speak in public.

How can you protect yourself from a massive loss of energy? The rest of this chapter offers protection and more—tips on how you can replenish your energy.

Three Ways to Balance Your Life

Middle-aged men especially need to understand the importance of balance in life. Imbalance is a major cause of midlife crisis; when career expectations aren't realized, too many people lose vision and hope for the future.

1. Identify Life Priorities

Imagine your life as a large, lush vegetable garden. (I know this may sound strange at first, but trust me—the word picture will help you better understand these concepts that have been of tremendous benefit to me and thousands of others.) Each type of vegetable represents one part of your life. For instance, the carrots are your relationship with your mate. The cucumbers are your role as a parent to your children. The lettuce is your career, whatever that may be. The green beans are the members of your extended family. The tomatoes are your friendships. Then add on your hobbies, your volunteer work, your homeowner responsibilities . . . and your spiritual life seems like sunlight and water.

Now, what I'm about to say may seem so obvious that you're tempted to skip to the next subhead, but stay with me. Far too many of us understand this intellectually but act oblivious to the obvious: *You won't have a very satisfying garden unless you plant several different vegetables.* And once you plant them, you need to nurture them carefully if you're eventually going to enjoy their taste. If you overwater or overfertilize some parts and neglect others altogether, the result can be one sick garden.

I've discovered that we usually need at least five healthy "vegetables" to keep up our vigor and love for life, even in the face of crises.

To help you find the five most important parts of your own garden, take a few minutes right now to think about the main parts of your life. How would you complete this sentence? I am a _____ . Come up with your five top responses. As I ask people to do this all over the country, the most common answers include:

I am a spouse.

I am a parent.

I am a friend.

I am a spiritual person.

I am a son or daughter.

I am a [name of vocation.]

I am a [name of avocation.]

I am a man or woman [a physical being.]

Some of those are my own answers, and they may be yours as well. Whatever your five "I ams" are, write them down:

I am a:

1. _____

2. _____

3. _____

4. _____

5. _____

Now look over your list and prioritize your five key areas. Which is most important, second in importance, and so on?

Why have I asked you to identify five top areas, not just one or two? It's a principle called *diversification*. A wise investor spreads his or her money—diversifies—over a number of different investments. That way, if any one or two of them is in the pits, the overall results can be helped by those that are doing better. If the investor held only one investment, on the other hand, and it took a nosedive, he could be wiped out.

You may have heard or read about the great famine in Ireland in the 1800s. More than one million people starved to death. Why? It had to do with the lack of diversification. Because of the climate and the soil conditions, potato farming flourished, and the peasant population thrived on a diet of potatoes—and not much else. When a fungus wiped out year after year of the sustaining crop, a small country starved.

Similarly (and unfortunately), some of us leave ourselves vulnerable in our personal lives by failing to diversify our interests. When one part of our lives is "hit by a fungus," we are susceptible to emotional starvation.

If we focus most of our energy and effort on just one or two areas of life—our careers and a hobby, for example—and something goes wrong there, we can be dumped emotionally, spiritually, and physically. But if we have five priority areas and a problem develops in one or two of them—like giving a speech that goes poorly and wondering if we'll ever be invited to do it again—our health in the other areas can lift our spirits and restore our energy.

If you're completely wrapped up in one aspect of your life and that area crumbles, you can feel as low as Gene, the small-business owner who committed suicide. How sad to think of all the men and women who can identify with his depression brought on by a career crisis! If you relate to his dilemma at all, it's time to diversify, to give some attention to the other key areas of your life.

Why do I suggest you list *only* five key areas? While life offers many good things, I've discovered there are only a few best, most important things. Those are the vegetables that both deserve and require my most careful attention.

The necessity of focusing on our top priorities can be illustrated visually. (I've actually done this demonstration before seminar audiences.) Take two large jars of the same size. One is filled almost to the top with uncooked rice. Each grain of rice represents one of the many good things we could make a part of our lives. The other jar is filled almost to the top with whole walnuts still in the shell. There are a lot fewer of them, and they represent the top-priority areas of our lives.

If you try to pour the walnuts into the jar that's already nearly full of rice, you'll manage to get in only a few nuts. However—and this looks almost like a magic trick—if you pour the rice into the jar that's virtually full of walnuts, all the rice will fit! Before your very eyes, the rice will fill in the many spaces under, around, and on top of the walnuts.

Here's the point: If we fill our lives and give the majority of our time and energy to *countless* good and worthy things (the rice), we won't have much room left for what is truly important. But if we devote ourselves first to those things that deserve top priority (the walnuts), we'll find we're able to enjoy the many other good things as well. They come as bonus energy-boosters.

2. Compare Expectations against Reality

For example, if the "cucumbers" that represent your relationships with your children could speak, what would they say? Would they tell you, "Hey, you're doing a great job here! We really appreciate all the careful attention"? Or would they say, "Hey, we're dying over here! You haven't watered us in days"?

You've named five key areas of your life—ways you identify yourself. By virtue of identifying these "I ams" as your top priorities, you've admitted that these parts of your garden are important to you. And if they're important to you, they are areas in which you want to do well. They encompass your high hopes. Those great expectations of life provide the happiest moments of our lives. But they also lead to our greatest disappointments—when expectations don't jibe with reality. And that gulf between expectations and reality means crisis.

Think about my son Greg's disastrous first speech. Why was it a crisis? Because his career goals—counseling and public speaking—are very important to him. He wants to do well long-term, and he expected to do well the first time out. After all, he had trained hard to be a good speaker, he had worked hard to develop a good talk, and then he had worked even harder to memorize what he was going to say. Everything was looking positive for an incredible first speaking engagement.

Then he ran into a brick wall called reality.

What Greg actually experienced was far different from—far worse than—what he had expected. As we already mentioned: The wider the gap between what we expect and the reality of what we experience in any important area of our lives, the greater the potential for discouragement and fatigue.

What is the second step in keeping your emotional and mental energy high, in surviving life's crises? Slow down and give your life a reality check. How do your expectations compare to your life's realities? What is the condition of your garden? How is each part doing? The effective gardener has to inspect all areas of his or her garden almost daily.

Another helpful way to picture this is to imagine that each of those top five areas of your life has its own thermostat. You might set the temperature at a comfortable seventy-two degrees in, say, the area of your marriage. In other words, you develop a set of nice, comfortable, satisfying expectations. Everything seems to go fine for a while. Before long, however, you start to notice that your home isn't as warm as you had expected. In fact, it's downright cold, and you reach for a sweater.

What's the problem? You're racing through each busy day without taking time to check the thermometer on the wall. And the fact is that the reality of your marriage isn't meeting your present expectations. Remembering where you set the thermostat isn't enough. You also need to look at the thermometer to see the actual temperature, which may be down around sixty degrees. The gap between the temperature you expect and the real temperature is a crisis that will drain energy from you every day. And that loss of strength will go on day after day as long as you're unaware of the problem.

There's a theory that helps explain this predicament and our need to check the temperature. It says that the human brain is always trying—always working—to close the gap between expectation and reality.[2] To match up the two, the brain labors feverishly to somehow reconcile them. If this theory is true, then it's obvious that the further our reality is from our expectations, the harder the brain has to work to try to bring them together, and the greater the energy drain. And in a crisis, when expectations and reality are very different, you can actually watch the strength drain out of a person.

Part of the process of checking reality against expectations may send you back to look at the way you've prioritized the parts of your life. Is your home life causing you stress—because you're spending too much time at the office and therefore distancing yourself from your spouse or children? If so, look at your priorities. When it comes down to the wire, is your job more important than your family?

Years ago I was forced to check my priorities—comparing expectations with reality. Like a lot of other people, I had gotten caught up in my career. Through church-related service work, I was "doing good"—helping others. I could point with pride to how well I was providing for my family. Fine. Great. Just one problem: In the process I was neglecting the emotional and relational needs of my wife and children, who should have held a much higher priority than my job. (If you'd asked me, I would have said they were my first priority. I would have said I wanted to be a good husband and father. But in reality? Well . . .)

I was finally forced to deal with the situation when our son Michael was born. Besides the extra work that's inevitable when another child comes along, Michael provided added stress because he was born with severe, even life-threatening medical problems.

Now, who do you suppose was suffering the greatest loss of energy during this period? That's right, my wife, Norma. She reasonably expected her husband to be at her side, offering emotional support and also extra help with the older kids while she cared for Michael. But I was still back at the office, absorbed in my job, imposing a reality far different from what she expected and needed.

This problem went on for some time, but gradually I became aware of what was happening and how my focus was almost exclusively on my work. Then I determined that I had to back off from my work somewhat and give more time and energy to my family. I had to find a better balance in the top areas of my life. And, with some effort, that's what I did.

Mind you, it's not that I started to improve my balance because I was some maturing husband or father who wisely assessed the situation and automatically made the necessary changes. Instead, Norma quietly confronted me one day and stated that either I helped her or she would have a complete nervous breakdown. In my line of work, that wouldn't have been good for business!

To this day, I'll say to Michael—who is now a healthy adult—"You brought me back to our family." Much to my surprise, I also found that I could still be effective in my work even while I made my loved ones a higher priority. In some ways, rearranging my priorities made me even more effective on the job.

I could give you example after example from my own experience of the need to check your expectations against reality. Another that stands out in my mind is the physical area of my life. My expectations are that I'm a trim, healthy fifty-something man with a long life ahead of me. Now for a little reality: As I said in a previous chapter, the men in the Smalley family have a tendency to develop heart trouble. A little more reality: A few years back a donut would have been the best symbol to represent my body.

You get the picture. So did I. At a periodic checkup I noticed that picture of the *Titanic* I mentioned at the beginning of the book. And that's when the doctor graphically warned me about the dangers of ignoring warning signals.

He had me right where he wanted me. I had been warned before to change my diet and exercise more, to get my cholesterol under control. I had been taking some pills and exercising almost every day, but considering the results of the tests and the shape of my body, that obviously wasn't working. How many warnings would I need before I made lasting, healthy changes? I wanted to be as strong as possible physically and to live a long life. Fortunately, this time he got my attention and made me slow down and look carefully at this part of my life. I doubled the medication and became more faithful in my exercise and eating habits. I've been doing this with the support of some close friends; I need the support and accountability of a "team" working with me.

When I compared my thermostat to the thermometer in my physical life, I saw they were far apart. And that, in turn, led me to the third step we all need to take to get and keep our gardens healthy, our lives in balance, and our energy high.

3. Align Your Expectations with Reality

There's a saying that if you keep doing the things you've been doing, you can expect to keep getting the same results you've been getting. I needed to relearn that lesson in my physical life. I couldn't go on enjoying the habits of Donut Man and expect my cholesterol level and other health indicators to move in the right direction. I needed to change both my expectations and my reality, gradually but steadily.

Change my expectations? Yes. A fifty-year-old body is not a twenty-year-old body, no matter what the family history is.

Change my reality? Yes. Even at fifty, I can change habits that are proven to affect my heart health. This idea applies in any area of potential stress. And there are many practical, workable ways to change habits.

One of the biggest energy-draining experiences most adults stumble through is a strained marriage. I think back over the number of times

Norma and I have been bent out of shape due to some disagreement. It's amazing how the tone of our relationship could get so dark so fast. One hour things would be great, and then instantly we'd be locked in an angry argument over some earthshaking situations like, "Oh, no, you didn't say that! You said you wanted to stop and eat there, so my mouth has been watering to taste their specialty. How dare you change your mind!"

One morning we were in our camper driving out of Prescott, Arizona. I wanted breakfast at this certain restaurant where Norma had agreed to stop, but as we got close, she remembered this other place and asked if we could eat there instead. We quickly found ourselves locked in a three-hour battle, and all kinds of things came out that had nothing to do with eating breakfast. The "discussion" created a gap between our marital expectations and reality, to say the least! After we ate at a completely different restaurant neither of us liked, we got back in the camper and decided to reexamine the marriage area of our respective "gardens."

I was wiped out, feeling like a failure and as if all our progress in being a loving couple had been washed away in one three-hour torrential downpour. We were never going to make it. In the middle of this type of crisis, my personality tends to see only the negatives. But Norma tends to put things in a more realistic perspective. I remember her saying, "Just look at all the things that go great between us, and this is only a small speck in the scope of all the years we've been married." That knack of pulling our expectations and reality closer together gives me more energy to continue the discussion.

We took a closer look at expectations and reality. Were our expectations unrealistic? Was our reality as bad as it seemed? As for reality, Norma had helped clarify that our whole relationship had not flooded away. She helped me take some of my own advice: Avoid extreme thoughts. No, Chicken Little, the sky is not falling.

As for expectations, we decided that some of my expectations about our marriage—that we would always be at peace—were just not practical or realistic. No couple can live each day without some disagreements or even major conflicts. Conflicts are inevitable and can even be healthy, as you'll see in chapter 13. Even if a couple can't work things out for a few days, that's okay. In our case, we had to develop new expectations, ones that were more pragmatic. And we had to remember:

Forever-love does not see doom in every gap between expectations and reality.

Driving down the highway, we both evaluated our marriage and began making a list of things we expected to receive and what we believed would be acceptable for a mutually satisfying relationship. And it's amazing how just talking and agreeing on those marital basics has increased our levels of energy and love for life and each other.

Remember, it's the gap between what we expect and what we get that drains our energy. When our experience is close to what we anticipated, we're stronger and more content. That bolsters our ability to keep on loving. But unless we talk about those things and bring our expectations to the surface, our mate may not know our wishes, and we may find ourselves facing an energy-sapping gap between our desires and our reality.

If you discover on inspection that your expectations and experience don't match up well in a particular area of your life, you need to determine whether you should try to change the expectations or the reality (or both). In my own life, I've often found that when I took the time to look at them, my expectations were unrealistic and had to be adjusted. What I wanted just wasn't entirely reasonable. But other times, I've seen that there were things I could do to improve my reality and raise it closer to my desires.

When your expectations in a certain area involve other people, a good way to make sure those expectations align with reality is to talk them over with all those concerned. This can be difficult and even a little scary if you're not in the habit of speaking with people candidly. It also seems to be human nature to simply expect that somehow our loved ones can read our minds and know what we want.

Many wives, for example, long to hear their husbands say "I love you" more often. Yet many of those same wives will go for years without telling their husbands that's what they would like. Rather than get upset with their husbands, those women can either lower their expectations or—much better—talk over their need to hear those three magic words with their men. The result can be a richer reality, a stronger marriage, better ability to weather life's crises, and more joy and energy for the whole family.

In my own family, we decided a number of years ago to write a family constitution that would spell out what was reasonably expected of everyone. (You can read more details about this idea in chapter 9.) In the process of writing our constitution, we had to talk through all the expectations each of us had that we each thought made up a mutually satisfying family. By the time we were done and started putting it into practice, we were all happier, because we all knew what was expected of us and that we were generally doing a good job of meeting those expectations. It wasn't perfect, but talking things through and getting our expectations out in the open was a big step in the right direction.

The Best Ways to Change

Before we leave this chapter, I'd like to draw your attention to four simple effective ways I've found to help me "stay the course" of lasting change.

First, I like to read several of the best recommended books on the subject at hand. Second, I find an expert or two in town and discuss the issue with him or her. I simply explain my goals and ask the expert to assist me in changing. Next, I gather three of four others who have the same goal, and we meet weekly for a number of months to give each other mutual support and, most important, accountability. For instance, I'm just finishing up a few months with Weight Watchers. It's the weekly weigh-in that keeps me losing weight. The others in the session are all supportive, which makes it easier to experience lasting change. Finally, but certainly not least, I always seek the strength I receive as I look to God in faith. Each of these four resources has given me the ability to keep going and growing. They help me close the gap between expectations and reality.

It's Always Your Choice

If you choose to take the three steps described in this chapter—identify your life priorities, compare your expectations against reality, and align your expectations with reality—you'll do two things: You'll maintain more of your inner strength in the midst of potential and actual crises. And when the inevitable crises do hit—expectations and reality will never totally align in this world—your balanced life will protect you from utter devastation. When a crisis strikes in one area, the health in the other key parts of your identity will provide balance that can soon restore your energy and *joie de vivre*.

In chapter 4 I suggested you list your personal strengths. Identifying five "I ams" has been the key to chapter 5. In the next chapter we'll look at one more aspect of the "Who am I?" question, this time asked in terms of "Who am I as separate from you?" It's a critical question—one that can stop others from robbing you of satisfaction in life and one that can help you enrich the lives of others.

Forever-Love Principles

Our list of forever-love principles continues from the previous chapter:

25. Forever-love is protected when it grows in a diversified garden.

26. Forever-love identifies and nurtures five priority concerns.

27. Forever-love inspects life—to compare expectations against reality.

28. Forever-love reduces life-strain by closing the gap between expectations and reality.

6

Avoiding Hurt Is My Responsibility

*That long [Canadian] frontier from the Atlantic to the Pacific Ocean, guarded
only by neighborly respect and honorable obligations, is an example to every
country and a pattern for the future of the world.*

—Winston Churchill[1]

If I could get you to read just one chapter in this book, it might well be this
one. I feel so strongly about it because the concept at the core of this chapter
has done more to change my life—my positive attitude, my wife's attitude,
and the health of our life together—than anything else in the last ten years.
Let me relate a disastrous scenario that awakened us to this powerful relational truth: When we are causing each other hurt and frustration, we both
are at fault. And we both have a responsibility for maintaining and respecting "neighborly" boundaries.

How to Ruin a Great Day

A couple of years ago, Norma and I were in Hawaii with a lot of our staff
members to do a live seminar. Norma was excited about being there—the
beach, the sun, the rest, and the relaxation. I always enjoy going there, too,
whether to speak or just to have fun, so we both started off in a good frame
of mind. Then I did it again—something I had done all too often in our
married life.

We had arrived on a Saturday, and now it was Monday morning. We woke up early, around six, and as I started to get going, I was thinking, *Hey, we're all alone, and we haven't had a good discussion for a long time. We've both been so busy. Now would be a great time!*

So I looked at Norma and said, "What do you say we work for an hour or so on our marriage goals for the coming year?" I assumed she would love the idea. We have periodic discussions about our future—a version of the "checkups" I mentioned in the previous chapter. Discussing goals helps us keep expectations and reality in line.

Instead, however, she answered, "No, I don't feel like doing that today."

Well, the word *no* is not one of my favorite expressions, so I persisted. "Look," I said, "we haven't had this kind of meeting for a while. We've always got people around, but here we are all alone for a while. What do you say? Let's do it."

Again she replied, "No, I really don't want to do that this morning."

Now her refusal started to get to me. I thought, *Wait a minute! I'm in the business of working on marriages, and we ought to be making sure our own is tuned up just the way it should be.* So I tried again. "Let's just get started on our goals," I said. "We can talk about them at length later, when we get home."

Norma still wasn't interested, and at that point I got a little upset. So what did I, the marriage counselor and seminar speaker, do? To my embarrassment now, I pushed right ahead against her will and said a few choice words under my breath that she didn't appreciate but that got her to give in. We had our talk, all right, but it was obvious the whole time that we weren't really working on our relationship goals.

Why didn't I recognize that I was doing a wrong thing? Frankly, I'm not sure. I know I was convinced that the subject was important and we needed to talk about it. At the time, I also thought it was getting urgent, because it had been way too long since we had last had a time like that to review our goals. Maybe I was even thinking, *This is hard today, but sometimes good things in life are hard, and you have to push your mate to do them.* That sounds good at one level, doesn't it?

Well, whatever I was thinking, after a couple of strained hours of that discussion, Norma's displeasure was unmistakable. She's really open and honest with me about everything, which I love, though this time it hurt.

"This is just great!" she said. "This is the day that Terry [one of our staff members] is going to ask Janna to marry him. It's supposed to be a happy, festive day."

That remark made me realize that I had wiped her out emotionally with our forced conversation. *Gary Smalley,* I thought, *why did you have to push it this far?* I knew she would walk out of that room, and the staff and our kids would take one look at her and then ask me, "*Now* what did you do to her?"

Sure enough, shortly after she left for breakfast without me, the story was out, and my son Greg came to me first and said, "Dad, I can't believe you did this! We're both counselors, right? . . ." and so on. One of the other wives also came and said, "Way to wreck our whole day!"

You can imagine how the rest of my day went! Norma and I weren't really speaking. I tried to be nice to her, to joke and warm things up a little, but nothing worked. She just wasn't ready to respond.

That night, Terry, our staff member, put up a big banner on his outside balcony asking Janna to marry him. It could be seen a long way off, from outside the hotel, and Janna saw it and said yes. So we were all excited and in a good mood, including Norma. I thought, *All right. She's getting warmer. There's hope for me yet. I only have four more days until my marriage seminar.*

A little later the whole staff spontaneously went out for ice cream. We were in high spirits, and I announced to everyone in the ice-cream parlor, "Hey, this couple just got engaged!"

All the people cheered, and the manager said, "All right! Free ice cream for you folks!"

After the ice cream was served and our group had finished eating, I was up at the cash register trying to pay, not sure the manager had meant to give us *all* free food. But she ignored me for the moment and looked instead at Terry and Janna. "Listen," she told them, "I don't really know you, but I'd like to give you some marriage advice. There's this television infomercial running right now by a guy named Gary Smalley. He's selling this video series on marriage, and I got it, and it's really been helpful. I think it would help you guys too. You ought to get it before you get married."

At that point, Janna looked at me, I looked at her, and I knew she was thinking, *Gary set this up.* So before she could say a word, I shook my head and told her, "No, I swear I didn't do a thing."

Janna turned to the manager and said, "Do you know who that is— trying to pay you?"

"No," the woman answered. "Should I?"

"It's Gary Smalley," Janna said.

The woman looked at me closely for a few seconds, and then her face broke into a giant smile. She ran around the counter and gave me a big hug.

It was a nice scene. But the clincher came as we were leaving, when Norma leaned in close with her arm around me and said, "You ought to order those tapes."

That day was a turning point in my life. The disaster helped Norma and me see an unhealthy pattern in our lives and our relationship: We didn't clearly understand the importance of personal boundaries. Today, I can see clearly that I was wrong to force Norma to discuss something she wasn't prepared to talk about that morning. I made a big mistake. But so did she. And the pattern we lived out that morning is repeated in home after home across the country.

My mistake was to barge into Norma's life without her permission. If you're a "Gary," in this chapter I'll give you a method that can help keep you from doing the same thing to your spouse or others.

Norma's mistake was that she *let* me barge in. For the "Normas" out there, I'll give practical advice for keeping others from storming into your life.

What's This Talk about Boundaries?

Let me answer that question by asking another: Do you know where you end and 'others' begin? The question doesn't have to do with physical bodies or skin. It has to do with your emotional being. Think of yourself as having an invisible property line around yourself. Imagine that a land surveyor marked off where you start and end with stakes. Inside the property line is everything that makes up who you are—your personality, your likes and dislikes, your goals and dreams, the various parts that make up your life—like the garden I talked about in the last chapter. That garden has a property line around it, but because it's invisible, others may not know where it is—they may not know if they're about to cross it, or if they have crossed it—unless you tell them where the line is.

Most of us want others to respect our property lines and not enter our gardens without our okay. I call this concept "No visitors without my permission." In short, we want people to respect who we are and see us as separate from them—but also as a loving part of them. We want them to respect the thoughts and values we have chosen that reflect our most personal selves, the part of us that is unique and special, like a fingerprint.

To reduce misunderstanding here, know that I'm not suggesting that a husband and wife should fence out each other or their children. I'm not talking about erecting a barrier so that others can't get close. I certainly support the enriching idea that a man and a woman can become "one flesh" after marriage. But oneness does not mean that one mate dominates the other or that the stronger controls the weaker. I'm also not suggesting that a shy person should use this concept to keep others at arm's length.

What I am suggesting is that each one of us, married or single, is a separate and unique person—worthy of two kinds of respect. (1) Respect from others. Others should treat us as separate people with our own likes and dislikes, feelings, hopes, and tastes. Other people should not cross our property lines unless they're invited to do so. (2) Respect from ourselves. We need to feel strong and whole enough to tell others when they are trespassing—trampling on our gardens.

When people insensitively force their way across our personal boundaries, we get very uncomfortable, frustrated, hurt, and, as a result, angry. If you've realized you've carried around deep-seated, unresolved anger, it may well be that someone in your past bulldozed his or her way into your garden. If you were young, you were particularly vulnerable and defenseless. Someone may be trespassing even now. You may think the border violations are out of your control, but there's hope.

Let's look more closely at how the dynamics work—first at my tendency to bulldoze and then at Norma's tendency not to stand her ground.

Confessions of a Bulldozer

Have you ever wished for something all your life, but you figured it would never happen, and then suddenly your dream came true? That's what took place for me, and it was great . . . for a while.

My dream was to drive a big, yellow, powerful bulldozer and build my own road. I don't remember if I played with toy bulldozers as a kid or what, but that driver dream was old and deep.

My opportunity came when my wife and I bought a small farm. Lo and behold, I needed to build a road about a block long down through some trees. So I got in touch with a bulldozer owner and arranged the date and time for him to come and clear the way for my road.

On the appointed day, I started salivating when I saw that gigantic machine on my own property driven by a burly, weathered guy. I thought, *Ohhh, I'd love to drive that bulldozer! But there's no way he'd let me do it. How many hundreds of thousands of dollars did he spend for it?*

The guy got the bulldozer off the flatbed trailer and fired up that huge engine. The ground shook, smoke filled the air, and I was a kid again!

I figured it was now or never. If I was ever going to have a chance of fulfilling my dream, I just had to ask. Besides, what did I have to lose?

"Excuse me," I said, "but I'd like to ask you a question before you start. Is there any way . . . I mean, I was just wondering . . . would you let me use your bulldozer and make the road myself? I'll pay the same amount. I'd really like to do it. What do you think?"

The guy scratched his head and thought about it. I held my breath, amazed that he was even considering the request. Then he said, "Sure, why not?"

Unbelievable! I thought. *Who would have thought?* I said, "Great! Show me what to do."

We climbed up on the bulldozer together, and he gave me about a two-minute lesson in how to operate the machine. "Here's your transmission," he said. "This lever raises and lowers the shovel, and so on. Then he climbed down, and I was on my own."

Was I excited! This was the thrill of a lifetime! You can keep your yacht; I'll take a bulldozer any day. I actually kept it for an entire week and smoothed down everything that needed smoothing all over my property.

A few days later on the following Sunday, I was sitting in my home with a friend when I heard a knock at the front door. I opened it, and there stood one of my neighbors with his wife and teenage son. "Hi, neighbor," I said with a smile.

Without any greeting or the usual pleasantries, he said, "We've got a problem."

"We do?" I asked.

"Yeah. One of your workmen bulldozed my fence and got into my rocks."

"Ohhh," I managed to say as the full force of his words hit me. As my face turned red and my legs went weak, I was tempted to say, "Yeah, those workmen! It's so hard to find good help today, isn't it?" That was my first instinct. But I forced myself to tell the truth. "You know, I need to apologize," I told him. "I'm the one who did that with the bulldozer. I thought I was smoothing my own land. I pushed down those trees and that fence, and I took those rocks. I really did think I was on my own property, and I'm really sorry. I'll be glad to bring the bulldozer back up there and try to fix things."

"No, no, don't bother with that," he said. "Just fix the fence so my horses don't get out."

We wrapped up the conversation, and he was very nice about it all. But as you can imagine, I was extremely embarrassed.

Here I thought I had done a good job of clearing a part of my land, when I had actually been rather careless, torn down a neighbor's fence, and taken something that belonged to him. That's how bulldozer-type personalities can think when it comes to another person's personal boundaries.

Bulldozer Reform

As I said earlier, the way I treated Norma that day in Hawaii illustrates a tendency I've had throughout my life. With my wife, my children, and my friends, I've often rammed my way into their lives, many times without regard for their feelings, and usually without even realizing what I was doing. I now see that my behavior was a classic example of a major way in which people are robbed of their contentment. True love never demands its own way but searches for ways of enriching the other.

My efforts at reform have not only made life easier for Norma; they have opened up my own "lighter heart." I carry less guilt for having "ruined a day." I see that we're both responsible for our own love and satisfaction. I see a way to reduce the frequency of our conflicts.

Though I use the word *bulldozer* to describe my own mode of operation, don't think that all boundary violators are as easy to recognize as a bright yellow earthmover. Some people are masters at "moving in" with subtle guilt trips: maybe a spouses's, "If you loved me you would . . ." or a child's, "All the other parents are . . ."

Soon after I gained new understanding about boundaries, I sent a letter to all three of our children trying to explain the dramatic changes that were occurring in me. Here's what they read:

Dear Kari, Greg, and Michael,

I woke up this morning thinking of you and thought I would send you a quick note about a very important lesson I've been learning as I prepare for my new video series.

You came to mind for two reasons. One is that without any choice of yours, you were born into our family. As I see more clearly the way I was raised, I can understand why I treated you and the other family members the way I did some of the time. There were many, many times that I was like a tank smashing down the important and sometimes fragile property line around you without asking if I could visit inside your life.

When you were younger, there were times I would "bulldoze" into your life even if for some reason you had asked me not to come in. In one sense, I could make you feel like, "Well, I'm coming in because I'm your father." I did the same thing with your mom and your siblings. But something happened yesterday to allow me to see these things I've done more clearly than I ever have. I now know that the way I was raised and my personality contribute to a lot of what I did.

If I could live my life over again, I would change a lot of things, but the one thing I would work on most is controlling what I say to others. I have crashed over people's property lines on so many occasions that I couldn't count them. When I think of the little and major things I have said to you over the years and the things I have uttered to so many people, it's scary.

The second reason I wanted to write you is that even though you will probably never do these things to people because of your maturity and loving nature, I just wanted to warn you that some of the things you may say to your classmates or others may come back to haunt you later in life. People are too precious to jump their property lines without permission. It may really hurt them, and many times we never know until years later.

Positive Role Model

In contrast to my aggressive ways, let me give you an example of someone who knew how to respect the property rights of others—my late mother. Without knowing any formal psychology, she greatly respected my property lines as I was growing up. I remember, for instance, that she did a lot of her family shopping in thrift stores because we didn't have much money. But I, as a typical high-school kid, was greatly embarrassed by this. Under the powerful influence of peer pressure, I had to have clothes with the right labels that came from the right stores. And I worked all the way through high school so I could do just that.

Mom didn't care about any of those status issues. But she did care about me, and she was sensitive to my embarrassment over her shopping habits. One morning she said to me, "I need to buy some shoes. Would you give me a ride down to the thrift store?"

"Mom, I really don't want to do that,"I answered.

"That's okay, I understand," she said. "Just drop me off a block away, and I'll walk the rest of the way. You can wait for me in the car and then take me home when I'm done."

"Nah . . . ohh . . . all right," I finally agreed.

Notice that she wasn't violating my individual feelings and needs; she wasn't walking in my "garden area" by making me do something that wasn't me. She got my cooperation, but she did it in a way that allowed me to maintain my sense of dignity. My feelings were valued and treated with respect.

How can we develop an attitude like my mom's with regard to others? As I already mentioned, the first mistake we can make is to invade another's territory without permission. That's what I had done to Norma in Hawaii and to my neighbor's property at home. But I've learned an effective way to slow down and respect the special "property rights" of others.

Respecting the Rights of Another to Pursue Happiness

This whole idea sounds a little like our country's Declaration of Independence, doesn't it? Our Founding Fathers laid down the truth there that "all men are created equal, that they are endowed by their Creator with certain unalienable rights," among which is "the pursuit of happiness."

With that God-given right of everyone to pursue happiness in mind, how should a person—especially a rather aggressive personality like me—approach others when there's something he or she wants? *It's basically a matter of asking for permission before entering someone else's "space" and then being willing to accept the answer you're given, even if it's not the one you wanted.* (This principle may seem obvious, but for many it's not practiced.) This is the thing I'm learning to do—the one thing that has most changed how I deal with people and has most improved my relationships.

Asking permission is critical, but so is the ability to hear a *no* or *not now* with grace. When Norma says "Not now," I need to respect myself enough to feel that she is not rejecting *me*. What does this mean? It means anger levels need to be low; we need to be constantly working through the principles presented in earlier chapters. If anger levels are low, we're best able to see a particular conversation as an incident unto itself; we're not dragging in excessive baggage from previous encounters.

Here's the approach I've now learned to use when I want to talk about something or do anything with Norma. I'll walk up to her and "knock" at her imaginary gate. I'll say something like, "Could we talk about next week's schedule tonight?" or "I want to go out tonight. What about you?" It can be any subject, feeling, or need I wish to address.

She's free to respond, "No, I don't want to talk about it right now. Maybe later."

Then I'll say, "Okay, when?"

She might answer, "I would love to talk about it later this evening. Or how about tomorrow?"

And I'll conclude, "Good. That's great. Then we go on to something else."

Believe me, my ability to operate that way and respect Norma's wishes—her uniqueness—is a big difference in my life. (And I don't want to misrepresent Norma: If it truly is an urgent matter that must be discussed now, she'll respect the issue and talk immediately.)

My gentler approach has also helped us deal with three or four particular subject areas we don't talk about often because it's so difficult. You and your spouse probably have similar subjects, the kind that get you heated up every time they're broached. It used to be that way when I wanted to discuss something explosive. We would just launch into the subject and hope for the best, and many times we ended up in a hurtful argument. Now we both ask for permission to bring up those topics, and we feel much more comfortable, safe, and loved.

Here's one final and very down-to-earth illustration of how to use this approach in a healthy way: Jim and Suzette, a couple from our support group and close friends of ours, were having lunch with us and practicing this concept one day. Suzette said to Jim, "Can I talk to you about something?" (Notice she's asking for his permission respectfully.)

Jim immediately responded, "Well, I've got a video camera security system on my property today." But he continued, "What do you want to talk about?" (He wanted to know more before he granted permission.)

"Just one thing," she answered.

"What is it? I want to know what you want to talk about before I decide to let you inside my gate."

"All right," she said, "I want to talk about what you're eating for lunch today."

"Okay, come on in and we'll discuss it," he told her, inviting her to come through his elaborate security system. (Remember, Norma and I are good friends with them, and they felt safe enough with us to have a discussion like this in front of us. I recognize that some couples can't imagine discussing a sensitive marital problem in front of others. But we've been doing it for so long it's now second nature, and it has been extremely helpful in both marriages.)

Suzette went on, "I know we've talked about this before, but when you order your favorite kind of spaghetti at this restaurant, by six o'clock at night you really have an unusual odor."

"What do you mean?" he said, surprised.

"Well, this garlic gets in your system, and you really . . . uh . . . smell. It's embarrassing to me when we go to basketball games or other public events. I'm very aware of it, so I find myself trying to keep you away from other people so they don't notice it."

Jim accepted that graciously, if reluctantly, and said, "All right, I won't order that today. If it really bothers you, I'll have something else." (Notice his sensitivity to her feelings and her uniqueness.)

Then Suzette decided to push her luck. "While I'm inside your garden," she continued, "may I talk about just one other thing?"

Now, realize he could have said no to that request. He could have said, "I really don't feel like two in one hour. Maybe later." But he answered, "All right, go ahead."

"Okay, one other thing," she said. "When we go to that high-school basketball game tonight, would you not yell at the officials and the fans from the other school? It really embarrasses me when you pick out a fan and start haggling with him."

"But I'm a coach," he protested. "I know how to work referees, so I do that. It's part of the game."

"Well, it really embarrasses me," she repeated, standing her ground. "You're a community leader, so other people are watching you. And it makes me feel like I want to wilt."

"All right," he said, choosing to be gracious again. "I'll try to be more aware of yelling tonight."

Here again, Jim had the freedom to decide. He could have said, "When I go to a game, I love to yell. That's just me. I can't help it, though I'll try not to be rude." But he had invited her comments, he was in a generous mood, and he gave her what she wanted. For her part, Suzette had respected his property line, asked for permission to speak, and then stated her case clearly. That's a healthy personal property line at work.

This first part of the chapter has covered the kind of mistake made by the Garys of this world, where the strong personalities tend to bulldoze the weaker. Now let's turn to the mistake Norma made.

Claiming One's Own Ground

Early that morning in Hawaii—the disastrous day that woke Norma and me to the reality of our border disputes—I was not the only person who made a mistake. Norma had a choice in how she responded to me. She and many people like her tend to blame their circumstances or others for their discontent with life. Each of us can and should take responsibility for how we allow others to "visit" us inside our "gardens" without permission. The Normas of the world need to understand that love does not always give in to every request, especially to intimidation.

Gaining Strength

As a human being in relationship to another human being, you are not a genie with this life motto: *Your wish is my command.* You have the ability to say no; you have a responsibility to say no if someone bulldozes over you. Allowing that bulldozer to tear down your fence and trees can cause resentment. You'll feel trampled and squeezed. (Think back to the "can of anger," where a dangerous substance was compressed, pressurized.) That unhappiness and unresolved anger you'll blame on the bulldozer. But wait. Have you let the bulldozer onto your property without as much as a warning sign? You are responsible for warning others and then lovingly standing your ground.

But, you say, saying no will cause an unhappiness of its own. "Making waves" is so uncomfortable.

Yes, bulldozers have a way of making it difficult to hold your ground. But let me give some advice:

Work through old unresolved anger. I repeat, if anger levels are low, we're able to see—and deal with—one incident at a time. You don't need to escalate a minor boundary infraction into World War III proportions. But that's what can happen when you've let someone squeeze you in for so long that one day you finally blow—pointing a weapon at someone and screaming "Get off my land!" That's what happens when you let a bulldozer's "few choice words" set off a minefield of emotion.

Remember, at the beginning of the chapter, we said that respect for others was half the boundary issue; respect for self was the other critical ingredient. As you claim your ground, speak in love. Speak with respect for yourself and the other person. Be reasonable but firm. And watch as a new self-respect counters your dis-ease.

A Revised Scenario

That morning in Hawaii, Norma could have claimed her ground and said, "Not now." She didn't have to give in to my intimidation.

Let's go back to that morning and ask what Norma could have done to defend herself from unwanted intrusion. Could she have done something practical to postpone our conversation until she was ready for it?

For one thing, after stating her objection, she could have tried to change the subject. She could have said, "Let's go to breakfast, and let's just have fun while we're here in Hawaii. This is Terry's engagement day, after all. What are you going to wear down to breakfast?"

But suppose I continued to push ahead with something like, "Breakfast can wait," or "Fine, we'll talk about it at breakfast." What then?

In that case, Norma could have emphasized her willingness to discuss the subject later. "Sure I'd like to talk about our marriage goals," she might have said, "but not now and not here. Let's just relax while we're here. This is supposed to be a fun vacation, and having a big, serious discussion now is not my idea of fun."

By that time I should have been getting the message, don't you think? But let's say I was still determined to talk about goals that morning. Then she would have needed to really dig in her heels and take the blunt approach: "What's that saying?" she could have recalled: "What part of *no* don't you understand? I really don't want to talk about marriage goals today."

At that point, even I would have understood. I probably would have been frustrated for a while, but that would have faded quickly as we got into the fun of the day and the joy of Terry's engagement. (For specific ideas on how to resolve conflict so that frustration doesn't turn to anger, see chapter 13.)

I'm happy to say that since the Hawaii incident, Norma has learned to defend herself much better. Awhile later, we went to Florida together for a conference and writing session. We were on the beach, close to the water where the waves could lap at our feet, and I was rehearsing what I would say in the part of my presentation covered in this chapter. I would ask her opin-ion of something I planned to say, and she would respond, "Try saying this and maybe this." She gave me a number of great ideas.

We went back and forth like that for about two hours, and I was really enjoying it. In fact, I wanted to keep going for another hour or so. But Norma had reached her limit, so she said something like, "I'm tired of talk-ing about this stuff. I came down to relax by the water."

Well, I was on a roll and I pleaded, "Just a little more?"

"My gate's closed," she said lovingly, looking me in the eyes. "I'd like to read for a while. I'm putting a 'Do not disturb' sign on my gate."

Fortunately, I had learned my lesson by that time, and I got the message. I was frustrated because we were right in the middle of the discussion as far as I was concerned, but I honored her as a special person with her own feel-ings and needs. I let go of my frustration and moved my chair down the beach a little way. Because I needed an audience and there was no one else around, I started speaking to the sea gulls! But even they didn't seem that interested.

Border Watch

How can you tell if the imaginary line around your life isn't being respected as it needs to be?[2] This is one area where your emotions may be a pretty good guide. For instance, have you been really angry in the last month, an anger that lasted more than a couple of days? Have you been frustrated over a period of time? Have you felt used or abused? Have you felt suffocated in a relationship?

If you're living with any of these negative emotions, your boundary may need to be better marked. Remember, your present quality of life depends upon the choices you make. Claim your ground. Except in cases of extreme abuse, I recommend that you choose to tell others when they're trespassing. (See "Tough Situations" below.)

One caution, again having to do with unresolved anger: If you find that everybody's always frustrating you, your old anger may be making your boundary unnecessarily broad. Remember, anger keeps you distant from others. Love builds bridges to others.

Tough Situations

What do you do if you're in a relationship with someone who con-stantly bulldozes into your life without permission and just won't take any form of no for an answer? Obviously, that's a tough situation, and there are no easy answers. I recommend that every couple be part of a couples support group. This might give you a safe place to discuss touchy things if your mate is willing. Professional counseling is another tool you might use for yourself or—even better—for both of you together. There are many helpful resources (agencies and counselors) available today in most cities.[3]

In extreme cases, especially where there is any threat of physical harm, you may have to physically separate yourself from the boundary violator. This might involve calling 911 and contacting legal authorities. No one should suffer physical abuse.

Perhaps you're thinking, *I want this person's love, so I had better just leave matters alone or he or she might leave me or harm me further.* Believe me, you're not the first person to think that way. But if you choose to ignore your circumstances, I've found the problem usually gets worse, not better. It's much better to alert an offender to your property line and insist that you will no longer allow trespassing. Take a stand, and defend yourself. In the short term, the other person will probably resist and may give you a hard time. But in the long run, he or she will respect you much more. It's your only real hope for a satisfying relationship.

Final Thoughts

As we've seen, clearly defining who we are is essential. It can make or break our love for life and the satisfaction we receive from relationships built on respect and honor. Learning this concept and beginning to respect the boundaries of my wife, children, and friends has literally changed my life, and I'm glad to say I'll never be the same as before.

But realize that keeping a "garden area" in good repair and defending it is hard work. For people with either tendency—to be too aggressive or too passive—the final word is *moderation.* An age-old rule of life and love is this: "Love your neighbor as yourself."[4] The two loves are intertwined in a tight strand of respect that can temper the aggressive, strengthen the passive, and make for long-lasting peace—with one's neighbor (spouse) and with oneself.

In chapter 7, I give one more warning—how you can avoid the biggest "iceberg" that threatens forever-love. When we quit pretending that our spiritual journey doesn't matter, we're on our way to availing ourselves of the power we need to love life and others.

Forever-Love Principles

Our list of forever-love principles continues from the previous chapter:

29. Forever-love respects another person's personal boundaries.

30. Forever-love never demands its own way but searches for ways of enriching the other person.

31. Forever-love asks permission before entering someone's garden.

32. Forever-love hears "no" or "not now" with grace—not with paranoia.

33. Forever-love is not a genie. "Your wish" is not "my command."

34. Forever-love can hold its ground against intimidation.

35. Forever-love knows the quiet, confident strength that comes with self-respect.

36. Forever-love equally respects self and others.

37. Forever-love tempers the aggressive and strengthens the passive.

7

Finding the Power
to Keep Loving

To make [things] your masters, to look to them to justify your life and save your
soul is sheerest folly. They just aren't up to it. . . . . Having ushered God out
. . . through the front door, the unbeliever is under constant temptation to
replace him with something spirited in through the service entrance.

—Frederick Buechner[1]

Where do we find added strength to keep loving and enjoying life when difficulties hit or when we just get tired of trying or when life turns into a boring
routine? I've found that one of the key truths lies in "sighting" and avoiding
a deadly cluster of "icebergs" that would block our spiritual journey.

Why is the spiritual journey so important? Marriage researchers are
finding a correlation between one's spiritual journey and one's satisfaction
in marriage. Howard Markman, Scott Stanley, and Susan Blumberg report
that religion has a favorable impact on marriage. They write that religious
couples "are less likely to divorce . . . show somewhat higher levels of satisfaction . . . lower levels of conflict about common issues . . . and
higher levels of commitment."[2] And in worldwide research Dr. Nick
Stinnett found six characteristics common to most happy marriages and
families—one being an active, shared faith in God.[3]

Though a recent Gallup poll revealed that over 90 percent of Americans
believe in God, many struggle to find a personal living faith. Most of us

realize that we don't have it all together and that we do need some outside strength to help us keep our love from fading or to endure the pain caused by others. But often, as I did for so long, we choose some course that drives us in a different direction from developing our spiritual dimension.

Out of my depression twenty years ago, I started learning about the obstacles that kept me disconnected from a personal God. As I've gradually seen how to connect, I've become keenly aware of how vital this spiritual area of life is for anyone wanting to experience greater satisfaction in life and lasting love.

In this final chapter of part 1, I will discuss four main factors that hindered my spiritual journey. I kept hearing that God was a God of love who could somehow give a person the ability to love others and himself or herself. But I couldn't find how this truth could be real *for me*. I seemed to need more than education and support from family and friends to keep my love for life and others alive and growing. I wanted supernatural help, but it wasn't there for me until I turned thirty-five and became very tired of hitting "icebergs."

In my thirties, feeling hopeless and isolated, my anger grew like mold in a damp basement. I distanced myself from my wife and kids, I didn't want to go to my job, and I was ready to quit the profession for which I had been preparing for years.

I felt as if I were floating in a sea of anger, and I kept allowing Norma and my kids to poke more and more holes in my leaky life vest. I realized I was sinking fast. I had to take some steps in a hurry and cry out for help.

It was like the time our family visited a wave-pool water park in Las Vegas; I went out in the deep end without a raft. Wave after wave came, and I finally tired. I was all by myself—the kids were already out of the water— and I decided to swim to the ladder at the side of the pool and climb out. But I couldn't make it! Every time I got close to the edge, another wave would push me away again, and I was too tired to fight it. I swallowed water, began to panic, and realized I was helpless. At that point my only thought was, *I'm going to drown here in Las Vegas in front of my family!* I was sure I was going down for good.

Fortunately, my family had seen what was happening. The next thing I knew, my son Greg was stretching way out, grabbing me by the arm, and pulling me toward that ladder. When I got to it, I wrapped my arms around it and hung on for dear life.

That's kind of what happened to me with God. I kept trying to reach out for some kind of satisfaction in life, but each time a wave of reality would push me back out, and I was sinking. I've heard alcoholics, the addicted, and many other hurting people who were just as miserable as I was, say this same thing. Each of us finally reached out and grabbed God's hand, which had always been there, outstretched and waiting for us.

It's been rewarding because I actually did find what I'd heard so many people say was possible, but had eluded me for so long. I found a way to tap into the spiritual realm and receive the ability to love God, others, life, and myself more. In other words, for the past twenty years my ability to keep loving has not been dependent upon the actions of others or my circumstances, but rather on my choice to stay connected to a personal God. This chapter is about how I was able to tap this supernatural force.

My own outstretched hand came in the midst of my depression and disillusionment. I recalled a verse from the Bible, Psalm 50:15: "Call upon me [God] in the day of trouble; I will deliver you, and you will honor me." I realized that was all I could do then, and it was what I needed to do. Sinking like the *Titanic*, I cried out to God for help, asking him to somehow rescue me from the mess I was in and show me he was real. And deep in my spirit, I kept hoping he heard me. Eventually I did find a personal connection to God, and it's been so rewarding I've never looked back.

Before I get to the four icebergs that kept blocking my ability to find a personal God, let me share what this chapter will *not* do. I obviously won't be addressing all the subtle meanings that you, my readers, bring to this spiritual area of life. I want to present my ideas so you see how wonderful it has been for me, yet I don't want to come across as preachy or saccharin and possibly cause some to further avoid its tremendous benefits. Also, I'm not trying to address all the various doctrines or great concepts about faith in God. I simply want to share the hindrances I encountered in my spiritual journey and why the lack of connection with a personal God affected my ability to love my wife, my family, and others—even myself.

You may have little interest in spiritual things because you've been wounded by someone who claimed to be a "religious person." Perhaps you've been hurt in a past church experience. Or maybe you've had close friends who claimed to be spiritual but lived out hypocritical lives. Well, I've been jerked around and hurt by a lot of "religious" people myself.

But I finally saw that denying the spiritual side of life because we've known some phonies is like refusing to go to a bank where they're waiting to give us one hundred thousand dollars because we know that some of the people who work there or deposit money there are two-faced.

In the spiritual arena, I've found truths that have meant the world to me. This area has been the most enriching part of my entire life's journey. I just couldn't write a book about making love last forever without talking about my faith. It would be like talking about sailing without mentioning the wind.

My faith has become like a powerful turbocharged engine in an old '57 Chevy. God has become like the warmth of a fireplace after being out too long in the cold. Before I found him to be real, I allowed myself to be spiritually hindered, even battered, by four icebergs that blocked my path.

1. My Doubts Kept Me from God

When I was seriously questioning the existence of God back in my college days, someone challenged me to open my mind to the possibility of a personal God by asking me three humbling questions. Those questions were healthy for me, because they caused me to develop my own personalized belief system. Here are those questions:

1. How much knowledge do you think we now have in the world out of all the knowledge that can be known (0 percent to 100 percent)? _____

2. How much of this knowledge do you think you know personally (0 percent to 100 percent)? _____

3. Do you think it's possible that a personal God could someday reveal himself to you through the remaining knowledge that you could gain (yes or no)? _____

When I ask these questions of others, the average person admits to having only a small percentage of the available knowledge. And most people then take the position that it may be possible to someday see and experience a personal God.

Again, for me, I was full of doubts about a personal God, and with my level of anger and guilt, even during my college years, there was no way I was going to "see" God. My anger kept him far from me.

I could fill an entire book with my elaborate doubts, many of which left as my anger and guilt subsided. You may not have a lot of doubts about

God's existence, and you may well be on your way with your own spiritual journey, but possibly telling my version of this vital area of life may further enhance yours. From my personal experience as well as that of thousands of others, I'm convinced that you can obtain the single, most important key to lasting love, one that nothing or nobody can ever take away.

2. Hypocrites Kept Me from God

I didn't start attending church regularly until I was a teenager. My older brother and sister got me involved.

At the very first church I attended, the minister was asked to leave because of some moral problem. That was a harsh reminder of the truth that no one is perfect. Nonetheless, I was fairly active in this first church—until I had a fistfight with one of the staff members! Shortly after that scuffle, my father passed away, leaving me in need of someone older to look up to. A new staff member with a sincere, loving nature kept me coming to church, and he proved to be genuine. I still deeply admire this man even though he, too, eventually left the church because of personal struggles. I used to wonder how this vital area of life, our faith in God, could survive with such inconsistencies among its believers.

In spite of the leaders I encountered, my faith remained alive during my college years, and then, as a graduate student, I was hired by a church to work with its youth. I was excited at the opportunity and looked forward to a satisfying, fulfilling ministry. To my dismay, however, the senior pastor never bothered to learn my name. In staff meetings he would call me "Hey, you." I thought, *That's incredible! People who say they serve a God of love are supposed to be more loving.* And I was scratching my head in wonderment a lot of the time.

My first meeting with the youth of this church knotted my stomach. The teenage leader was asked to pray before a noon meal. He rose respectfully to utter these words: "Rub-a-dub-dub, thanks for the grub. Yea, God." Then he sat down amid giggles from the other kids. One evening awhile later, that same teen admitted in a formal youth business meeting that he couldn't find God as a meaningful experience. Several others in the meeting expressed their disbelief as well, along with the adult sponsors. Everyone else seemed to get into the confessional mood, so I joined them. That night after the meeting, I told my wife that I would probably be asked to leave the church because I had just admitted that God was not real to me. I believed God existed; I just couldn't find him to be personal. Nothing ever came of my confession, but the experience certainly motivated me to find out what kept blocking my ability to know God.

My wife's childhood church experience also fed my growing disappointment with "religious people." In her first church, the pastor ran away with Norma's best girlfriend's mother. The church-family members were devastated, and so was the child who would become my wife.

Following graduate school, I worked for a religious organization with which I grew disenchanted, and I finally left that place as a discouraged man. Then, despite my spiritual condition and disillusionment, I went to work—briefly—in another church. I was hired to guide the congregation in setting up a counseling center. But within months that pastor was asked to leave because of marital infidelity.

I stayed there to help out for a while, and when I left there I started my own work teaching a marriage seminar, along with writing books about how to stay happily married. I've since had many wonderful experiences being a member of various churches—but for more than fifteen years I've not had the opportunity again of being a staff member.

You may be wondering how I stayed on a spiritual journey with all I had experienced. I had plenty of reason for skepticism, and you may as well.

I came to realize that I wasn't responsible for the wrongs of those other people. Then also, I wasn't going to let their irresponsibility rob me of my future love for life. I held on to a baseline faith in the "God of hope."[4] I chose to heed the advice of an old friend who reminded me, "If you draw close to God and continue to seek after him, you will find him."[5] And I listened when someone said, "God is still enriching the lives of those who find him." I always wanted to know if it was possible to experience God. I got to the place where I no longer cared how hypocritical the "bank tellers" or the others who "deposited" at church were; I was going to keep up my own search for his treasures and his power.

Powerful Lessons

I finally saw the major hindrances for me in knowing a personal God. I can best explain it by asking you to imagine a life-size baby doll in a store and picture this doll moving and even speaking a limited vocabulary. In her back a battery pack opens up; it holds three D batteries to supply the power so she can function as she was designed to—so she can be all she was meant to be.

We're all somewhat like that doll. God made us capable of doing many good and wonderful things, but we need power to operate. He intends for us to get the main power for living—and the primary things we need in life—from him. If we let him, God can empower our love; it's like having all three D batteries in place. He fits. I find that many people, like me, have had this vague emptiness in their lives; they don't know what will fill it. We can feel a need to be connected to a personal God, a longing for wholeness, or a desire to gain control over our emotions and struggles.

Our spiritual problems only increase when we try to stuff things other than God into our battery packs, hoping these things will fit and empower us. I've found that if we try to gain completeness, strength, love, and joy from any substitutes for God, they don't bring a lasting fulfillment. In fact, when you look closely at negative emotions of hurt, frustration, and fear, they often come as we expect God's creation—rather than God—to "charge" our life.

We can simplify this idea by seeing that these substitutes generally fall into one of two categories: what we expect to get from other people (like AA batteries) and what we expect to get from our jobs (like C batteries). I tried to stuff people and my job into my battery pack for years, and all I kept getting was the very emotions I didn't want—hurt and emptiness.

I'll never forget the day I realized that my lack of connection with God was primarily the result of my own decision to remain angry. My main anger source was my expectations that people and my job would fit nicely into my battery pack, that they would provide me with energy, love, and satisfaction. Unfortunately expectations bring the hurt and frustration leading to anger. People and the things our jobs can bring are great batteries, but just the wrong size for us.

On this particular day, I was casually reading a section of Scripture and my eyes stopped at a verse that seemed to scream this message at me: "If you remain angry with anyone, you'll lose your ability to walk in the light of God and thus the ability to know the love of God."[6] Very angry people seem to be spiritually blind and unable to draw near to God.

3. Expecting Too Much from People Kept Me from God

We try to fit friends and loved ones into our battery packs. We think, *If only I had the right mate. If only I had some good friends who would stand by me and support me, no matter what. If only I had parents who believed in me. If only I had kids who made me proud instead of embarrassing me every time I turn around . . . then I could set the world on fire. I'd have it made.*

We rely on one person or a group of folks to meet our needs for love, purpose, excitement, fulfillment, ego gratification . . . And you know what happens? They eventually let us down because they are human. Their love often proves to be conditional rather than without reservation. Life with even the best mate is boring at times. And no one lives forever—what then? Our kids have a will of their own and may choose words and actions that hurt us rather than fulfill us. A best friend might betray us or just move away to another part of the country in our time of deepest need.

Remember, our supply of energy for dealing with life's daily demands depends on how closely our expectations match the reality we experience. Well, when friends and family let us down, when we've been counting on them, we can suffer a huge energy loss.

This is what happened to me in my period of great discouragement after graduate school, when I went to work in the field of counseling with a reputable religious organization. I thought I had it made. Not long after I joined the staff, however, I grew uncomfortable with what I saw. I felt that top administrators were involved in highly questionable activities. And I developed a special animosity—a hatred, really—toward one individual in particular.

Eventually I had so much anger toward some of my coworkers that there were days I couldn't make myself go to work. I would call in sick. And I distanced myself from my family too. For instance, I couldn't bring myself to sit and eat with them. I hid myself away in a bedroom for days on end. Our kids were only three, seven, and nine at the time, and they needed their daddy, but emotionally I couldn't be there for them.

Norma grew concerned, not only for my health and the family's, but also for our finances when I started talking about resigning.

"But you can't do anything else," she said pragmatically. "You've been trained only in this kind of work."

Her words were like a bucket of ice water thrown into my face. It was painful to acknowledge. I had a graduate seminary degree. What good would it do me if I left the religious milieu? I had no skills I knew of that would get me a job outside the fold. "You're right," I had to admit.

In that moment of realization, I went deeper into discouragement and depression. As Norma walked away, her hand slipped out of mine, and in a sarcastic tone I said, "Thanks for your encouragement."

It was so debilitating, that sense of anger mixed with hopelessness. In every area of my life at the time, including my marriage, my expectations were far from my reality.

Coworkers I had greatly admired eventually disappointed me—a huge difference from what I had expected. So without even realizing it, I leaned more heavily than ever on Norma to meet my needs. But she didn't understand all I was feeling; she was busy being a mom to three young children, and she had only so much left to give me at that time.

That's my point exactly: Some friends and coworkers simply weren't interested in meeting my needs. And even my closest family member, who has a heart of gold and wanted to help me, couldn't supply my need. As someone has rightly observed, spouses make lousy gods. They don't fit our "battery packs," and they simply can't meet our deepest needs or keep us happy all the time.

So I was losing massive amounts of energy, and that was contributing to my depression. Years later I came to realize that going through that trial opened me to a new, deeper compassion for people who are hurting and discouraged (one of my pearls from that sand storm).

As a result of this crisis, I also made massive strides in my own spiritual journey. We've said that anger distances us from God. In time, through forgiveness and pearl-counting, I was able to take inventory of my relationship with God—a God who dwells in a sphere beyond human hypocrisy. And, again, I've found God more than adequate; he supplied far above what I expected from others. Today I'm actually grateful I walked through all that hurt and depression, because it was the main motivation leading me to discover a personal God.

There are many good reasons to forgive the wrongs of others, but the most rewarding is to use it in our spiritual journeys. Consider the words of what came to be known as the Lord's Prayer: "Forgive us our trespasses as we forgive those who trespass against us." This indicates his forgiveness of us is connected to our forgiveness of others. It's because our unforgiveness blocks our ability to receive his strength and love.

Unforgiveness is a sign that we're expecting power from a "false battery." If we're trying to stuff other people into our battery packs, the result is usually anger when they disappoint us. (People are good at not allowing us to use them.) But if we're not trying to use them to somehow energize us—if we know the true source of power, if we know that only God gives the best things in life—we can forgive them and consequently relax our expectations of them. As we understand the limitations of people fulfilling us—they can't compare to what God can do when it comes to energizing us—we can sincerely desire the best for others. That's genuine love.

So if people offend us or let us down, we can release our anger to God and allow the hurtful experience to remind us of our dependency on him.

As we do this, we find freedom—and power—to help others on their own spiritual journeys. Again, that's genuine love.

To summarize this idea, one of the main blockages to our spiritual journey is expecting others to meet our deepest needs, and this sets us up for being hurt and getting angry. But we tend to relax when we realize that God can meet our deepest needs. Then as we actually experience God meeting our needs and doing things that could only be described as miraculous, we gain a peace and happiness that's beyond what we had imagined gaining from other people.

I believe the key to maintaining love and satisfaction in life is not expecting lasting satisfaction and love to come from God's creation. Keep those expectations for God alone. Allow him to be the main-battery power source and expect everything else to be "overflow."

That's not to say I never experience down times anymore. Like you and most others, I still have anger and other defeating feelings at times. But the difference for me is that when I experience those normal negative emotions, I find myself "rejoicing," which means returning to the source of my joy. I'm willing to admit that my anger is a result of expecting to use others for my satisfaction instead of enriching them.

4. Expecting Too Much from My Job Kept Me from God

The other "false battery" I used to squeeze God out was looking for fulfillment and energy in a job.

Think of all the places we can go and the things we can have because of our "positions." The money we earn makes all those things possible. We may think, *If only I had a bigger house or a more modern house . . . If only I lived in the right part of town . . . If only I could vacation in Cancun instead of Cleveland . . . If only I could live in Florida, where I'd never have to shovel snow anymore.*

But once again, this type of expectation is bound to disappoint. In reality, a bigger house means higher costs, more work, and more worry. And when you get right down to it, all homes are just wood, bricks, and mortar. Vacations, as great as they are, are only temporary breaks from the demands of daily living. And Florida, as warm and beautiful as it is, also gets hurricanes and is the land of large roaches.

No matter where we are, we face the challenges and difficulties that are universal to humankind. No matter how big our house, the folks inside have all the failings of the human race. When you stop to think about it, can any home or other location take the place of God in filling our battery packs and meeting our deepest needs? I haven't found any place that rejuvenates as he does.

We may also think, *If only I had a lot of money in the bank . . . If only I could drive the right car or wear the latest designer clothes . . . If only I had a higher-paying, more prestigious job, one where I was considered invaluable by all my superiors . . .*

Perhaps you've seen the bumper sticker that says "He who dies with the most toys wins." Well, I've been able to enjoy a few nice things in recent years, and while they provide pleasure for a while, they also rust, break, get stolen, or just wear out. And, according to the hundreds of people I've spoken with, when you have a sick child or a troubled marriage, the size of one's bank account doesn't bring the satisfaction one once expected. The more accurate bumper sticker is the one that says, "He who thinks that having a lot of toys brings fulfillment is already dead."

I know rich and poor people alike who are at both ends of a scale of contentment; some are very happy, and some are miserable. Money doesn't seem to be the gauge for happiness. I can honestly say that no amount of money has ever kept me satisfied or in love. Only if I'm allowing God to meet my needs and empower me with his love, joy, peace, and contentment every day am I truly happy regardless of my circumstances.

Nonetheless, our natural human tendency is to expect fulfillment (a personal battery-charge) from friends and loved ones or from what our jobs can buy—where we live or visit and the things we own. And they inevitably disappoint us, leaving us frustrated and angry.

Practical Ways by Which I've Drawn Closer to God

I have talked at length about my crisis twenty years ago and what precipitated my feeling distant from God—how anger had blocked my relationship with God.

To cover the next twenty years of my life in detail, especially how God made himself real to me, would require another book, a book I wrote several years ago titled *Joy That Lasts.*[7] But I can briefly summarize the two main lessons I have learned that have made my journey more than worthwhile. These two truths were first planted in my heart during my college years. But in my midlife-crisis years they really took root, and they form the essence of my faith in God. Actually, these two truths have become the centerpiece in every area of my life. They are the soil that nurtures my marriage, my relationships with family and friends, and my work. But they didn't become personalized until after my discouragement.

These truths are captured in this quick summary of all the biblical laws: "Love God with your whole heart, and love others as you love yourself."[8]

Can We Really Love God?

When I read that commandment as a college kid, I wondered, *What in the world does that mean? Love God?* It was embarrassing even to say it out loud. You can love your wife, your girlfriend, fishing, or golf, but how do you love God? It seemed too ethereal, too strange. But it was a lifesaving truth I recalled in my depression, and then it began to make sense. I certainly don't know how God does it, but he somehow makes himself real to those who wholeheartedly seek after him. I'll try to explain this as I've come to understand it.

I came to realize that the word *love* is an action verb that indicates you're doing something for someone because that someone is very valuable to you. It is closely connected to a word I've used extensively in my seminars and writing and counseling, the word *honor*.

To honor someone means you choose to see a person as being very valuable. In your eyes, he or she is the heavyweight champion of the world, the best, of the highest value possible. *Dishonor*, on the other hand, is when you consider somebody as nothing more than mist from a teakettle; it disappears and is gone and has little value. (I'll share more about this concept in chapter 8).

This word *honor* has helped me draw close to God. As I have established God as my highest value in life, God has miraculously reached out and made himself real to me in many ways. I don't understand how he does this anymore than I understand how my computer works, yet I go on typing . . . And in my spiritual life I still go on honoring and believing, and God continues to make his presence known to me.

Let me illustrate what I mean by "making God my highest value." Imagine that you and your mate are at a concert with thousands of fans, waiting to hear one of your favorite female singers, Crystal Gayle. As you sit and wait for the concert to begin, you think about how all your life you've wanted to meet Crystal and get her autograph.

Your seat is in about the fiftieth row, and once the show starts, you and the thousands of other people listen for hours, just spellbound. Several times you mentally thank the friend who gave you the ticket, and you feel especially valued because this friend gave up his own seat—for you.

And Crystal—you've got all her music, and you're yelling and clapping and treasuring this time with her. She is of great value to you, and you're honoring her with your presence and enthusiasm. That's what the word means.

Now let's go further. Let's say that just before the concert is over, an usher in a tuxedo comes down and points at your seat number, M-52. An announcer calls out, "Would the person in seat M-52 step out and follow the usher at the end of the show? The friend who gave you the ticket wrote Crystal and told how much you like her music. She would like to meet you personally in the green room after the concert."

Well, your heart practically explodes. You just go nuts. For the rest of the show, you're thinking, *This can't be happening. This is too good to be true.* You don't really hear the final songs because of your excitement.

The concert ends, and you ask the usher, "Is this for real?"

And he knows your name! "Crystal got the letter that talked about you," the usher says, repeating the announcer.

So you go backstage and meet her. She asks about you and thanks you for being such a big fan, and the two of you hit it off. You even go out with her whole entourage for something to eat afterward. Then, to your amazement, she says she'd like to see you and your spouse again the next day, so you spend the afternoon together. At the end of the day, to top everything off, she says she'll pay for you and your spouse to take a two-week vacation with her because she really enjoys being with you. So over a period of months, you get to know her; she becomes one of your close family friends, and you just shake your head in wonder at your good fortune.

That's kind of what happened to me in my experience with God. I was like a groupie with God as my idol. I had valued him ever since I was in college. Nothing meant more to me than him and my relationship with him. But I certainly wasn't able to do what I thought he expected of me—love him and others as I did myself. I fell way short of his standard. I needed not only his forgiveness, but also his strength. But having such high honor of him, I was drawing close to him and loving him even when I wasn't aware of it.

I've learned that as I honor God, I learn to love God. As I've sought after God, I've found him. As I set aside the anger that keeps me distant from him, I am ushered into his presence; I am able to experience him in my spirit.

I have hundreds of examples of how he has made himself known to me. Many involve inner assurance—peace and comfort and wisdom—in the midst of crisis, a rejuvenating joy, and an increased desire to love others. I didn't have to work at these things; they seemed to be given to me without effort on my part. All I did was draw closer to him by honoring him. As I honored him, I got to know him and trust him.

This contentment came as I, in faith, experienced the fulfillment of biblical promises such as "My God will meet all your needs according to his glorious riches in Christ Jesus."[9] All the things I will ever need, God can supply! That's quite a promise, especially since a lot of my emotional needs had been going unmet for years, my work had been disappointing rather than fulfilling, and I was wondering how I would provide for my family in the months ahead. But as I got to know God better, I came to trust him more, and I found that he's as good as his Word. Time and again, he has miraculously met my deepest needs in very practical ways.

Can We Love Others?

As I recovered from my crisis, this new awareness that God was taking care of me allowed me to spend more time and energy thinking about the needs of others. It was like, "Well, I'm taken care of, so now I can do more to take care of the needs of those around me." This attitude allowed me to concentrate more openly on the second truth. Remember, the summary commandment was, "Love God with your whole heart, and love others as you love yourself."

When I no longer felt distanced from God, I could better love others (and myself). When I started increasing the value of others—honoring them—my desire to help them increased. It's been said, "Where your treasure is, there your heart will be also."[10] As I treasured people, I loved them. I didn't have to work up a love for people; it just grew as I honored them more.

Practical, Specific Steps

I'd like to present some steps that I take each day to maintain my relationship with God. It's not a rigid set of procedures but just some ideas that help me in a practical way.

I recognize that God's creation can't ultimately give me the kind of contentment that only God can give. So I use my natural negative emotions to remind myself to let him be that source of power for me. Whenever I'm fearful, worried, or angry because someone or something has failed to meet my expectations, I admit it to God. (That's another way of saying I confess my error of seeking contentment from people or the things money can buy.) For example, if I'm angry, I say, "Lord, I'm thankful that I'm angry right now. It shows me how easy it is to expect your creation to charge my battery pack. It also shows me that I've been looking in the wrong place for my fulfillment, because I haven't been looking to you. I haven't been honoring you as the source of my power and life."

Then I tell God, "I'm going to take the time right now to pull that non-God thing out of my battery pack." In other words, I make a conscious decision that I'm going to stop relying on people or my job for fulfillment. I'm not going to keep expecting them to provide my happiness, contentment, and love.

Next, I say to God, "I now invite you to take full possession of my battery pack." I realign myself with God, acknowledging that only he will never disappoint me. I start looking to him, and him alone, as my source of energy and joy. And when I'm aware of how I've "missed his mark" by acting in an unloving way, I seek his forgiveness. That keeps our relationship open.

Finally, and this is the hardest part, I tell God, "I honor you and your ways that are beyond my knowledge. Lord, I'm willing to wait until you 'charge my battery.' I know it may take awhile before I'm content with what you provide rather than secretly expecting my spouse or my house or my job to meet my needs. But I want you to be the source of my life, the source of my strength, my power to love others as I should."[11]

I've found that in praying this way consistently and sincerely, God has been faithful in revealing himself to me. If we're putting anyone or anything other than God into our battery packs, expecting people or jobs or things to energize us and make us happy, we're going to be disappointed—and often. Those people and things simply can't take his place. *The reality is always going to be less than our expectations.*

Can you imagine what it would be like to have two people in a marriage who are both relying mainly on God to fill their "happiness packs"? Then they would both try to outdo the other in meeting one another's needs. They would be following what Jesus called the greatest commandments: Love God with all your heart, and secondly, love others as you value yourself. I don't know of anything better.

Heeding the Warnings to Steer Clear of Disaster

Our spiritual journey concludes the first part of this book. We've seen how our choices in five major areas can make the difference between hitting an iceberg or taking a route that can lead to a deeply satisfying love for life that undergirds a love for our mate. It's our choice:

- To move beyond unresolved anger and learn to forgive,

- To seek the highest value in all of our trials,

- To gain strength from more than one or two life areas,

- To lovingly claim and respect personal property lines, and

- To allow a loving God to meet our deepest needs to empower us to love for a lifetime.

Next, in part II, we'll focus on eight of my favorite ways to enrich relationships, especially with your spouse. I'll show you how you can make a few adjustments in your own life that can transform your marriage. Even if your mate is unwilling to travel this route with you, you can still greatly influence your marriage for good. And the basis for part II is that second truth that has transformed my life: Love others as you love yourself.

Forever-Love Principles

Our list of forever-love principles continues from the previous chapter:

38. Forever-love relies on God as its enduring source of power.

39. Forever-love doesn't ask the impossible of a truelove: "Be my power-pack."

40. Forever-love knows that power isn't in positions and titles.

41. Forever-love gives God the highest value in life.

42. Forever-love admits its failures and asks for grace.

Part II

Forever-Love Principles: How to Stay in Love with Your Spouse

Looking for the secret of growing old alongside your spouse? After fifty years of marriage you hope you'll still be smiling when he walks in the door? Still reaching for her hand in the movies? Still eager to snuggle up on the couch or between the bedsheets?

Stay tuned. Part 2 focuses in on the intricacies of personal relationships, especially marriage. How do you learn to balance what you know makes you happy with the things that satisfy your spouse's needs? How do two people maintain their energy for life and their excitement for each other? From the ABCs of effective communication to the XYZs of good sex, the following chapters present principles for making a solid marriage that is defined by the vows made on one's wedding day: to love and to cherish till death do you part. Together forever as partners in love.

Keep in mind that these forever-love principles work to the extent that both parties are trying to live out the love-for-life principles presented in part 1. Two people at peace with themselves have more energy to be at peace with each other. Think about the possibilities: living with a mate who has so much fun in his or her own life garden—and you in yours—that, when you're together, it's overflow. I personally can appreciate the scenario, because it is the kind of relationship my wife and I have cultivated and grown in our garden of love.

I see a different scenario altogether if one spouse has shut the door on the love-for-life factor. For example, a spouse who is spraying unresolved anger at anyone and everyone may not be able to receive a mate's loving words or actions. Why? Because anger can repel love and keep others at a distance.

Having said that, I assure you that there is hope for virtually any relationship if even one party is taking responsibility for his or her own contentment, quitting the blame game, and choosing to go for love in the relationship. Ultimately love-for-life and lasting love for each other are based on the choices we make—choosing our responses to circumstances and to people. *The buck stops with each one of us.*

I urge couples to read part 2 together, if possible aloud to each other, pausing here and there to discuss an idea or its application. If your mate resists the thought of improving the relationship, remember that even small changes by you can make a huge difference in your marriage.

Part 2 presents the tools that have worked best to renew my own marriage and the thousands I've been able to help. Here's how these "tools" are shared in this second half of the book:

- Chapter 8 gives five signs that indicate a healthy relationship and symptoms of relationships that are not healthy.

- Chapter 9 discusses seven ways to enrich your communication, making it possible for you and your spouse to understand each other's meaning and feel each other's emotions. Here you'll see how you can move beyond the superficial levels of communication and get to the deeper levels of intimacy. This is the key to staying lovingly married—meaningful communication.

- Chapter 10 shows how anyone can make himself or herself more lovable—by understanding and working to bring out the best in your own natural personality tendencies.

- Chapter 11 sheds some additional light on five ways you and your mate are different from each other. One of these areas is the fascinating topic of gender differences. How can you bring out the best in your maddening mate?

- Chapter 12 is a high tribute to women in general. Here's how to read a woman's built-in marriage manual. A woman intuitively knows what small steps could be taken to make for a better marriage. To me this is a spectacular insight.

- Chapter 13 describes how normal, everyday conflicts can be used to strengthen your relationship. Instead of tearing you down, they can actually prove to be benefits. You'll see how to reduce the frequency of conflicts and use them to enrich your intimacy.

- Chapter 14 reveals that good sex has four equally important elements—and only one of them is physical.

- Chapter 15 discusses the most powerful way I know to divorce-proof your marriage. You might call the concept "no deposit, no return."

- Finally, chapter 16 describes the best kind of love, the kind that may give you more satisfaction than receiving love from another.

I challenge you to read part 2, "Forever-Love Principles," carefully and discuss which tools would be most useful to you at this time. Then review the book later, as new challenges arise.

And as you read, know that many of these principles will enrich all your relationships at work or at home, especially the potentially explosive relationships with children and teens.

At this midpoint in the book here's the challenge I place before you: Make forever-love your aim, have patience, and watch the fruit of your marriage grow.

8

Five Vital Signs
of a Healthy Marriage

*Love is an active power in man[kind]; a power which breaks through the walls
which separate man from his fellow men, which unites him with others; love
makes him overcome the sense of isolation and separateness, yet it permits him
to be himself, to retain his integrity. Envy, jealousy, ambition, any kind of greed
are passions; love is an action, the practice of a human power, which can be
practised only in freedom and never as the result of a compulsion.*

—Erich Fromm[1]

Are my relationships healthy? Maybe you can hear someone asking the question of a counselor. Maybe you've asked the question yourself. What does the question mean? What does *health* mean in terms of a relationship?

Here's what I'm learning about what's healthy. It's a relationship where each person feels valued, cared for, safe, and loved. Each person is relatively content with life and is growing toward maturity.

In every relationship, especially in marriage, there are at least five generally accepted indicators, or vital signs, of the health of that relationship.[2] In this chapter we'll take a close look at those signs. To make love last forever, marriage partners must learn how to read their relationship's vital signs.

Symptoms of Ill Health

If we can identify signs of health, we can also see symptoms that indicate "something's not right here." Let's look at some of those symptoms in the story of Jack and Sherry. At one point, all their vital signs were negative. Their marriage seemed to be a terminal case.

About ten years ago, after several years of marriage, Sherry got so fed up with the shape of things that she decided the marriage was over. "This is it!" she said. "I'm not going to put myself through this emotional roller coaster anymore!" Packing a few things, she fled the house.

"I didn't have any mama to run home to," she explains, "so I went to our houseboat and locked myself in."

In a way that boat symbolized the root of the couple's problem. Jack's father, an alcoholic, had never hung on to a job for very long. "I was hell-bent to be the antithesis of that," says Jack, who became a classic workaholic, toiling long hours to build a successful business and provide financial security and comfort for his own family. One of those comforts was the houseboat. He enjoyed this luxurious "toy" and others, paid for by his long days and professional preoccupation. And he assumed Sherry appreciated the boat as much as he did.

She may have enjoyed the boat and what it represented, but it did not satisfy any inner restlessness. What did Sherry want? In her mind she pictured and longed for a loving marriage. Central to that image was a husband who made time for her, talked with her, and cared for her. No comfortable home or big boat could take the place of a loving husband's presence and attention.

Sherry's frustration increased when she knew that Jack was at least somewhat aware of her dissatisfaction. Wanting to be a better husband, he agreed to go to marriage conferences and counselors. They even joined a small group devoted to building up the members' marriages. He would hear some piece of advice—such as a reminder that they needed to spend more time together—vow to Sherry that things would improve, do better for a while . . . and then revert to his old workaholic ways. Sherry, who'd never had a great relationship with or trust in her dad, grew more resentful.

When it came to affection, Sherry felt as if she were living in a perpetual drought. She'd get no rain for months. Then a few sprinkles would drop, and she would think, *Oh, this is so refreshing!* She wanted the sprinkles to turn into a shower, but she was never too hopeful. *No, no, something is going to happen, and he'll stop again.* Those negative thoughts made it impossible to enjoy even the sprinkles. Then sure enough, she soon found herself back in an emotional drought.

Jack's tennis-playing became a particular sore point. He used the game to relax, something he really needed after working such long hours. But to

Sherry, tennis was an intruder competing for her husband's attention. And when he would make space in his schedule for a match and not for her, she grew increasingly jealous.

Sherry's resentment built up over the years. It was hard for her to express her thoughts and feelings to Jack. When she did try, he shamed her into silence. "Why, you have everything wonderful!" he'd insist. "What are you complaining about? We've never had it so good!" And her emotional needs remained unmet, her feelings unacknowledged.

The tension and pressure built until Sherry decided she couldn't take it anymore and ran to the docked houseboat.

Their son Jim came after her as soon as he found out about her disappearance. Knocking on the door, he said, "Mom, I only want to pray with you."

She refused to open the door and let him in. "I knew that if Jim prayed for me, I would start crying and give in," she says, "just like I'd always done with Jack." So she told Jim, "No, I don't want to do that right now. I don't want you out here. I really need some time alone."

Jim respected her wishes and went home. But then Bob, a member of their small group, showed up. He was almost like a son to Sherry, and she had always been able to be open with him in the group setting. When he knocked on the door and identified himself, she still held her ground. "Go away! This is it. I don't want to talk."

"Sherry, I'm not going to try to change your mind," he said. "I just want to be here and make sure you're okay."

"No, I can't see you!" she maintained. "Just go away!" And that, she thought, was the end of it. Nothing more was said, and she assumed Bob had left.

Half an hour later Sherry needed to use the rest room, which meant leaving the houseboat. It was February and bitterly cold—only seven degrees above zero that day—so the water on the boat was turned off. Sherry opened the door to go out, and there sat Bob—no coat, shivering, starting to turn blue! He had never left.

Sherry couldn't believe it. And in her concern for Bob, she immediately forgot her need for a bathroom, dragged him inside, and gave him a blanket. They started to talk, and before long she was pouring out all her frustrations and resentments. She told him every lousy thing Jack had ever done. Bob just listened—no criticism, no defensiveness, no denial of her feelings. He simply gave her the gift of an attentive ear.

As Sherry talked, an amazing thing happened. Having someone listen and understand her frustration "uncorked" her hurtful feelings, and they seemed to drain away as she spoke. Finally, she couldn't think of any other negative things to say about Jack. She sat there for a while in silence. *What's this?* she thought as she sensed a subtle shift in her spirit. By emptying herself of the clutter of negative emotions, she had discovered a residue of positive feelings. She remembered a few of the good things Jack had been doing and the small but hopeful changes he had made. She saw ways he had been trying, in his own way, to reverse the habits of a lifetime to be more of the kind of mate she needed. He was far from perfect, but he was making an effort to improve. She felt a new appreciation for him and, without fully understanding it, a fresh hope for their marriage.

Within about an hour her feelings toward Jack and the potential for their marriage had turned around. After talking to Bob a little longer, Sherry said, "I think maybe there's hope for us after all. I'm going home to work things out."

Since then Jack and Sherry have experienced the normal relational bumps that any couple can expect. But her retreat to the houseboat was a real turning point, and I've watched their marriage continue to grow and flourish right up to the present. They're such an inspiration to me and so many others.

Before this momentous day their marriage exhibited the two most common characteristics—symptoms—of unhealthy relationships: (1) Too much distance between the partners, and (2) Too much control being exerted by one person. When both are present in the same relationship, as they were in Jack and Sherry's case, disaster is almost inevitable.

Too much distance can occur when the husband and wife are not talking enough for both to feel "connected." One person is too often silent, unable to share deep feelings or simply closing the other person out of his or her private life. Often a couple gets too busy to stay in touch emotionally; one's job may require too much time away from home. If even one person feels this "distance," resentment can spread like a cancer.

In a situation of overcontrol, one spouse is dominating the other—choosing where the couple will live, go to church, and take vacations, making everyday decisions, and so on. The one being controlled can lose a sense of personal identity and eventually not know clearly what he or she wants or who he or she really is. This person's personal boundaries can be violated until he or she feels squeezed into a little box. And in that box anger is quickly compressed.

Unless they're recognized and understood, these problems—of distance and control—can become deeply ingrained in a marriage. That's exactly what happened with Jack and Sherry. Jack failed to understand that his controlling nature created distance between him and Sherry, who learned not to discuss her negative feelings; rather, she buried them. Until the crisis at the houseboat, neither of them recognized the warning signs of a problem potentially deadly to their marriage.

Now let's turn from ill health to the vital signs of health in a relationship. We'll continue to refer to Jack and Sherry and their "new" relationship to see how several of these signs function. (I thank my friend and psychology professor Dr. Rod Cooper for his insights in this discussion.)

Vital Sign 1: All Feel Safe to Think for Themselves

In any healthy relationship, people have the freedom to think for themselves. Think of a converse situation. If a spouse says things like "That's a stupid idea!" or "Just do what I say and don't ask questions!" the mate soon learns that it's not safe to think for himself or herself. It's not long before that berated person learns to belittle his or her own thinking or grow resentful (or both).

In the case of Jack and Sherry, he routinely made it clear that if she didn't see things his way, there must be something wrong with her. If she said he was working too many hours, he told her she was failing to appreciate the sacrifice he was making for the financial good of the family. If she claimed he was giving tennis a higher priority than time with her, he insisted she was refusing to recognize his need for recreation to relieve the pressures of his job. In short, he communicated that her thinking must be flawed.

In healthy relationships, on the other hand, we encourage others to think. We want our kids to verbalize their plans, ask questions, and then learn to make their own decisions. We want our spouses to use their creativity and intelligence to complement our own. As someone has said of marriage, if both of us think exactly alike, one of us is unnecessary.

I have to admit, with embarrassment, that I was somewhat insensitive to my wife's thinking process in the early years of our marriage. I believed many stereotypes about the female "emotional" way of thinking; at times I would discount her ideas because of my desire to have everything be "perfectly logical." I foolishly assumed my way of thinking was superior.

Now, having been married for more than thirty years, I've learned, not only to listen to Norma's ideas about everything, but also to draw out her thinking as much as I can. That's because I've so often seen her intuitive and logical thinking processes work wonders and keep me out of messes.

Vital Sign 2: All Are Encouraged to Talk and Know Their Words Will Be Valued

In a good relationship, you have not only the freedom to think, but you also are encouraged to talk, to express yourself. When you talk, the other—your spouse, parent, friend, boss, or whomever—listens with the attitude that what you are trying to express is greatly valued, even if the two of you disagree.

(Please understand that I'm not saying it's okay to speak disrespectfully. With freedom comes responsibility, and everything we say should be honoring to those we're addressing. Even strong opinions can be stated in a way that's clear and yet respectful.)

In a lot of homes, unfortunately, spouses and children are literally to be seen and not heard. Or perhaps when they do speak, they're constantly interrupted. Or they know certain subjects are taboo and are raised only at their peril. Getting shut down like that can produce a lot of buried, destructive anger.

Whatever type of communication was used in your childhood home, that's the pattern of communication you'll tend to use as an adult. If you weren't allowed to talk as a child, you'll tend not to give your spouse or children that freedom, either. If you were encouraged to speak, you'll probably give others the same right.

Did you have a distant or controlling parent? Were you never allowed to speak candidly? Were the words "I love you" seldom heard? If you now find yourself repeating such an unhealthy pattern, I have a recommendation that has worked for many of my clients. Go to your husband or wife (or your kids or close friends) and say, "I wish I were talking to you more and listening to what you have to say, but I wasn't raised like that so it doesn't come naturally to me. It's hard for me. But I want to break that habit, that generational pull. Will you help me?" When the people we love begin helping us love them more, they are usually much more tolerant of our ways and forgiving of us.

I've asked for help a lot as a husband and dad. I've had to, because just as soon as I would tell myself I would never jump on Norma or the kids and shut them down again, I would turn around and do it once more. It helped them to understand why I sometimes reacted the way I did, and it helped me to know they were holding me accountable. It also gave us a basis for asking for and extending forgiveness when I "slipped."

In Jack and Sherry's case, he had learned a very unhealthy pattern from his alcoholic father; in turn, Jack was an expert at shutting down Sherry's attempts to express herself. You'll recall that his weapon of choice was shame: "How can you complain? Look at how good you've got it!" So Sherry kept silent and grew more angry and more frustrated until she had finally had enough and ran away.

Anytime I see parents controlling their children in unhealthy ways, I don't think, *What rotten people!* Instead I usually think, *I wonder what kind of parents they had.* Almost always, their negative parenting habits can be traced back to the way they were reared.[3] Based on research presented in their book *Family Therapy*, Irene and Herbert Goldenberg have concluded that the communication skills we learned as children tend to be the ones we use as adults. Again, it's the generational effect: What we got as kids, we tend to give to our mates and kids.

The encouraging evidence for us today is that the pull of our pasts can be broken. And as I suggested above, one of the best ways to accomplish the break is by making ourselves accountable to our loved ones.

To convey acceptance of others' words, I recommend a gentle touch. Whenever you're listening to your spouse or your children, remember to put an arm around them or a hand on their shoulders. That tender touch communicates that you love them, that they're important to you, and that what they're saying is valuable.

Eye contact is also vital, especially with children. When we make the effort to set aside whatever else we may be doing and look them in the eyes, they know they have our full, undivided attention. But if we're trying to talk at the same time we're doing something else, they know we're not really listening.

A friend tells of the time he was looking at the newspaper and his little girl wanted to talk. "Daddy, are you listening to me?" she asked.

"Uh-huh," he said, continuing to read.

Whereupon his daughter reached over, took his face in both her hands, and turned his head so he had no choice but to look her directly in the eyes. "Look at me when I'm talking to you, Daddy," she pleaded.

She knew how to be sure she had his attention. But why wait until someone makes such a desperate plea? Why not make eye contact on your own and show someone—young or old—respect?

Body language can also convey interest and acceptance. Leaning toward the person who's speaking, occasional nods of the head—these are some of the subtle signs of active listening that encourage people to talk.

Vital Sign 3: All Enjoy a Sense of Safety and Value in Sharing Their Feelings

In a healthy relationship, you not only know your thinking and words will be valued, but you also have the freedom to share your feelings, knowing they will be respected. In an unhealthy situation, on the other hand, any attempt to share feelings may be met with a denigrating statement: "Oh, grow up!" "Lighten up!" "You're making a mountain out of a molehill." "Give me a break!"

Recently I was with a husband and wife as they packed the car for a trip during which they were leaving their high-school-aged son with some friends. They hadn't spent a lot of time away from their boy in the past, and the wife expressed some feelings of regret about leaving him behind. "Who's going to make his lunch in the morning?" she said. "Who's going to fix him a snack when he gets home from football practice?"

The husband responded, "Come on, lighten up! We're only going to be gone a few days. I can't believe you're making such a big deal out of this!"

Being a friend of the couple, I put my arm around the wife's shoulder. As I looked at the man to make sure I had his attention, I asked her, "How do you feel about what he just said?"

"It makes me feel silly and like my feelings aren't valid," she said, staring at the ground.

"Would you rather not go on the trip?" he asked, embarrassed.

"No, I want to go," she replied. "But I would love it if you would just let me say what I'm feeling without criticizing."

Then I put my other arm around his shoulder and asked, "Do you hear what she's saying?"

"Yeah, I hear it," he said with a sheepish look.

Do you think he realized what he was doing when he made that harsh comment to his wife? No! He had no idea he was controlling her by belittling her feelings. He was like so many of us who can fail to realize what we're doing unless it's pointed out to us.

I've been in that man's place more times than I care to remember. Norma would express her feelings, and I would reply sarcastically, "I can't believe this! Here we go being sensitive again." If she would cry, I would roll my eyes in frustration and do all I could to win the argument quickly so we could get on to "more important things." For much of our married life, I didn't realize how unhealthy that kind of response was. But as I've learned, I've given her more freedom to share her feelings, and she has grown safer in doing so.

Because the tendency to belittle her feelings has been so ingrained by my background and personality, however, this will probably always be an area of struggle for me. Several years ago, when our kids were pretty much on their own and we had a little extra money for the first time, I said to Norma, "We have the rest of our life together. What do you want from me more than anything else, so that if I gave it to you, you would say, 'This is the best gift you could have given me; I need this most of all'?"

Without hesitation she answered, "I want you to be soft and gentle with me, to understand my feelings and listen to me, not to lecture and be so hard on me."

You see, I was still doing a lot of the controlling things I had learned from my own father, things that were natural for me, considering my personality style. But I told her, "If that's what you want, that's what I want to learn to give." And since that time, I've made it my goal to be the person with whom she feels the safest sharing her feelings. I'm still learning and I still goof up, but I know I've made a lot of progress, too.

I tell the story in another of my books about the time Norma sheared off part of the roof of our mini motor home as she pulled away from our garage after a shopping trip. If I had still been reacting like my father at that point, I would have gone ballistic the way he did one time when I had an accident with his car. In the early years of our marriage, I was capable of saying something like, "That was stupid! Weren't you looking where you were going?"

But because I had been learning and growing a little in this area, I knew Norma felt bad enough already and didn't need a lecture from me. (I also knew that she had already told the neighbors across the street, and they were looking to see how I was going to respond!) She needed me to understand her heart and reassure her I didn't think it was the end of the world. So I put my arms around her and told her I loved her more than campers. We even managed to get the roof fixed within a couple of hours.

How safe do you feel sharing your feelings with your spouse? How safe does he or she feel with you? How safe do you and your kids, your neighbors, your fellow church members, and your coworkers feel with one another? This freedom to share feelings and know they'll be heard and respected is one of the clearest indicators of the health of a relationship.

Vital Sign 4: All Feel Meaningfully Connected

What are the best ways of knowing if you're "connected" to the ones you love? You're connected when you regularly share your deepest feelings with one another, when you're enthusiastic about seeing one another at the end of a long day, when you enjoy being together and doing things with one another. The opposite of this is a situation where a partner is either neglectful—perhaps a workaholic—or controlling. Neglect or control creates distance rather than connection.

The desire for connection is a basic human need. It's so powerful that when people don't feel connected, they're far more likely to develop addictions. The pain of empty relationships is so great that they go looking for some way to medicate the hollow feeling, to cover it over with some numbing pleasure. They get their sense of connection, not from healthy relationships, but from some unhealthy addictive substance. Or even food. Pam Smith, a nationally recognized nutritionist, notes that some compulsive overeaters "eat to 'fill the gaps' in their lives. Food becomes a friend and companion who is always there no matter what. When we're lonely, eating seems to fill the emptiness. It can substitute for love, attention, and pampering."[4]

Think again of Jack and Sherry. Because his alcoholic father had been unable to connect with his children, Jack didn't know how to connect either. (From my experience, it appears that alcoholism disconnects people.) And because Sherry had had a poor relationship with her dad, Jack says, "Some of the suspicions and lack of trust of me didn't come from what I was doing but from her memories of her father." So neither Sherry nor Jack knew how to connect. It's no wonder they had an unhealthy relationship for so long!

Remember, too, that unresolved anger disconnects people. It makes a person want to withdraw, not draw close. If your spouse hates his parents, he's going to have a harder time connecting with you. Hidden anger sabotages a lot of relationships, and that's one of the reasons it's so important that we deal with our anger the right way, through forgiveness and pearl-counting, as we've discussed previously.

How do we build better connections with others? Through shared experiences, intimate conversations, meaningful touch, and—one of the best ways I've discovered—shared crises. As Norma and I look back over our years of marriage, we both realize that one particular type of shared experience was the key to our family being so "connected." Namely, we took time for a lot of outdoor family activities. We did everything from skiing to scuba diving. But of all the things we did, the best one for emotional connecting was our camping trips.

Camping has a way of creating a crisis—hopefully minor—in every outing. And we discovered, by trial and error, that any time a family experiences a common crisis, if the people can overcome the inevitable accompanying anger, they're drawn closer together after the dust settles. At the end of two weeks of mosquitoes, rain, and cold sleeping bags, folks are either more closely connected or very angry at each other! But as soon as the anger subsides and forgiveness is experienced, the shared crisis has driven everyone into close bonding.

Let's take another look at Jack and Sherry: As part of their eventual effort to develop a more healthy sense of connection, they scheduled more activities together. Recently they went boating on a lake and stopped for a romantic picnic on a remote part of the shoreline. By the time they started back to the dock where their car and trailer were waiting, night had fallen. Suddenly, as they were driving through the water, they collided head-on with an unlighted boat. Their boat was thrown about ten feet into the air! Miraculously, no one was hurt. But the whole day, from the romantic meal to the near tragedy in the boat, became an experience that drew them closer as they remembered and retold the story in the weeks that followed.

Just a few months later, Jack and Sherry took a caving trip in Arkansas. As they were climbing out of the deep and long cave, Sherry slipped and fell headlong about twelve feet. She was rather seriously injured and needed two months to recover. But this experience, too, as Jack rescued her and then cared for her as she healed, multiplied their feelings of loving closeness.

I'm not suggesting you have to go on dangerous outings to stay connected, but I do encourage you to plan regular activities that have the potential for minor things to go wrong. Then watch how any shared crises bring you and your mate into a deeper sense of closeness. You don't even have to go on an outing; crises and bonding can occur in your apartment or backyard. The key is to go through the crises together however and whenever they happen.

Connection is healthy. Lack of connection, or distance, is unhealthy. How connected do you feel to your spouse, your children, and other members of your family? Or better yet, how much distance are you putting between yourself and those you love? Just like Jack and Sherry, you can plan activities that you have discovered bring you and your loved ones into closer connection.

Vital Sign 5: The Personal "Property Lines" of All Are Respected

The fifth vital sign of a good relationship is respect for each other's personal "property line." We discussed this in detail in an earlier chapter, so I won't say a lot more here. But honoring and protecting others' boundaries is crucial to the health of both the individual and the relationship.

Let me give you a couple of new word pictures to illustrate the importance of this. One of the primary functions of physical skin is to protect a person's internal organs. If you cut it, disease and infection can get in and threaten the whole body. Now think of your mate's property line as a sort of skin around his or her personality and feelings. Violating it can cause a crack that lets in emotional infection, especially anger, that threatens every area of the person's life.

Or think of your loved one's property line as a fragile robin's egg. If you care for it and nurture it, you'll see a beautiful, healthy bird. But if you're careless and crack it, the growing bird inside may die.

All five of these vital signs are important if you want your relationships to remain healthy. But one of the most important threads running through each of these five signs is a concept that is hidden throughout this entire book, and I believe it is the most important concept of all healthy relationships. When it comes to life itself, think of this concept as the very air you breathe. It's that vital.

Honor: The Weighty Foundation of Good Health

Honor is to any growing and loving relationship as diamonds are to jewelry. For the ancient Greeks, something of "honor" called to mind something "heavy or weighty." Gold for example, was something of honor because it was heavy and valuable. And the word dishonor actually meant lightweight "mist" . . . unimportant things.[5]

If we honor someone, that person carries weight with us, like the "Heavyweight champion of the world." That person is valuable to us. Honor is so weighty and significant in relationships that I've dealt with it at least briefly in every book I've written. It's the theme in all eighteen marriage videos we offer through our national television show.

When we honor someone we give that person a highly respected position in our lives. Honor goes hand in glove with love, a verb whose very definition is doing worthwhile things for someone who is valuable to us.

What's the relationship between honor and love? We first honor—increase the value of—someone, and then we feel the desire to love—do worthwhile things for—the person. Love is honor put into action regardless of the cost. Honor provides us with the energy to stay in love.

Consider the ancient truth: Whatever you treasure, that's where your heart is.[6] When we highly value something, such as a job, car, friend, toy, rifle, or a coat, we enjoy taking care so as not to lose it or harm it. We enjoy "being with it." I've found that as I increase the value of my mate and family, it's easier to love them. I want to be with them, and I feel as though I'm "in love." The feeling of love is simply a reflection of my level of honor for them. So how do you retrieve lost feelings of love? By choosing to increase the value that person has in your mind.

There's a little trick to honoring someone. You can feel as if you're showing honor or doing someone a favor, but your intentions can go awry if you're not listening and communicating well. (Hold on. Communication is the topic of the next chapter.)

Just recently, though I had the best honoring intentions, I actually managed to communicate dishonor to my mate. Here's how it happened: Besides being the keeper of our home, Norma runs the day-to-day affairs of our business. She gets up at five each morning to accomplish everything, and I thought I saw energy draining from her because of overwork. In addition, since she was doing our financial reports manually and not using a computer, I wasn't getting some information I thought I needed.

So I figured I would kill two birds with one stone by suggesting she get some accounting help. That would lighten her workload and get me the financial data I wanted. A good idea, right? I thought so when I proposed it to her.

There was just one problem with my plan to help Norma: It wasn't what she wanted or needed. "Gary," she said, "if you think that's what would make me happy, you haven't been listening to me. I enjoy what I'm doing. I like getting involved in financial details, even if it makes for a long day. In fact, a total high for me would be if all three of our kids [who are all married now] would call a family conference and ask me to sort out their finances and set up budgets for them."

She was right. I don't ever remember hearing just how much she enjoys working with numbers. She really didn't want anyone else taking her jobs away. Then she gave me a word picture that made her feelings crystal clear. "What you're trying to do for me," she said, "is like my suggesting that you have someone else write all your books—the content, stories, word choices, and everything else—because you're working too hard." Since I love communicating the insights I've gained to as many people as possible and books are a great way to do that, I understood immediately what she was talking about. Even if it might lighten my load, I wouldn't want someone else doing my work.

As I said, I started that whole affair with the best intentions. But because I didn't ask Norma what she wanted and what was best for her—I just assumed I knew—I ultimately failed to honor her. Instead of giving her more energy and fulfillment, my idea would have been draining energy away from her.

In one sense, however, I was honoring Norma. I'd made the suggestion to get help because I consider her valuable. But if I value and respect her, I need to ask what she wants and then listen carefully. I can't make decisions that affect her without first getting her input and approval. She's a unique and special person, and I prove she's these things when I listen to her and understand her.

If you consider the principles presented in part 1, you can see that honor and forever-love for your mate grow best out of a healthy respect for yourself. When you have high regard for yourself, you can more easily and energetically—with greater focus, clarity, and insight—do the things that help your mate feel valued.

Many of the things we've already discussed in this book will help you value yourself in a healthier way. For example, draining anger out of your life will increase your sense of self-worth. Pearl-counting can always raise your awareness of personal benefits. As you work to align your expectations with reality in your life garden, you will be renewed—better able to love your mate and your children. This, in turn, honors them and makes you feel more worthwhile as a person. And as you'll see in a later chapter, accepting and appreciating your own unique personality, as well as your mate's, is still another way of valuing and honoring both of you.

Time for a Checkup

Like you—and like Jack and Sherry—I want my marriage to be healthy. I want my family to be healthy. I want my friendships and working relationships to be healthy. And healthy means giving others the freedom to think, to talk, to feel, and to connect with us. Healthy means showing honor by respecting each person's uniqueness.

But let me remind you that we all make mistakes. No one is perfect as a spouse or parent, so don't kick yourself mentally or dismiss yourself as a failure every time you blow it. I hate it when I hear some presentation about relationships and the speaker makes me feel ashamed and guilty. We all struggle in one area or another, and we all need to help each other develop healthy habits. But even if we fail a thousand times along the way, with the help of others new habits can be formed. We can choose to pick ourselves up when we fall. We can choose to check our marital vital signs regularly and make adjustments to move from ill health toward health.

I suggest you use the "Parental Effectiveness Scale" rating system shown on page 138 to take inventory of your life in light of the five vital signs of healthy relationships discussed in this chapter. Where are you? What's healthy about the way you do things, and what's unhealthy? When you've done that, join me in deciding to break those habits from our pasts and to start a new way of life for ourselves, our mates, and our children. Let's launch a wave of healthy relating that will carry generations to come into a positive future.

A big part of launching this relational revolution is learning how to be a better communicator. The next chapter deals with the part of marriage where couples say they need the most help. If we don't know how to communicate effectively, any relationship is jeopardized. According to Drs. Howard Markman, Scott Stanley, and Susan Blumberg, one communication method you'll read about in the following chapter has the potential for erasing the four main causes of divorce.[7] I call it "drive-through talking."

Parental Effectiveness Scale:
Rating the Way You Were Raised

As we've discussed, unhealthy relational patterns tend to be passed down from generation to generation—unless one makes a conscious effort to change course.

Consider again the line of Abraham Lincoln: "If we could first know where we were and whither we were tending, we could better judge what to do and how to do it."

The ten questions in this inventory will help you judge where you've been so you can better judge where you are and where you should be in terms of relational health.

On a scale of 0–10, use the following statements to rate the way you were reared by your parents (0 = not at all; 10 = all the time).

My parents were:

_____   1. Like dictators, wanted obedience.

_____   2. Rigid, forceful with strict rules, values, beliefs, and expectations (shamed us if we differed).

_____   3. Critical, judgmental with harsh punishment. ("I felt abused emotionally, sexually, physically, mentally, or spiritually.")

_____   4. Closed to talking about certain subjects: sex, religion, politics, feelings.

_____   5. Poor listeners about my thinking and feelings.

_____   6. Like a machine with many demands ("you should" and "you should not").

_____   7. Degrading with names such as "stupid," "lazy," "no good."

_____   8. Cold and indifferent toward me.

_____   9. Resistant to changes and learning new things. (It was not easy to disagree with them and stay "safe.")

_____ 10. Distant (not close friends, and I was not invited to do things with them regularly).

_____ Total score. Add up the numbers of your ten responses.

The higher your score (the closer it is to the max of 100), the higher the potential for your having been raised in an emotionally unhealthy home.

Questions for further thought: How much "old baggage" do you still carry? Do the statements reflect your current relationship to your spouse or children?

Forever-Love Principles

Our list of forever-love principles continues from the previous chapter:

43. Forever-love is handicapped by too much distance between partners and/or too much control by one over the other.

44. Forever-love allows others to think for themselves.

45. Forever-love encourages conversation, listens well, and values the words of others.

46. Forever-love is not afraid to ask for help to break bad habits learned in childhood.

47. Forever-love does not belittle the feelings of others.

48. Forever-love makes a truelove feel safe.

49. Forever-love looks for ways to connect with a truelove.

50. Forever-love thrives on shared, minor crises that, when remembered, prompt laughter.

51. Forever-love highly values a truelove. "With me, you carry weight!"

52. Forever-love is honor put into action regardless of the cost.

9

The Number One Request:
Better Communication

The small-talk of everyday life can be a genuine road towards contact, a way of getting to know somebody, a prelude to more profound exchanges, a simple and natural approach. But, let us admit it, it is also often used as a means of avoiding personal contact. It is like a prologue that goes on so long that the play never begins. It allows us to be friendly and interesting with people without touching on subjects that would compel us to enter into real dialogue.

—Paul Tournier[1]

At most of my live marriage seminars, I ask several hundred couples to name one thing they believe could improve their marriage above everything else. Without exception, in more than twenty years and from more than three hundred thousand people, the answer has come through loud and clear: "We need better communication!"

The quality of our communication affects every area of every relationship we have. Review the vital signs of a healthy relationship, and you'll find effective communication at the heart of all five of them. It even influences our physical health. Effective communication reduces occasions for anger to be buried inside. And, as we saw in chapter 2, unresolved anger can disastrously affect one's health. Learn how to be a better communicator, and everyone wins.

Why such a high priority on communication? Because good communication is the key to what all of us who marry basically want . . . to love and be loved. We want to share our lives with someone who loves us unconditionally. We want to grow old with a mate who has valued us, understood us, and helped us feel safe in sharing our deepest feelings and needs. We want to make love last forever. And this type of loving relationship is most often attained by couples who have learned how to reach the deepest levels of verbal intimacy.

Communicating—at What Level?

Marriage researchers have helped us understand that there are five levels of intimacy in communication, moving from the superficial to the most meaningful.[2] The more often a husband and wife reach and remain on the fourth and fifth levels, the more satisfying their marriage.

When we communicate on the first level, we speak in clichés: "How did your day go?" "Fine." "Give me five!" "What's happening?" Think about it. Does conversation at this level mean much? A question like "How are you?" may be more than a cliché, especially in marriage, but it's often asked just as superficially in a domestic setting as it is by a store clerk you've never met before. Some couples who are afraid of conflict spend a lot of time at this "safe" level.

At the second level of communication, we share facts—just information. "Hey, it looks pretty wet today, doesn't it?" "Watch out for that new road construction." "Did you hear the latest about the president?" Like level one, this is pretty shallow communication, and it's still relatively safe. Not many major marital wars start this way.

At the third level, we state our opinions. Here is where communication feels a bit more unsafe and conflict may arise. "How can anyone vote for that person? He has no experience." If we feel insecure in our marriage, we tend to steer clear of this level. Though most couples do get to this level, most of our conversation, even with family, rarely goes beyond it to the deeper levels.

The fourth level is when we say what we're feeling. "I was really hurt by what my father said on the phone last night." Opening up this way can be scary, but we can reach the deeper levels of loving and being loved only when we put ourselves at risk of having our feelings misunderstood or ridiculed. In fact, one of the healthiest questions we can ask is "What are you feeling right now?"

The fifth level is where we reveal our needs. "I just need for you to hold me for a few minutes," you might say after hearing about the serious illness of a good friend. To risk at this level of verbal intimacy, we have to feel secure in the relationship. Let's see how a couple with a strong marriage and good communication skills might work their way quickly to this level.

Suppose, for instance, that a conversation starts at the third level with the husband saying to his wife, "Hey, you're drenched! Why don't you ever remember to put your umbrella in the car?" That's an opinion that his wife should keep an umbrella handy.

She responds at the fourth level by saying, "Do you know how I feel today? I feel like somebody ran over my foot at work. It's been a tough day! And with that cute comment, you're now standing on my foot!"

Instantly he knows how his spouse feels. He can now encourage her to move to the fifth level by asking, "What do you need tonight? What would it take to make you feel as if your foot is being massaged and soothed? What can I do?"

She might respond by saying, "You know that movie we were planning to go see? I don't really feel like going tonight. I'm beat! I would love a hug, and I just want to talk and be with you. But first, I would like to be alone for a while, to relax and kind of cool down."

Those are needs, and expressing them is the deepest level of verbal intimacy.

If the environment is really safe and healthy, the husband might say, "Okay, let's do that. I wanted to go to that movie, but we don't have to go tonight. We can go tomorrow. What do you think?" That's a mutually satisfying relationship, where both people's needs are expressed and they have the flexibility of give and take.

Our goal as a married couple should be to go into those fourth and fifth more satisfying levels of communication more easily and frequently. But again, the key to deep verbal intimacy is feeling safe to share our feelings and needs and sensing that our feelings and needs are valued by our mate. Having the self-control to listen lovingly without overreacting or misunderstanding keeps the lines open. The caution I would interject here is that we need to speak in love, measure our words carefully, and only make requests that we can reasonably expect our mate to respond to favorably.

About ten years ago, a good friend of mine brought up the subject of weight with his wife. He said he really needed her to lose a few pounds. It made perfect sense to him and seemed reasonable because they had both been talking about ways to improve their marriage. But his wife wasn't able to respond positively to this fifth-level request. She was hurt and frustrated, because all her previous attempts to lose weight had ended in failure. She felt trapped. She wanted to please her husband in this way, but she couldn't.

What she wanted from her husband was comfort—not the sense of rejection she felt now. She had been trying for some time to find the underlying reasons for her overweight condition. Some were probably inherited, she concluded, while others were learned. But she couldn't overcome all the various "pulls" she felt to control her eating habits, and his request only seemed to increase her problem. So again, my caution is that you allow honor to regulate when and how your communication goes to the fifth level of verbal intimacy. Sharing needs that require your mate to make too great of a change can be hurtful and actually weaken the relationship.

Now let's take a look at five effective communication methods that can enrich a marriage and help you move into those deeper levels of intimacy more often and with greater ease. Over the years Norma and I—and our children—have tried many communication methods, and I consider these five my favorites. To help give you the flavor of them, I've given them names that relate to eating in a restaurant.

Practice Drive-through Talking

Drs. Howard Markman, Scott Stanley, and Susan Blumberg report that this first type of communication I'm going to describe is the key to overcoming the four main reasons couples divorce.[3] For me, it's the absolute best method I've ever learned. My wife and I use it as a couple and with our family, and our company profits by it as an organization. Communications expert Dr. Dallas Demitt, of Phoenix, taught me this approach several years ago.

I call this first method of communication drive-through talking. Let me explain. I've just driven to one of the fast-food restaurants and pulled up at the speaker. I'm ready to place an order for my whole family. The clerk comes on the intercom and says, "Welcome to the Good Life Cafe. May I take your order, please?"

"Yeah," I say, "I would like three hamburgers, a cheeseburger, three Diet Cokes, one Pepsi, three fries, and one order of onion rings." Then I ask my family, "Is that it, guys?"

They say, "Yeah."

The clerk comes back on the intercom and says, "We have three cheeseburgers, one hamburger, three Cokes, one Pepsi, three fries, and one onion rings."

"No," I say. "That was three hamburgers, one cheeseburger, three Diet Cokes, one Pepsi, three fries, and one onion rings."

The clerk says, "Okay, I think I've got it. Three hamburgers, one cheeseburger, three Diet Cokes, one Pepsi, three orders of fries, and one onion ring."

"You've got it!" I answer. "Thank you."

"Drive through, please," he says.

Then I drive up to the window, get our order, check the bag, and say, "This isn't even close to what I ordered!" And I start all over again.

Have you ever had that frustrating experience at a fast-food place? We all have, I imagine. And it illustrates the best way to communicate what's on your mind. Drive-through talking is when you say something to someone and you wait to hear it repeated back exactly the way you said it. If the other person gets it right—if he or she can tell you accurately what you just said without somehow missing your meaning—you respond, "Yes, you understand me." If it isn't right, you say, "No, that's not what I said," and you repeat your message until the individual gets it right. Once the other person reflects an understanding of what you meant to convey, you know you've communicated.

This method can be especially effective when you're communicating feelings or needs. An incident that took place during the early years of our marriage shows how drive-through talking could have helped Norma and me avoid a misunderstanding. I was jogging early one day, and during the run my mind wandered in a number of areas. Then I thought, *Why don't I do something loving for Norma today?* You know, it was one of those thoughts that can come to a man's mind on rare occasions. Anyway, I started wondering what I could do for her. Then it occurred to me, *We're going camping later today. And she loves to go to breakfast with Helen. I could volunteer to pack the camper while she goes out for breakfast with her. Then, when Norma gets home, we can jump in the camper and be off.*

Now, I want to ask the guys reading this: Don't you think that sounds like a loving, sensitive thing to offer? Yeah? It did to me too. I didn't see anything wrong with it. So when I got home, I told Norma, "Hey, I've got a surprise for you."

"What's that?" she said.

"How would you like to go to breakfast with Helen while I pack the camper? And then, when you get back from breakfast, the camper will be ready and we can go." I added excitedly, "What do you think?"

To my surprise, Norma wasn't very enthusiastic about the idea. And I thought, *Wait a minute! What's wrong here?*

But do you know what she was thinking? Because her personality makes her want to be sure things are done "correctly," she figured I had planned a creative way to get her out of the house so I could finally pack the camper "my way." But that's not what I was thinking. I didn't care one way or the other about how the camper was packed. Her response irritated me. I felt like saying sarcastically, "Okay, you pack the camper, and I'll go to breakfast with Helen." Have you ever had such feelings after you do something that you think is loving and the person nails you for it?

Well, those negative feelings would never have happened if Norma had used drive-through talking. Instead of assuming I had an ulterior motive, she could have repeated my message like this: "Now, let me understand. You're saying you want to pack the camper. And you want me to go to breakfast with Helen. Then when I get back, it's all done?"

I would have said, "Yeah, that's exactly it," because that's what I said and that's what I meant.

Next she might have asked me to confirm the feelings or needs behind the words. "But are you really saying that you want to get me out of here so you can pack the camper the way you like it?"

Then I would have said, "No. That wasn't what I meant. [That's not the order I placed.] I'm really just trying to make your life easier and give you a good time with Helen." In such a scenario we would have been moving back and forth between the fourth and fifth levels of communication. At this level of intimacy, I valued her feelings while she valued my need to be helpful.

This method of communicating—taking the time to repeat back what we think we've heard (or what we think the real meaning was behind the words)—eliminates so many unnecessary hostile episodes. You can practice it with your mate, your kids, your coworkers, and I promise you'll be amazed by the results. You'll understand each other more clearly and feel so much better about the relationship.

Recently I was with a couple who in more than twenty years of marriage had never once tried drive-through talking. When I had them sit together and start practicing it, they were instantly pleased with the results. At first this confirming feedback might seem awkward. But try it. It's the best method I know to enrich communication—with anyone.

Write a Marriage or Family Menu

My second favorite and effective communication technique involves listing the most important "foods" on your marriage menu. It can be like a marriage or family constitution. Sounds like a chore? Keep reading to see the rewards.

What is a marriage or family constitution? It's a written listing of the most important things you and your loved ones want out of your relationship every day. It objectifies your feelings and needs, and it sets guidelines for your family the way a federal constitution sets guidelines for a nation. When you read a restaurant menu, you know what the establishment is all about. You can say the same for a marriage constitution.

My wife and I wrote our own constitution for our relationship, and we order our life according to it. We feel great about it because we each know that our crucial feelings and needs—critical to intimate communication—are understood and in writing. It has evolved over the years and today lists eight items, but yours could have three, five, ten . . . whatever fits your situation.

To give you an idea of what might be in such a constitution, let me summarize ours.[4] We listed eight items significant to our lives together:

- **Honor.** The greatest thing in our relationship and in our parenting is that we honor each other. Honor is woven through all our constitution. It's the foundation, the basis of everything we do, including our communication. Remember, I have defined honor as "choosing to attach high value, significance, and worth to someone or something." When we highly treasure someone, we are honoring that person. We've continued to discover that our lasting feelings for each other follow our honoring of each other.

- **Personality traits.** We want to understand each other's personality traits and value them, especially when they're very different from our own.

- **Resolving anger.** We want to keep unresolved anger out of our house. So we wrote a short paragraph that describes how we will deal with anger. It fits us and our personalities. Briefly, we simply try to resolve any hurt feelings, frustration, or fear before the next day, if possible. We listen carefully to each other, and when necessary, we seek or offer forgiveness. (Chapters 2 and 3 show how to reduce levels of anger; you can write your own paragraph based on what you learned there. See also chapter 13, on conflict resolution.)

- **Touch.** We want a lot of tender, meaningful touch. How many times does your mate, particularly a wife, need to be touched each day? Just recently we were updating our constitution, and I asked Norma, "How often?" A written answer to that question is only a guideline, however; touch shouldn't become a mechanical action. Remember that each person is different. You may need twenty affirming touches a day. Another person may need only five. And each day the need may vary.

- **Communication.** We also want regular and healthy communication. Just how much and what kind do we need? That's spelled out in our constitution.

- **Bonding experiences.** We also place a high priority on bonding experiences—doing fun things together.

- **Finances.** What about our spending, giving, saving, and other financial issues? We have an agreement on those in our constitution as well.

- **Spiritual issues.** Our spiritual life is a vital part of our marriage. So our constitution also states what we agree on here.

A family constitution forces couples to the fourth and fifth levels of intimacy. But it's also the best method I know of in training and disciplining kids. As I go into more detail about how a constitution helps make for a mutually satisfying marriage, let me show you how it works with kids as well.

A Constitution Brings Unity

First, a constitution brings a couple—or a family—into unity. There's terrific strength and consistency when you're united on a course of action that you all believe in and are committed to. When a young couple writes a constitution, it's theirs, both the husband's and the wife's. When a family writes one, the kids have ownership too. Let me illustrate this from my own family's experience.

Our kids helped to write our constitution. That meant the rules it contained were truly family rules and not just a code imposed by Mom and Dad. This caused the kids to become very committed to the whole approach. And then, for more than three years, we had a meeting at our dinner table every night where we reviewed our constitution, which was printed and hanging on the wall. We would just read through it and see how we all did that day.

At that time our constitution included about a half-dozen requirements for the kids, such as, "How well do you obey Mom and Dad in things, like when they tell you not to go up the street?" We had some things about cleaning your room, chores, manners, and honor. (If I had it to do over again, I would put honor at the top, and all the others would be subpoints to honor.)

Finally, our children agreed on three character qualities they had to have to some degree before they dated. (Because a lot of people have asked about the three qualities, I've listed them in the appendix at the end of this book.) Then, when they got to the age where they were about ready to date, they would say, "Can I date? Can I date?"

Norma and I would answer, "Well, remember you agreed that these three qualities need to be present."

And they would have to say, "Oh, yeah." Our constitution saved us a lot of arguments that way.

Likewise, a constitution helps keep everyone together on what the consequences will be when family rules are broken. Just as a restaurant menu lists rules such as "No shirt, no shoes, no service," so a family has rules to meet its needs.

Let's say one of your marriage constitution items is "We'll spend at least twenty minutes a day in meaningful conversation with each other." And it's your turn this week to be the initiator. But by the time you get ready for bed, you haven't fulfilled your commitment. That's when your spouse says, "You were supposed to do this before 10:00 P.M., but you forgot."

Once you're caught, the agreed-upon consequence kicks in. You can choose various penalties for violations of your constitution. Pick things that are realistic but still mildly painful if they're to be effective. For example, you might agree not to watch a favorite TV show or to do extra chores or do something with your spouse that he or she enjoys but you could live without, and so on.

In writing this part of our constitution when our kids were younger, we had them list about fifty things they would be willing to lose for twenty-four hours if they violated one of the rules. Then I said, "Okay, do you guys agree with this?"

"Yeah," they said, and they signed their little names.

I remember when Greg said, as we were working on the consequences, "If we violate the first rule, no dinner for a month." You know how some kids can be harder on themselves than their parents would be.

"No dinner for a month, huh?" I said. "That sounds pretty severe. I don't think I could do that to any of you. Maybe we could make it no dinner for one night."

"Okay," he said. "That's pretty weak, but I suppose it will be all right."

Guess who was the first one to violate that particular rule: Greg, of course! So he was in the next room salivating while we ate dinner that night. Norma was fidgeting the whole time, and finally she said, "You know, this is more punishment for me than it is for him. I'm the one who's hurting. I don't think this is a good consequence."

"I don't like it either," I told her. "It makes me real uncomfortable." We had agreed that if we didn't like the way one of the consequences was working out, we could have a meeting immediately and revise it. So I said to the kids at the table, "Hey, do you like this consequence?"

"No, we don't like it at all," they answered.

Then I called out to Greg in the other room, "Greg, do you like this consequence?"

"No, I hate it!" he yelled back.

"Come on into the kitchen then," I said, and during the meal we picked a different consequence for him to have that night. He didn't get out of being disciplined, but we revised the constitution right on the spot. That's being flexible, which is healthy. Too much control, or rigidity, on the other hand, is unhealthy.

A Constitution Reminds You What's Important

A relationship constitution also helps you concentrate on and stay committed to your most important values. We hung our constitution right on the kitchen wall so we could see it every day. It reminded us of the values we had all agreed were crucial to us.

As I said earlier, our highest value was honor. When our kids were little, we would be driving through town with them, and I would say right out of the blue, "What's the greatest thing in life?" And they would say, "We know it's honor, Dad. Don't keep asking us. It's honor." But today my children— all in their middle and late twenties—agree that honor is their highest value.

A Constitution Acts As Police Officer

A written constitution is vital for a third reason: It becomes the police officer in your home. When you have it in writing, there's no dispute over what the rules are or who agreed to what, because you don't have to rely on anyone's memory. In marriage, for example, it's not uncommon for a couple to be a little angry and distant for a while, but you don't want it to continue for long, and breaking the ice after a conflict is never easy. A marital constitution can help return warmth to the relationship if it contains an article something like this: "We, the Smith family, do hereby swear that we will open up and discuss any hurts within twenty-four hours after the hurt occurs." You may want two or three subpoints to help clarify how things will be resolved, but make sure they're easy to remember or they become useless.

With our kids, I remember a night when Michael was about four years old. We were going down the list in our constitution, and we got to the rule about the kids keeping their rooms clean. "Mike," we said, "how is your room today?"

"Great!" he said. (Everything was always great with Mike.) "My room is spotless."

But Norma said, "Mike, just before dinner, I looked, and it wasn't done."

"I know I cleaned it up, Mom," he said with conviction.

"Well, why don't we just go look?" she suggested.

So we all got up and walked into his room. It was a mess! "I thought I cleaned this up," he said.

We went back to the table and checked the constitution, and his consequence for failing to clean his room was no TV for twenty-four hours. When she saw that, Kari said, "Mike, do you know what night this is? This is *Little House on the Prairie* night!"

"Oh, no!" he said. "Of all the days not to do my room!" He paused for a moment, and then he said, "Oh, I don't care. There's too much sex on that program anyway."

We hoped he didn't know what he was talking about, but you can see how the constitution served as the policeman enforcing the rule in that case. Norma and I were free to hug him and say, "Bless your heart. We love you, but no TV tonight."

That constitution saved us over and over. It cut down on the need to even think about spanking because it became the policeman, and it was in writing, right in front of all of us.

For the constitution to do this part of its job effectively, the key once again is flexibility. Couples in a healthy relationship feel safe to introduce any revisions. And parents especially need to be flexible. When Greg was ten or twelve, he would come and say, "You know, I don't like this constitution idea. I was a little kid when you started this. I think you're taking advantage of us kids, and I think we ought to change it."

"You want to change some part of this?" I'd say.

"Yeah, I'd like to change part of it."

"Which item?"

"Well, I don't know, but I'll give it some thought."

And you know what? He never came up with anything. Just knowing we were flexible was enough to convince him the rules were fair.

Go for an All-You-Can-Eat Buffet

A third effective communication method is what I call an all-you-can-eat buffet. You can use this in a marriage, certainly, but you can also use it in parenting, in a friendship, or in any other relationship. It is like giving someone a huge injection of energy—feeding someone a gigantic meal. Here's how this worked with the Smalleys: We would pick out one member of the family, and then for sixty seconds all of us would barrage him or her with praise. We would say anything positive we could think of and as much as we could think of. After sixty seconds, the person was "stuffed."

To the individual being praised, it was just overwhelming. You would sit there and say, "Oh, oh, okay. Thank you a lot. Okay. I believe that one. Oh, that's a good one." It's fun and very enriching.

I remember interviewing dozens of women years ago and asking, "How often do you need to be praised by your husband?" And I was amazed to hear repeatedly, "As often as he wants to praise me." Almost all women say, "I have a bottomless capacity to be praised."

From those interviews and other evidence, I've concluded that we don't need to worry about praising people too much. Some people say, "If we praise them too much, they'll get a big head; they'll get conceited." But just the opposite is true. If people aren't praised and don't feel valuable, that's when they appear to be conceited. You really can't overdo genuine, meaningful praise, because most of us can't remember to give it as much as we should.

Make Your Spouse Thirsty

What I call the salt principle is a communication method by which you can be sure you have the full attention of the person you want to talk with. This fourth method is great when you're wanting to say, "Hello in there. Is anyone listening? Is anyone home?" I especially recommend this method to wives because I've repeatedly heard wives complain that their husbands don't listen to them. (I've found that it's just naturally harder for many men to connect verbally than it is for women.)

Using the salt principle, you don't try to make your point to someone unless you have that person's full, undivided attention. To get that attention, you pique that person's interest until he or she is "thirsty."

You know the old saying that you can lead a horse to water but you can't make it drink? Well, that's not true. If you dump a lot of salt into its oats before you take it to the water, it will probably be very thirsty. That horse will suck it up as fast as it can. And a wife or husband can do the same sort of thing with a mate. I'm not talking about manipulation here. I see manipulation as a selfish tool, something done to get one's own way. The salt principle could be used to manipulate, but it won't be if honor is the guide and you're trying to com unicate for the benefit of the relationship.

Consider how my wife got my attention and motivated me to listen to her one time: She had a desire—or need—she wanted to communicate to me. She wanted me to spend more time with our children. So she came up to me and said, "I talked to Greg's teacher today. I found out that he's not doing well in reading and spelling. The teacher said part of his problem is that he hasn't developed his hand-eye coordination well enough. That's a real serious thing." Immediately she had salted my interest with the word *serious*. And then she said, "It could cost us a lot of money in the future."

"A lot of money in the future," I repeated, engrossed now.

"Yeah," she said, "because we would possibly have to get some tutors. So the best thing to do is to nip it now." (That's a whole can of salt.)

"What do we have to do?" I asked as I "thirsted."

"I've been thinking about it," she continued, "and I think it would be good, if you're interested, to start playing catch with Greg regularly so he can develop that hand-eye coordination."

"Football, you mean?"

"Yeah."

I thought, *Hey, hey! Saving money in the future and helping my son. Where's the football?* And I started playing catch with him right away. In high school, Greg was a receiver on the football team (not just because I played catch with him, of course), and he's also a great reader, a good writer, and a good speller today. But notice that before Norma made her request that I play catch with Greg, she first got my interest.

This salt principle can be effective in almost any relationship, even when the person knows it's being used. See if the following story doesn't create some "thirst" within you.

Peter Cartwright was a circuit-riding preacher back in the 1800s. When he arrived in a town, news would spread: "The preacher's here; there'll be a meeting tonight." One day he and his horse were both exhausted. Though this wasn't a scheduled stop where he had a loyal congregation, he "parked" his horse and went to an inn—actually a saloon—to get something to eat. A band was playing. The clientele was dancing and boozing it up. As he watched this, Cartwright thought, *I wonder if there's some way I could give my message to these people? But how do you get people in a bar to listen to you, especially if you're a preacher?*

He was sitting there thinking about what to do, his head down, when he felt this warm hand on his. He looked up, and there was a pretty young woman. "Would you be my partner for the next dance?" she asked.

"I'd be honored," he said, and the two of them went out on the dance floor.

Just before the music started, Cartwright said something to the woman. In an instant she dropped to her knees, confessing a newfound belief in God. His words were also heard by others in the room, and several of them—even in the band—walked up to Cartwright thanking him, and God, for changing their lives.

Now, if you're like most people, you probably want to hear the end of this story; you're thirsty for more. What could Cartwright have said that would make such an impact on the patrons of a bar? It amazes me how even simple stories like this one can create a thirst to hear more. But unfortunately I'm in the same boat as you. Because the person who told me the story wouldn't give me the whole ending. If he knew it, he wasn't telling! Like me, you'll have to guess what Cartwright did. You might mull over the story to remind yourself of the power of the salt principle.

Have you ever found yourself telling your spouse, "I've said this to you fifty times! You never seem to remember"? Maybe his or her interest level hasn't been high enough. That's the key. Try dumping some salt in the "oats." Your partner is more likely to say, "Yes! Give me this information. Tell me what you feel. Tell me what you need." You might think that would never happen with your husband or wife, but I've seen it work time and again.

Creatively Title the Recipes

A fifth and powerful method of communication calls for the use of emotional word pictures. Most of us use these already. The poets among us might call them metaphors or similes.

Ever been to a restaurant where a hamburger wasn't just a hamburger but a steamroller? Or read a magazine where a recipe for tuna-noodle casserole was called "Fish 'n' Worms"? (Maybe not.) A cook is giving you a word picture.

In a relationship, word pictures might work like this: When you meet somebody who seems a little off, you might say, "That person seems one taco short of a combination platter." If you've had a really tough day at work, you might come home and tell your spouse, "I feel as if I've been run over by a truck." A little earlier in this chapter, we had the example of one spouse telling the other, "I feel as if you're standing on my foot."

Those are simple word pictures that help one person quickly understand what another is thinking and feeling. Why is this method is so powerful? It helps us "step into the other person's shoes" and experience something emotionally close to what he or she feels. It can move us into and keep us in the fourth and fifth levels of intimacy.

Let me give you another example of how a word picture can help a couple move into the intimate levels of communication. Friends of mine—a husband and wife—have a pretty good relationship. But the husband had a habit that really annoyed the wife. When they had a disagreement, he wouldn't lose his temper and yell at her; he would switch into a lecturing tone of voice that made her feel he thought she was stupid. He wasn't even aware he did it, but it bothered her to no end every time it happened.

Finally, she decided to use a word picture to make him aware of his habit and how it made her feel. The next time he spoke to her that way, she stopped the conversation and said, "Do you realize what I see when this happens? I see you gritting your teeth and speaking deliberately, as if I'm stupid and can't understand you otherwise. I feel like a little girl being lectured by her daddy."

"Really?" he said. "I had no idea I was doing that or that it made you feel that way. But now that you mention it, I can see how you could take it that way. I'm sorry."

And ever since, though the wife says he occasionally needs a "you're doing it again" reminder, he has tried to be much more careful about how he speaks to her in times of conflict. Her word picture helped him see and feel clearly, in just a few words, how dishonoring his way of speaking had been.

Word pictures are powerful. I actually call word pictures the male language system. As a woman, why use more words when one "picture" can open up a man's heart? More times than I can count, I've seen one word picture stop and change people like that husband. If you'd like even more examples, Dr. John Trent and I have created more than three hundred that anyone can use in any relationship; we share them in our book *The Language of Love*.[5]

My son Greg uses a word picture on me that works every time. In an earlier chapter, I described the big moment when he got up to address a large audience for the first time and forgot his speech about halfway through. He was mortified. Neither of us will ever forget it. But now he can simply say to me, "Dad, when you say or do this or that, I feel like I've just forgotten my speech." I instantly feel with him and apologize if I need to.

An effective variation on emotional word pictures relies on a scale from zero (very low) to ten (very high) to rate how you feel or what you need in a particular area. Men especially appreciate how this approach clarifies many relationship situations. And like other kinds of word pictures, it immediately lets your partner know how you're feeling. For example, you can say, "On a scale from zero to ten, this need is an eight." Obviously, that's a strong need. "I only need this at a three level" would indicate a need that's not so urgent.

This rating tool really helps when a couple desires a marital growth spurt or when the relationship is in decay. In either case, husband and wife can ask each other, "Zero to ten, where are we today in our communication . . . touching . . . anger level?" Then they can follow up with the golden question: "What would it take today (or over the next few weeks or however long) to move each area of our marriage closer to ten?" Even in the middle of a conflict with Norma, I've stopped and asked where that dispute had moved us, zero to ten, and what it would take to resolve it.

Go for the Best

There are many other effective communication methods, but the five I've presented in this chapter are my favorites. My family and I have used them all, as have many people I've counseled and addressed in my seminars. I know these methods work.

Try them out, practice them, and improve your communication skills. Remember that your goal is to move through the first three somewhat superficial levels of verbal communication and get down to the more intimate fourth level, where you find out what your mate feels, and finally to the fifth level, where you discover what he or she needs. The more you do this, the healthier your marriage and all your relationships will be. In fact, they'll come alive! Don't settle for anything less. Go for a love that will last forever.

Communication can be a particular challenge if you and your spouse have differing basic personality types, which is usually the case. But an understanding of temperament types leads to more effective communication. The next chapter—about temperament types—can help you understand why your mate behaves in a particular way. It gives insight into why you both get under each other's skin from time to time. You'll also see how making small adjustments to temper the extremes in your personality styles can quickly improve your relationship.

Forever-Love Principles

Our list of forever-love principles continues from the previous chapter:

53. Forever-love is built on communication that gets to the heart of what both people feel and need.

54. Forever-love takes the risk to ask, "What are you feeling right now?"

55. Forever-love thrives on flexibility.

56. Forever-love measures words carefully and only makes requests that are within the realm of reason.

57. Forever-love communication repeats back what has been heard and then asks, "Have I understood your message and motive?"

58. Forever-love clarifies priorities and sets guidelines for the relationship to eliminate unnecessary guesswork and help align expectations and reality. This might be called a family constitution.

59. Forever-love looks for things to agree on.

60. Forever-love communication creates a thirst—piques an interest—for "tell me more."

61. Forever-love communication uses vivid word pictures to make it easy for a truelove to understand feelings and needs.

10

Understanding Personality Types: A Key to Lovability

Almost without exception, our weaknesses are simply a reflection of our personality strengths being pushed to an extreme.

—John Trent, Ph.D.

We're all a blend of four basic personality types, but most of us have one or two dominant styles. Our individual blends make us unique, like fingerprints. And one of the best ways to improve our relationships is to bring balance to any of our traits that we've neglectfully or subconsciously pushed to an extreme. If you're already familiar with one or more categorizations of personality types, stay with me. In this chapter I present a short course in how we can "take the edge off" the extremes that make us less lovable than we could be.

Many unhappy spouses are just like Sam, whom you're about to meet. They create problems for themselves simply because they don't see that their greatest personality strengths pushed just a bit too far out of balance can become their biggest problems when it comes to relationships.

A person's basic blend of personality tendencies seems to be natural or innate. But as we grow older, we can get into the habit of pushing one or more of our natural traits to an extreme that can strain our marriage and hurt others. It's just harder to love some people who push their natural strengths to the limit.

Understanding why people behave a certain way is a great help in working through anger or conflict. And in the same manner, better understanding of the motivations and actions that grow out of our basic personalities can help us achieve personal and marital satisfaction. Sam didn't have that basic self-understanding and self-control, and it was about to cost him his marriage.

The Lion King

One day several years ago, when I was still counseling regularly, Sam called my office. When my secretary buzzed me and said there was a man on the phone who insisted on talking to me directly, I immediately had a clue as to what kind of personality we were dealing with. And when the secretary put the call through, Sam's voice came booming—even barking—over the line.

"My name is Sam, and my wife is getting ready to leave me," he said, getting right to the point. "I'm miserable and depressed. So I need to see you, and I'd like to see you today, if possible."

"I'm sorry," I answered, "my schedule is full for the next two weeks. But I could see you after that."

"You don't seem to understand," he said in a commanding tone. "I have to see you. I'll come over after hours, I'll come to your home, or I'll meet you early, but I won't take no for an answer."

Faced with his aggressive personality and the fact that I really did have a full schedule, I decided to try an approach I had never used before. "Sam," I said, pausing and getting aggressive myself, "I have to tell you that you're one of the pushiest people I have ever talked to! I don't know why your wife is leaving you, and I certainly don't condone it, but I have a strong suspicion I know her motive!"

The phone line was silent for what seemed like a long minute as my words sank in. Finally Sam replied, "I'll call you back later," and he hung up.

A few days went by, and after he had had a chance to cool down, Sam called again, saying, "No one has ever spoken to me the way you did—but it was exactly what I needed to hear. I'm too pushy with my wife and others. I'm too controlling. Would you help me overcome that tendency?"

Sam did become one of my counseling clients, and as I got to know him and his background and present circumstances, we established that his domineering behavior was just an outgrowth of his basic personality. He wasn't carrying deep-seated anger; no one had seriously violated his "property line." But he had a type of personality that I call the lion style (more about that shortly). With no understanding or even awareness of his natural temperament, he had allowed it to get out of hand, and his wife was suffering the bad, sad results.

You Know the Type?

All of us have distinct personalities—not just the aggressive lions—and all of us can, without knowing it, push some of our inborn characteristics to an unhealthy extreme that can wreak havoc in a marriage.

In the late 1970s, Tim LaHaye and Florence Littauer helped me understand, through their books and lectures, that there are four basic personality types.[1] And while all of us reflect a combination of styles, one or two styles usually dominate a personality. LaHaye feels that wives tend to understand their husbands' personality styles better than husbands understand their wives'. But in the many years since I first started talking about personality differences, I've seen too many husbands and wives misunderstand their mates, causing a lot of relational damage.

Then in the mid-1980s, I gained further insight from a personality inventory—a tool for learning what your personality type is—given to me by my dear friend Dr. John Trent. It's called Performax. Thanks to Dr. Trent's personal touch and advanced understanding of personality styles, we were able to write our own inventory and test it on thousands of people. And in 1990, we did an entire book on the subject titled *The Two Sides of Love*. Dr. Trent is still teaching an excellent seminar on understanding how personality affects one's marriage and especially parenting skills.[2]

More than thirty different personality inventories are available today, and you may have already taken one. But because self-knowledge in this area is vital, if you haven't taken a personality inventory in the last six months, I invite you to turn to the end of this chapter and take the inventory. People usually stay pretty much the same for most of their lives, but retaking an inventory can show if you're more balanced than you were the last time. You'll find that taking the evaluation is quick. You can see the results easily and clearly.

You might also encourage your spouse to take the inventory. One word of caution: Use the inventory to strengthen your relationship, not as a tool for criticism or as something to throw in your spouse's face.

Dr. Trent and I came up with a way of describing the four personality types using four animals that capture the common traits of each style.

First come those people we call lions. Our friend Sam, whose story began this chapter, is a classic lion. These folks are like the king of the jungle. They're usually the leaders at work, in the civic group, or at church. They're decisive, bottom-line-oriented, and problem solvers. They build big buildings and organizations, and they command armies—but they're normally not intimate conversationalists.

Next come the otters. If you've ever seen an otter frolicking in the water, you'll know why we chose this animal to describe those people who are basically fun-loving and playful. Human otters are essentially parties waiting to happen. They tend to be the entertainers and networkers (they love to talk!), and they're highly creative. They're also good at motivating others.

Then we have those people who are the most sensitive and tender in the world; we call them golden retrievers. Just like that special breed of dog, these folks are unbelievably loving, nurturing, and loyal. They'll stick with something or someone forever. These are the people who buy all the greeting cards. I like to call them the nerve endings of our society. They're great listeners and real encouragers.

Finally we have the beavers—those people who like to do things right and by the book. These folks tend to be hard working, and they actually read instruction manuals! (Those manuals were probably written by beavers to begin with.) They're excellent at providing quality control in an office or factory, and they shine in situations that demand accuracy. They're also the bankers and accountants of this world. They like quality things, too—no junk for a beaver.

Perhaps you've already got a good idea of your basic personality type and that of your mate from your own previous study or from these brief descriptions. The four animals capture the four styles in a way that's easy to understand.

But remember, the same traits that make each type of person unique and valuable often get taken to an extreme, and that's the source of a lot of unhappiness for everyone involved. We may be born with one or more characteristics; even so, the characteristics can be controlled. Want a happily-ever-after marriage? Consciously work to become more aware of your natural tendencies. Go for a healthy balance, tempering any extreme problem area. Focus on the strengths of your dominant characteristics and learn to cultivate the strengths of your less-dominant areas. Let's look at how you can tame the extremes of your dominant personality trait.

Taming the Lion

Lions who push their strong, decisive leadership qualities too far can become overbearing, hyperaggressive, domineering people who trample anyone who gets in their way. They're used to getting what they want, and sometimes they're none too diplomatic in how they go about it.

These traits can start at a very early age. Three-year-old Steve was a lion; his father was not. One day, Dad ducked into the bathroom for a quick shower. As soon as he finished, while he was still toweling off, Steve demanded, "I want my bike out of the garage."

"In a minute," Dad said. "I just got out of the shower."

That wasn't good enough for Steve. "I want my bike now," he insisted.

"You'll have to wait a few minutes," his dad said. "I have to finish drying and get dressed."

But Steve kept pushing and just wouldn't take no for an answer. Finally, Dad decided it was easier to give in than to keep arguing. He threw on the all-purpose terrycloth robe that hung on a peg inside the bathroom door, and without even taking the time to tie it, ran out to open the garage door.

Unfortunately, as Dad began to pull up on the door, the bottom of the robe caught on the lock. As he continued to slide it open all the way to the top, his robe was pulled up and over his head! There he stood, facing the street, arms in the air, fully exposed! Both dad and son learned an important lesson that day about what can happen when lions demand and always get their way.

Bobby was a six-year-old with a lion for a father. One morning as his mom was driving him to school, he blurted out, "Mommy, where are all the idiots?"

His mother was shocked. "Where did you learn to talk like that?" she asked.

"Yesterday Daddy drove me to school," he said innocently, "and we saw six idiot drivers on the way."

Sam, the lionlike husband whose wife had left him, had a lot of what Bobby's dad and Steve had. He had gotten in the habit of demanding what he wanted from everyone in his life. To say he was overly controlling toward his wife is a major understatement.

As I worked with Sam, however, he became more aware of his tendencies and learned to control that natural bent of his. He actually learned all over again how to date his wife, and little by little, she warmed to his efforts at being softer and less demanding. His desire to honor his wife led to a change of actions. It didn't happen overnight, but after watching him for several months, she did decide to come back. I saw that it wasn't easy for him, because natural tendencies are so ingrained, but she eventually did start trusting him again. Yes, she was concerned that he would revert to his old ways, but she responded as he reined in his tendency to control and push and balanced it with some tender golden retriever qualities.

Many lions need to make a conscious decision to relax their control over others. Again, this won't be easy, and it will take some time, but as Sam's case shows, it can and must be done. And one of the best ways of relaxing your grip on others is to look at the best traits of the golden retriever and practice using those same strengths.

Lions also may need to learn that meaningful communication takes time. They need to slow down and discuss decisions with others, not simply charge ahead on their own. For a lion, that's a secret of getting along with people and being enjoyable to live with.

Slowing Down the Otter

Let's-have-fun otters can push their natural tendencies too far as well. As a card-carrying otter myself, I'm a master at getting into trouble. It was a big moment for me when I realized I was 100 percent responsible for my choices and needed to get a handle on some of those traits that created problems for me and others.

We otters are always ready to take chances. Our attitude is *Hey, this will be fun! Let's go for it!* We don't always carefully think through the entire situation. I could give you all kinds of illustrations of this from my own life, but there's a particular incident that stands out in my memory.

Not long ago Norma and I were in Scotland, celebrating our thirtieth wedding anniversary and having a good time. While we were there, Norma decided to tint her hair using a dark brown/reddish dye. The next day some friends were flying in from the States to be with us, and Norma, who also has some otter in her, suggested to me, "Why don't you color your hair too? Then when we go meet our friends at the airport tomorrow, we'll see if they recognize you without your gray head!"

"That's a great idea!" I said without a second thought. So Norma dyed my hair, and everyone enjoyed the gag the next day. It was otter heaven.

The fun didn't last, however. Just a short time after we got home, I was scheduled to speak at a big university in front of several thousand students. Posters had been put up all over campus advertising the event, and they featured a picture of me with my naturally gray locks. You can understand, then, why I didn't want to show up with—and have to explain—my reddish-brown hair.

When I tried to get the color out of my hair, however, I discovered I was in trouble. The box said it would come out in twenty washes at most, but after twenty shampoos, my hair looked the same as before. So I tried Tide, Amway cleanser, and anything else anyone recommended. Nothing worked.

Finally, I ended up going to Norma's stylist to see if he could get the dye out. The process took several hours, during which my scalp was burned and my hair changed colors several times. At one point it was orange, but I didn't know that, and I asked the guy if he was done yet because Norma wanted to go out to dinner.

"Sure, you can go out—to McDonald's," he said. "You look just like Ronald McDonald!"

Well, I decided not to go out right then, and I didn't leave when it was yellow, either. At last he got my hair pretty much back to normal—normal, that is, for a woman in her eighties with that bluish-gray tint. I was able to speak at that university without being embarrassed. At the time I write this, though, you can still see about four different colors in my hair if you look closely. Only an otter would get himself into such a mess!

Otters also love to challenge authority. As far as we're concerned, rules were made for other people. A restaurant menu, for example, is just a group of suggestions to us. Norma will dutifully order number 5 off the menu, but I'll ask the waiter if I can get this part of number 5, half of number 3, and another item out of number 8. "Why can't you just order by the number?" Norma will ask in frustration.

"Because it's no fun that way!" is my standard answer.

As an outgoing, outspoken otter, I love to bargain too. That can be irritating to an accompanying spouse, or it can get someone like me in trouble all by myself. A few years ago, I was speaking in Wichita, Kansas, during a bitter winter storm. When I arrived from warm, sunny Phoenix, I realized I had forgotten to pack my overcoat.

"Well, let's get you a new one," one of my staff members suggested. Our host told us about a factory-outlet store with a large selection of coats, so off we went.

A factory outlet is made to order for a bargainer like me. And as soon as we entered the store, I saw a beautiful navy blue topcoat that I wanted. The tag on the sleeve said the original price—$450—had been cut to $129. That was a great deal, but the otter in me decided to see if I could push it. "Watch me get this coat for $99," I bragged to my friends.

I walked over to a salesman and said, "Excuse me, I'd like to speak to the manager."

A couple of minutes later, an older man came up to me and identified himself as the store manager.

We had exchanged pleasantries, and then I got down to business. "I'd like to buy this overcoat. But look at the condition of it. There's a button missing [it was in one of the pockets], and it looks as if someone has already worn it. It doesn't look quite new anymore."

The manager sighed. Obviously, he wasn't enjoying this game as much as I was.

But since I was far away from home and not worried about seeing anyone I knew, I kept pushing for a special deal. "What do you think, how about this coat for ninety-nine dollars—considering its condition?"

"Normally we wouldn't do that," the manager replied politely. "But I'll let you have it for ninety-nine dollars, Mr. Smalley. My family is watching your videos."

He had recognized me! I was so embarrassed! I assure you I have not tried to work a price down like that since.

As I said earlier, some of my biggest marriage problems and greatest dissatisfactions in life have come from my mouth—talking too much or too quickly without first thinking through what I was going to say. The otter in me saying things spontaneously, attacking verbally when under stress, or talking about people's problems without their permission has sometimes deeply hurt others and me.

To deal with such tendencies, my fellow otters and I need to develop some golden retriever and beaver traits, such as sensitivity to the feelings of others and weighing the consequences of our words or actions before we jump into something. My vow never to embarrass anyone in my seminars is a sign of my growth in this area.

If you have a lot of natural otter tendencies, what do you do that gets you into trouble or irritates those closest to you? To become more balanced, you might consider taking on some of the traits in one of the next two personality types.

Building Backbone in the Golden Retriever

Thank God for golden retrievers! Their love and loyalty are a blessing to us all. But they, too, can push their good inborn traits to an unhealthy extreme.

Norma is primarily a golden retriever, and our family is much the richer for it. But there are times when she needs better balance. For example, she loves and feels so deeply—her empathy for her family is that great—that when I or one of our kids is disappointed or discouraged, she can get very disappointed or discouraged herself. That means her emotions are being too controlled by others, and she is learning to take more responsibility for herself and not just reflect what her loved ones are feeling. Her retriever's concern is wonderful, but she needs to remember that she's not responsible for my happiness or that of her children. She's responsible only for her own. This is a truth all retrievers need to learn.

Sometimes Norma's sensitivity toward others frustrates the otter in me. I remember the time recently when we attended a concert near our home. Norma, a real fan, was especially excited to see this particular popular singer. We were able to get good seats close to the stage for the big event.

I enjoyed myself immensely that evening, and I could see that Norma was having a great time. But then, as the concert neared its end, my otter nature asserted itself. I leaned over close to her and said, "Let's sneak out during the last number and beat all the traffic." Fun-loving otters don't like being stuck in the parking lot!

Norma, however, wasn't on the same wavelength. "No!" she said emphatically.

"Why not?" I asked, genuinely puzzled.

Her answer was pure golden retriever. She didn't want to offend the performer. "She's looked at me several times this evening and smiled, so she'll notice, and it could hurt her feelings to see us walking out on her before she's done."

I just rolled my eyes.

From her many years of experience with me, Norma knows how much of an otter I am, and usually she'll go along with my impulsiveness. But if she thinks someone's feelings will be hurt by my suggestion—well, that's a different story, and she can dig in her heels with the best of them. I've never seen anyone so stubborn as a golden retriever who is protecting someone else's feelings. In this situation, since I know her as well and didn't want to make us both unhappy, I didn't push to leave early but dutifully stayed until the concert was over.

Golden retrievers are often indecisive too. That's why it's rare to find two golden retrievers married to each other—neither of them could have made the decision to get married. A golden retriever will often marry a lion. The retriever likes the lion's willingness to lead, and the lion likes the retriever's willingness to listen and follow. It can be a good match as long as both of them keep their natural tendencies under control. But this combination is the one I've seen most often in my office for counseling. They can have a great marriage, as they grow to be tolerant and forgiving and self-controlled—and these qualities generally come as a result of understanding themselves and each other.

Golden retrievers also can be so eager to please others that they have a hard time saying no. The result can be overcommitment, fatigue, and putting too much time and effort into things that aren't really their highest priorities.

If you're a golden retriever and this is a problem for you, you may need to balance your personality with more lion and otter tendencies. I suggest, for example, that you actually practice saying no. It may be hard at first, but the more you do it, the better you'll get at it and the more you'll enjoy the feeling of freedom and control over your own life. So stand in front of a mirror and say it out loud with several different inflections: "No. No. No." You'll probably never feel comfortable doing that, but keep practicing it with your spouse or another friend. It's one of the simplest yet most helpful skills you can develop.

That skill—the ability to say no—can help you set the boundaries essential for your own well-being, as we saw in chapter 6. And it can balance some of the extreme lion or otter behavior that wounds or pains others, especially the sensitive golden retriever. Sometimes people say or do things that unintentionally offend others; they don't know the effect of their words. But a golden retriever's willingness to articulate feelings and then say no can make others—lions or otters—aware of the pain they may have caused.

Yet another characteristic of golden retrievers is that when they get under pressure, they do the most amazing thing—they slow the pace of whatever they're doing and may even deny that things are as bad as they are. Just becoming aware of this tendency will help a golden retriever overcome it, as will a conscious decision to develop some lionlike determination to push ahead and some beaverlike commitment to getting the job done.

Easing Up on the Beaver

Beavers are the best at getting the details done or even seeing what needs to be done. They seem to be able to spot the smallest piece of dirt in the corner of the room. The room may look okay to everyone else, but not to some beavers if it's not just right.

Overly rigid and organized beavers can make life uncomfortable for others. Take Bonnie, for example. She was single, but if your husband or wife is a strong beaver, you'll identify with Bonnie's friend:

Bonnie had a lot going for her when she came to me for help. An attractive woman in her late twenties, she had a fulfilling career in banking. Yet she was very unhappy and looking for answers.

"I continually have a problem in my friendships," she told me.

"Describe it for me," I said.

"It seems to me that my friendships only go so far, and then my friends pull back," she explained.

"What do you mean, pull back?" I asked.

"Well, we appear to get along fine until I start making suggestions . . ."

"What kinds of suggestions?"

Bonnie looked embarrassed, but she took a deep breath and went on. "My friend Arlene is a good example. I really care about her as a friend, so it bothers me when I'm over at her apartment and I see dirty dishes in the sink and laundry left unfolded. Rather than attacking her, I offer to help her straighten things up, but she always seems offended by that."

"Can't you just enjoy yourself at Arlene's without making an issue of the unfinished chores?" I asked. But I already knew the answer.

"To be honest," she said, looking me in the eyes with a mixture of resolve and resignation, "no, I can't."

"Do you know why you can't?" I asked.

"Why?"

"Because that's an important part of your personality. You thrive on finishing jobs and doing them right. On the other hand, you're frustrated when things go unfinished."

"You're right," she said.

Bonnie is a typical beaver, but her natural desire for neatness and seeing work completed was pushed to such an extreme that she was alienating all her friends. As a result, she was feeling rejected and lonely. The same traits that helped in her career were ruining her social life. And this same trait can put unnecessary strain on a marriage.

I explained the four personality types to her, and she immediately recognized herself. Then I asked, "And what personality type is Arlene?"

She thought for a second and then replied, "Based on what I know of her, I think Arlene is an otter."

"I would agree," I said, "and that's why it would be good for both of you to continue pursuing your friendship. You can really help each other grow."

"How?" she said with a puzzled look.

"Arlene may need someone like you to help her learn the importance of finishing things. Just remember not to be pushy and to offer your help only if she wants it or, better yet, asks for it."

She smiled and nodded her understanding.

"And Arlene can help you," I pointed out. "As an otter, she knows how to relax and have fun. You need someone like her to keep reminding you to lighten up and not take yourself so seriously."

"That's a good idea," she agreed.

Shortly after that, Bonnie and Arlene gave each other the personality-evaluation inventory, which confirmed what Bonnie and I had already determined. They had a good talk about it and a lot of laughs, and their new understanding allowed them to be more honest with one another as well. They really were able to help each other grow and develop better balance.

If you're a beaver like Bonnie, you may have trouble deciding just how much of each personality style you have. After all, you must be accurate. But your focus on doing things right, if carried too far, can hurt you. For example, I've found that beavers have more stomach problems than any other personality type because of the pressure they put on themselves.

Like Bonnie, then, beavers need to develop some otter and golden retriever characteristics. If you're a beaver, relax and have fun with your spouse! It's okay for your closet to be a little messy now and then too. And it's okay if your family and other loved ones don't do things exactly the same as you. Save your stomach, your marriage, and ultimately, your smile.

Tempering Your Natural Tendencies

Let me close this chapter with a couple of final suggestions for each personality type. If you take no other advice away from this discussion, applying these tips can still make your life more pleasant and your marriage more enduring (and endearing) as you take responsibility for tempering your natural tendencies. And if you want more of an in-depth study on personality development, please read my book with John Trent, *The Two Sides of Love*.

Lions: Be softer and more gentle, and include others when making decisions.

Otters: Think before you speak, and consider the consequences before you act.

Golden retrievers: Practice saying no and making firm decisions.

Beavers: Learn to relax, and don't expect others to do things just like you.

Understand that I am not suggesting that you deny your dominant temperament. I've found that if you try to become too different from your natural tendency—from the personality with which you were born—you ineffectively use or drain off an excessive amount of energy. But if you accept yourself as you are and work to accentuate the positive aspects of that temperament while tempering its extreme manifestation (and if those closest to you praise you for that—we'll get to this point in the next chapter), you'll find that you're constantly being energized.

In this chapter we've focused on ways you can improve your marriage by making yourself easier to live with. But when it comes to two unique characters sharing a life, "How can I temper my extremes?" is only half the equation. Another question is just as important, and its answers are just as rewarding for a happy marriage. The question? "How can I bring out the best in my maddening mate?" That's what we'll discuss in the next chapter. But first, take the personality inventory to identify your own strongest temperament characteristics.

Personality Inventory

How to Take and Score the Inventory

1. For each temperament type, circle the positive traits (in the left column) that sound the most like you—as you are at home. Do not score yourself as you behave at work. (If you want to evaluate

your "at-work" tendencies, take the test again later, with that environment—or any other—in mind.) *For now, ignore the right-hand column.*

2. For each trait, add up the number of circled traits (in the left column) and then double that number. This is your score.

3. To graph your temperament "mix," mark your score for each temperament type on the graph with a large dot. If you want, draw a line to connect the dots.

I give special thanks to Dr. John Trent and Dr. Rod Cooper for their insights and help in working on this inventory.

Lion Temperament	*Characteristics*
Likes authority.	Too direct or demanding
Takes charge	Pushy; can step in front of others
Determined	Overbearing
Confident	Cocky
Firm	Unyielding
Enterprising	Takes big risks
Competitive	Cold-blooded
Enjoys challenges	Avoids relations
Problem solver.	Too busy
Productive	Overlooks feelings; do it now!
Bold	Insensitive
Purposeful; goal-driven	Imbalanced; workaholic
Decision maker	Unthoughtful of others' wishes
Adventurous.	Impulsive
Strong-willed	Stubborn
Independent; self-reliant	Avoids people; avoids seeking help
Controlling	Bossy; overbearing
Persistent	Inflexible
Action oriented	Unyielding
"Let's do it now!"	

Lion score (double the number circled):_____

Otter Temperament	*Characteristics*
Enthusiastic	Overbearing
Takes risks	Dangerous and foolish
Visionary	Daydreamer
Motivator	Manipulator
Energetic	Impatient
Very verbal	Attacks under pressure
Promoter	Exaggerates
Friendly; mixes easily	Shallow relationships
Enjoys popularity	Too showy
Fun loving	Too flippant; not serious
Likes variety	Too scattered
Spontaneous	Not focused
Enjoys change	Lacks follow-through
Creative; goes for new ideas	Too unrealistic; avoids details
Group oriented	Bored with "process"
Optimistic	Doesn't see details
Initiator	Pushy
Infectious laughter	Obnoxious
Inspirational	Phony

"Trust me! It'll work out!"

Otter score (double the number circled):_____

Golden Retriever Temperament	*Characteristics*
Sensitive feelings	Easily hurt
Loyal	Misses opportunities
Calm; even keeled	Lacks enthusiasm
Nondemanding	Weakling; pushover
Avoids confrontations	Misses honest intimacy
Enjoys routine	Stays in rut
Dislikes change	Not spontaneous
Warm and relational	Fewer deep friends
Gives in	Codependent

Accommodating . . . . Indecisive
Cautious humor . . . . Overly cautious
Adaptable . . . . Loses identity
Sympathetic . . . . Holds on to others' hurts
Thoughtful . . . . Can be taken advantage of
Nurturing . . . . Ears get smashed
Patient . . . . Crowded out by others
Tolerant . . . . Weaker convictions
Good listener . . . . Attracted to hurting people
Peacemaker . . . . Holds personal hurts inside
"Let's keep things the way they are."
Golden retriever score (double the number circled):_____

Beaver Temperament   *Characteristics*
Reads all instructions . . . . Afraid to break rules
Accurate . . . . Too critical
Consistent . . . . Lacks spontaneity
Controlled . . . . Too serious
Reserved . . . . Stuffy
Predictable . . . . Lacks variety
Practical . . . . Not adventurous
Orderly . . . . Rigid
Factual . . . . Picky
Conscientious . . . . Inflexible
Perfectionistic . . . . Controlling
Discerning . . . . Negative on new opportunities
Detailed . . . . Rarely finishes a project
Analytical . . . . Loses overview
Inquisitive . . . . Smothering
Precise . . . . Strict
Persistent . . . . Pushy
Scheduled . . . . Boring
Sensitive . . . . Stubborn
"How was it done in the past?"
Beaver score (double the number circled):_____

	L	O	GR	B	
40					40
35					35
30					30
25					25
20					20
15					15
10					10
5					5
0					0

How did you do? Remember, this isn't a pass-fail test. This evaluation simply shows your tendencies and traits. As you look at your charted score, you may see a blend of all four categories. That's fine. Or you may see two scores significantly higher than the others. Or you may have one category that's head and shoulders above the other three. No one pattern is "correct."

Now note the right-column extreme for each of your circled characteristics. This might be how your positive trait is perceived by your family or friends.

Forever-Love Principles

Our list of forever-love principles continues from the previous chapter:

62. Forever-love understands how personality type influences interpersonal dynamics.

63. Forever-love isn't afraid to look inside and ask, "What characteristics of mine do others find most irritating?

64. Forever-love tempers temperamental extremes and cultivates the strengths of less-dominant characteristics. "For you, my truelove, I'll rein myself in and go for balance."

65. Forever-love knows that meaningful communication takes time.

66. Forever-love does not charge ahead, making unilateral decisions.

67. Forever-love weighs the consequences of words and actions and doesn't lash out when under stress.

68. Forever-love is not so desperate to please that it says yes to every request.

69. Forever-love knows that life will never be perfect.

70. Forever-love doesn't feel the need to "fix" everything about everybody.

71. Forever-love strives for self-control but knows the grace of self-forgiveness.

72. Forever-love knows that natural temperament doesn't need to control life's temperature. "I can temper my control."

11

How to Bring Out the Best in Your Maddening Mate

Many women could learn from men to accept some conflict and difference without seeing it as a threat to intimacy, and many men could learn from women to accept interdependence without seeing it as a threat to their freedom.

—Deborah Tannen[1]

I trust some of my readers remember that old love song with one unforgettable line: "You say to-may-to, and I say to-mah-to." That simple phrase can describe the wonderful—and yet maddening—differences between you and your mate. When you were courting, those fascinating qualities may have intrigued you, attracted you. But now, after living in the same house for twenty years—even two years—fascination has turned to frustration; intriguing characteristics are now idiosyncrasies. You may appreciate the more drastic word picture that titled a best-selling book: *Men Are from Mars, Women Are from Venus.*

If you and your spouse are so very different from each other, how do you maintain your energy for love? That's what we'll discuss in this chapter. Again, an understanding of the issues is the basis for a breakthrough in the relationship.

To illustrate differences between Norma and me—differences that go beyond our natural, dominant temperaments—let me walk you through a moving experience we had not long ago.

We were out driving together on a Sunday afternoon, and we both started extolling the virtues of another state thousands of miles from our home in Phoenix. After a bit, she said, "Why don't we just move there? I mean, why are we staying here in Arizona when we both love it so much over there?"

"Great idea!" I said.

So far, so good; we were in agreement on the general idea. But then a lot of the basic differences between us started to come into play. The moment we said we would like to move, I was ready to pack my bags, load the pickup, and hit the highway! I get going in a hurry when I decide to do something. In fact, within two months of that day, I was already living in the Midwest.

Norma, on the other hand, moves more slowly and cautiously. Before she does anything, she thinks of all the ramifications and makes a plan to cover every detail. It took her another eight months to close down our business, sell the house, take care of all the changes of address, and complete the move.

Before she moved east, we had bought a small farm and begun remodeling the house to suit our needs and desires. She had flown out three times to check the building plans and make changes, but by the time she arrived to stay, the renovations were only about half-done. I remember an exchange we had right after she'd moved. She walked into the farmhouse, and with great anticipation I asked, "Do you think we captured what you wanted with the kitchen?"

She took one look and said, "I don't like that. I thought I had explained how I wanted it done, and that's not it."

"Yeah," I said, "we tried to get close to what you wanted. Doesn't it look nice?"

Well, it was obvious from the look on her face that she was not pleased at all. "I have to get out of here for a while and think about this," she said.

"But you need to stay," I insisted. "We should figure this out."

"No, I have to go," she insisted. "I have to be alone." As she was getting into her car, I urged her to stay because decisions were needed the next day. I yelled my last words at her car as she was driving away: "Stay! It's safe. I'm a marriage counselor!"

Clearly that was a time of real stress for us. With my extroverted nature, I wanted us to stay together and work out what to do. But Norma, being much more introverted, needed to get by herself to think things through. I'll say more about this extrovert-introvert difference shortly.

The story goes on. One early afternoon as we were walking around our small farm (we'd moved in and the remodeling was almost complete), she said, "Wouldn't it be great someday to have animals out here—chickens and turkeys and maybe a little lamb?"

"That's a terrific idea," I told her. "Why don't we go get them now?"

"Can we?" she asked.

"Sure," I said with confidence. "There are farmers around here that sell animals—I think. Let's go!"

We impulsively hopped in the pickup, making no provision for carrying animals home. I assumed the farmers would have boxes—or something. So we found a place, bought a few turkeys, chickens, guineas, and a cute baby goat, and put them in a makeshift pen in the rear of the pickup. Actually, we had to put the goat in the cab with us; Norma held it all the way home. And, of course, on our way back, Norma named all the animals.

To say the least, we didn't know how to keep or protect our "pets." As soon as we got home, the goat escaped—gone. Norma felt bad about the loss of her newly named friend, but I just shrugged: "Well, he'll come back when he's hungry, won't he?" Too soon every animal we bought had escaped from the barn or the chicken pen. Most we recaptured.

But then we discovered we had neighbors—foxes, coyotes, and wild dogs—who suddenly made their presence known. They quickly started picking off our birds; if the birds didn't get up in a tree for the night, they were gone by morning. Norma was pretty upset by this. But I took it in stride. "Oh, that's too bad for those precious little animals. I guess we'll have to build a pen."

I recall the day we were walking our new dogs in the woods. Unleashed and roaming nearby, they came back to us dragging this turkey carcass. "That's Carl!" Norma exclaimed.

"Oh, that's Carl," I repeated with considerably less grief.

Fortunately, some of our animals have survived up to the present. Norma loves them. I tolerate them. We're different that way and—as the whole story illustrates—in many other ways too.

It shows the uniqueness of our personalities, our extrovert-introvert tendencies, and the major distinctions of being male or female. After we were married, those and other distinctions irritated both of us for several years. But gradually, with new understanding, we learned to appreciate the other's uniqueness.

Changed Perspective

Part of my goal in this chapter is to have you see your mate's maddening differences from a new and positive perspective. Impossible, you say? Consider this lighthearted story of a church secretary and a rich Texan. Watch how quickly her view changes.

The Texan called the church office in the middle of the week and said to the secretary, "Hello. I'd like to talk to the head hog of the trough."

"Excuse me?" the secretary said, annoyed.

"You heard me, ma'am," the Texan said. "I want to talk to the head hog of the trough."

"Are you referring to our senior minister?" the secretary asked.

"That's what you call him," he said. "But I call him the head hog of the trough."

"Well, sir," the secretary said stiffly, "I'm sorry, but he's out of the building right now. May I take a message?"

"Yeah," he said, "I visited your church last Sunday, and I was real impressed. I see that you're having a building fund drive, and I'd like to give a million-dollar gift if I could."

The secretary hesitated and then answered, "Sir, I think I hear that big old pig coming down the hall right now." Her whole perspective on the Texan changed when she suddenly saw some value in him.

You may not see it yet, but there is great value in your mate's uniqueness. That's because natural tendencies that may be fundamentally different from your own can *enrich* you and your marriage.

In this chapter we'll look at five areas that make people different from each other. We'll briefly consider how natural temperament, birth order, and personal history can affect one's relationships, especially marriage. Then we'll look more closely at two additional areas: extrovert-introvert and male-female differences.

The Sixty-Second Boost

As you learn to understand various differences between you and your spouse, you can spark appreciation for qualities he or she has that you lack. Verbalize that appreciation, and you can bring out the best in your spouse. Try praising your spouse and see what happens. Praise is like a shot of adrenaline that energizes a person. It gives a quick, sixty-second boost to any relationship. Dr. John Gottman says that long-lasting "in-love" marriages enjoy a regular dose of five positive experiences to one negative.[2] Praise brings a very positive experience to any marriage.

How do you energize, motivate—bring out the best in—your mate? Give the gift of praise. Think about it. When someone praises you for some attribute, like being a thoughtful person, doesn't that instantly give you a lift and make you feel better about yourself? When you're praised for some action, like cooking a delicious meal, doesn't that make you want to do more of the same? It takes only a few words to praise your mate, only a few seconds of time, but the impact can be monumental.

The opposite of praise is criticism. Think about what criticism does to you. If you're like most people I talk with, criticism drills a hole in your emotions and through that hole your energy flows out. Along with it goes most of your motivation to try to do better. Remember the concept covered in chapter 5: The further we are from what we expect in any area of life, the more energy we lose. Criticism causes us to feel that we've let someone down. We haven't met that person's expectations or our own, because we expected ourselves to be pleasing or acceptable to the other.

Criticism isn't always blatant; it can be subtle, as with the wife who wakes each morning and right off gives her husband a honey-do list ("honey, do this; honey, do that"), no hugs, no smile, not even a good morning. No thank you in the evening. She's telling him each day: "I'm not happy unless you're performing. I'm not happy even when you *are* performing." You can imagine how that implied criticism and lack of love and appreciation makes that guy feel.

But praise, on the other hand, energizes us because it helps to meet two of our most basic human needs: (1) a deep need to feel significant—to feel that we matter, that we're important somehow, that we're needed; and (2) a great need to feel secure in our closest relationships, to feel that no matter what happens, we belong to each other and will be there for the other.

We can give that gift of praise at any time. Don't worry that your spouse will get tired of being praised. When I ask seminar audiences, "How many of you would like to be praised more often by your spouses?" everyone in the room raises a hand. It's just something we can never get enough of.

Let's look now at five things that make each of us unique, areas in which we can look for natural things to praise and energize one another.

In Praise of Personality Differences

You'll recall that in the previous chapter, we labeled the four basic personality types as lion, otter, golden retriever, and beaver. I trust you took the self-test and identified which one (or maybe two) of the four is your dominant type. Maybe your spouse also took the test.

We all need to be appreciated and affirmed for the strengths inherent in our dominant types: if a lion, for decisiveness; if an otter, for spontaneity; if a golden retriever, for being kind and steady; if a beaver, for being careful and detailed. Pointing out your mate's uniqueness in this area and expressing appreciation will give him or her a real energy boost.

Even if your spouse's dominant type is the same as yours, the degree of dominance and the overall mix of all four types will vary between any two people.

In Praise of Birth-Order Differences

Research shows that your place in the birth order of your family has a great deal to do with how you live with and relate to others. If you were the firstborn of several children, for example, you probably tend to be a leader type, because you learned to take charge of the other kids. Secondborns are usually somewhat competitive and insecure, because they had to prove themselves—measure up to big brother or sister. On the positive side, middleborn children are good negotiators and adaptable; they often feel little need to "control." And third or lastborn children are often very sociable, knowing how to deal with people.

This discussion hardly scratches the surface of this interesting topic. But can you see birth-order influences in your spouse? Are they similar to or different from yours? Consider discussing your varied family experiences in terms of birth order. This topic can get a couple to that intimate "expressing-feelings" layer of communication. As you better understand your spouse, can you look for a characteristic to praise? Try it—discover its effect in energizing your mate. If you'd like to know more about this subject, I recommend *The Birth Order Book* by Dr. Kevin Leman.[3]

While I urge you to understand these categorizations, again I warn against using them as a weapon against your mate. Instead look for the positives.

In Praise of Personal-History Differences

We all have a unique personal history. That means you. It means your spouse. Was your spouse raised by just one parent? Raised with several brothers and sisters, only sisters, or only brothers? Was your spouse abused? Raised in a tough home? Rejected as a child? All these things made a lasting impact and contributed to the person your spouse is.

And his or her history is different from yours. How can these differences draw you together?

Again, honor and communication are key starting points. Talk about your pasts—events, feelings, resulting needs. Look for positives to praise. How does your spouse's past enrich your relationship? Suppose, for example, that your wife was raised with a couple of brothers. As a result, she may have some understanding of how important sports are to most guys. Perhaps she even likes to shoot baskets with you. Put yourself in her shoes for a minute. Wouldn't it make you feel good to hear, "You know, I'm so lucky to have you. You play this game better than I do! I'm glad you understand me and love my world as much as I do." Sweet music! The positive energy pumps through her system! *Yes. Yes!*

You can also take the hardships your mate endured and together "count pearls." As you see more clearly what your mate learned from past hurts and how those hurts matured him or her, you can reinforce the resulting good through praise.

In Praise of Extrovert-Introvert Differences

As you may have noticed in the opening story of this chapter, Norma has a lot of introvert in her, though she's fairly balanced, while I'm an off-the-chart extrovert. Whichever you are, you need for your spouse to know that part of you, appreciate it, and praise you for it (and vice versa).

Extroverts like to be with people. Even if I've been with others all day, I still like to be with people at night because I get energy from interacting with them. But if introverts have been with others all day, they'll often need some time alone at night. They've had enough of people for one day. A lot of times Norma will come home at the end of a workday (I work out of our house now while she runs the business office), and I'll want to spend time with her right away. "No, just give me a little time by myself first," she'll say.

I used to be bothered by that until I understood this basic difference between us. She's much more steady than I, and part of that trait comes from her desire to be alone and process things by herself. She doesn't have to run from thing to thing or person to person. I'm much more spontaneous, and I like to tell her, "Honey, I love it that you naturally calm me down."

As an extrovert, I'm also happy to tell almost anything to almost anyone. I've been known to reveal our bank balance to perfect strangers! (That really bothers Norma, so I've learned to restrain myself a little.) But introverts like Norma don't like to divulge personal things to people they don't know well. They're just not very open except with trusted friends. Even today, there are some great stories from our marriage that I would like to tell in my books and seminars, but Norma isn't ready to let the world hear about them, so . . . you'll have to wait.

Furthermore, as an extrovert, I love to think and plan out loud. I like to have others around so I can bounce an idea off them and ask, "What do you think of that?" I actually need to think through something by talking to someone. For a long time, however, Norma thought that I fully intended to do whatever I said out loud. Then if she didn't like my ideas, she would react strongly. So we were getting into conflict just because she didn't understand the way I process ideas.

She, on the other hand, likes to think things through on her own for hours or even days. I'll want to talk an issue out with her, but she'll say, "I can't do that." When we were first married, I used to think it would take her a week of "consideration" before she'd do anything "spontaneous," and that really irritated me. But it doesn't anymore, because her more careful, introverted approach has saved me from trouble many times over the years.

I used to feel like one of those clay pigeons they use in skeet-shooting. I'd come flying out with a new and exciting idea, and *boom!*—Norma would blast it out of the sky with her shotgun. "Why do you always do that to me?" I'd ask in frustration. But now I recognize that it's only because of the way she thinks. Can you imagine the trouble I'd be in if I had followed through on all the ideas I've come up with off the top of my head? So now I praise her for her caution.

For her part, Norma praises me for my spontaneity and very visible creativity. Over the last couple of years, we've concluded that she's a dream-maker, meaning she loves to get with me and ask, "What are you dreaming this year? How would you like to be able to help singles or couples or families?"

I'll respond, "Well, I've always wanted to do this or that." So I get to be the idea person.

Then she'll say, "Great, give that to me. Let me go figure out how we can make that happen."

What a match we've turned out to be! And this difference that used to divide us is now one of the things in our relationship for which I'm most grateful and most eager to praise her. Our strengths complement each other and make for a great team.

In Praise of Gender Differences

The first four areas of difference we've considered in this chapter aren't gender specific. But now I want to look at some of the things that research indicates do tend to distinguish men from women. I'm aware of the dangers in stereotyping people, but my hesitation to speak in generalizations is offset by the new understanding that can come as we identify behavior patterns of men and women that do follow certain norms. Not every man and every woman will fall neatly into the categories I'll cover in this section, but from both the present research and my own observations, the majority certainly do. In fact, I find the generalizations to be true 70 or 80 percent of the time, so if you're a skeptic, I ask that you humor my generalized statements that "men do this . . . women do that." It's amazing how our nation is enjoying all the new information about gender differences, and that's because it rings true.

For more than twenty years, I've been speaking and writing about gender-based differences. Some of my most hilarious anecdotes come from those differences. I've actually made my living off the way men and women tend to view life and operate day in and day out. But as I look back over those years, I can see now that I've only been scratching the surface of the vast differences. Research coming out today from specialists like Dr. Deborah Tannen[4] and Dr. Bernie Zilbergeld,[5] along with popular books such as Dr. John Gray's *Men Are from Mars, Women Are from Venus*,[6] are helping us discover that most men and women are in different worlds, and we tend to be confused and sometimes irritated by those differences.

There are thousands of differences between men and women. Here's just one scientific-medical example: In a recent study, brain monitors revealed strong gender differences in brain activity when the subjects were told to "think of nothing."[7]

I could mention many gender-based distinctions that do not need brain monitors for detection. But I'd like to summarize five of my favorites from my own study and observations, hoping that, as you increase your understanding of your complementary strengths you'll have more ammunition with which to praise your mate. Look for the positive; discover the value of variety! After a general look at these differences, I'll give you several specific suggestions in praising your mate.

Difference 1:
Men Love to Share Facts—Women Love to Express Feelings

Men, even in close friendships, tend to be into gathering and expressing facts. Women in the same sort of relationship tend to be better at and more interested in sharing their feelings. This is no rigid rule, remember. Both genders can and do share feelings and facts, but the scale seems to be tipped in favor of facts for men and emotions for women.

A wife might say, "Honey, we need to talk tonight." She is expressing a need, no doubt based on a feeling of "disconnection" from him.

He may answer, "About what?" He wants the facts.

"How are you feeling about your job?"

He scratches his head, wonders where that question came from, and responds, "I feel fine." He isn't as in touch with his feelings or as interested in them as she is. And he thinks his answer finished their talk.

Then she might change the topic and express her need to discuss their older daughter's twelfth birthday party four months away.

It's obvious to him that she's continuing the conversation—but on a new subject—and he wants to know where their conversation is headed. So he asks her, somewhat annoyed, "How long is this conversation going to last?"

She may be offended and suggest he doesn't love her anymore.

Now he's really confused. How did this conversation take this turn? How did his question—asking for facts—turn into "I feel as if you don't love me"?

This differing fact-feeling orientation does not have to tear down a relationship. But it's important that both men and women understand the other's propensity. Your mate is not necessarily irritating you on purpose. Usually the behavior that bugs or frustrates us is just a reflection of the way our spouse is. He or she is not trying to strain the marriage but is just being natural and normal.

Remember, men, we are healthier when we become better communicators. Thank God for your wife. When's the last time you paused and thanked her for wanting to talk about emotions?

Difference 2:
Men Tend to Be Independent—Women Tend to Be Interdependent

A second big gender difference is that men tend to be independent while women are more *inter*dependent. This shows up clearly in the way young boys and girls play and disagree.

Have you ever wondered why it takes millions of sperm and only one egg to make a baby? Maybe it's because not one of those little surfers will stop and ask for directions!

In contrast, girls tend to form small groups or pair off to play games where they share things face to face. In other words, the girls go for community. Female interdependency is evident in the common situation where several women in a group get up together to go to the rest room, something men rarely do.[8]

I realize some men will be more community minded than others, and some women will be more independent than the norm. The key is for you and your spouse to figure out where the two of you are in this area and work together in an understanding way, praising each other rather than ragging on one another for the things that make you unique.

Difference 3:
Men Connect by Doing Things—Women Connect by Talking

This third difference—men connect by doing things together while women connect by talking together—is closely related to the first two: facts/feelings and independence/interdependence. A fascinating aspect of this difference is the way the two sexes define the word *intimacy*. Over the last few decades, women have played the major role in defining intimacy for our culture, with the result that many men have concluded it's just not for them. That definition always includes "talking and touching"—that's what women want when they say they want more intimacy.

What's the male definition of intimacy, according to the latest research? Doing something with another person.[9] There doesn't have to be any talking at all. A couple may just be watching TV together, but the man will think that's getting close or being intimate while the wife is sitting there thinking, *When are we going to say something?*

A woman at one of my recent seminars told me how she used this insight to get her own needs met. "I found that when I wanted my husband to open up verbally," she said, "I could suggest that we do something together, like take a drive or a walk. As soon as we started doing it, he would start talking." Another woman for whom this worked too well told her husband with tongue in cheek, "I roast at baseball games; I freeze at football games; I get bitten by mosquitoes when we're fishing. Why do you always have to do everything with me?"

Most men like just being with someone else. But they tend to avoid togetherness if the woman is critical or insists on communicating the entire time, because that's not their idea of intimacy.

Let's look at how this difference—women connecting through words, men through actions—can affect a typical conversation. Over dinner, after a rough day at work, the wife says, "I hate my job!"

How might a man respond? "Why don't you quit then?"

"No," she says, "it's just that there's so much work to do and not enough people."

"Well, then, tell your boss to hire some help for you."

"Oh, why can't you ever just listen to me?" she asks, getting frustrated.

And he, genuinely confused, says, "I *am* listening to you. If you didn't want my advice, why did you bring up the subject?"

What's going on there that neither of them may understand? By expressing her feelings about her job, the wife is really saying, "I want to *connect with you*. I want to get into community with you. And I do that through conversation. I'm not trying to get anything solved." When the husband fails to respond in keeping with her need to connect, she concludes he isn't really listening to her.

From the man's perspective, however, his response is consistent with his view of intimacy. He wants to *do something* with her. He wants to fix things with her. In this case, that means offering a logical solution to her problem. His comments are factual and aimed at helping with her dilemma.

His comments may also be a reaction to the male fear of being controlled and losing his independence. A conversation focusing on emotions can make him feel inadequate, less in control. So he may try to assert control with a verbal attack and not even realize what he's doing to her.

How can we get past this misunderstanding of one another to develop the connection both partners need? What I'm about to suggest may sound unrealistic at first, but Norma and I have learned to handle such a situation in a way that seems to work. If she complained about her job and I suggested she just quit, she might come back with something like, "I see what you're trying to do. You're doing something with me—helping me, right? You think quitting my job would help, don't you? That's an interesting idea. I appreciate the fact that that's part of who you are. But I'm not really looking for a solution tonight. I just want to talk and connect with you. Is that okay?"

And then I might think, *Oh, I see what's happening. I was trying to help you and at the same time feel significant myself.* But I can respond by saying that I appreciate the way she wants to connect with me; I know that's good for both of us. I might even ask straight out, "Do you feel disconnected from me right now?" If she says yes, I could then ask, "What could we do—or talk about—tonight to get more connected?"

For her part, she might ask me, "What would it take for you to feel significant and helpful to me? How can I best respond when you offer your well-intended fix-it suggestions?" If a wife praises her husband's attempt at trying to be "helpful" when he's giving unsolicited advice, it can push the relationship forward a long way.

In this way, we respect one another's different needs and understanding of intimacy.

Difference 4:
Men Tend to Compete—Women Tend to Cooperate

This difference is very important to understand, because it can help explain why a male may all of a sudden start an argument over something the wife had no idea would lead to a fight.

Why do males tend to be competitive while females tend to be more cooperative? You can see this in the kind of pets the two sexes like. Most men prefer dogs to cats. Think about it; dogs don't engage us in a contest of wills; most dogs are loyal, obedient, and easy to train. They come when you call them. We men want to win and feel we're in charge.

Women, on the other hand, tend to prefer cats. When you call cats, they give you a look that says "bug off" or "I'll come if and when I feel like it, which will be when I want something from you." Women by and large are more willing to tolerate a pet that has to have its own way. Why? They like to stay in harmony whenever possible. It goes back to their concern for community.

Male competitiveness extends to just about every area of life. It certainly applies on the job, where it's vital that a man feel as though he's doing well. If he doesn't, he can be discouraged and experience a massive loss of energy. Wives, one reason we're so sensitive about your jokes concerning our jobs is that much of our identity is wrapped up in what we do. (This may be a reason why many men become ill after retiring.)

My male competitive nature hurt my family from time to time in the early years. When our kids were little and I would play games with them, Norma would get upset with me because I "couldn't" let them win. It was hard for me to bring myself to lose on purpose. "It's terrible that you have to win against your own children," she would say accusingly, sometimes with tears.

I'd try to defend myself with, "Well, they've got to learn that this is a tough world, you know."

But she would insist, "I just can't believe you could treat the kids like that." She was seeing the whole thing from the "community" viewpoint, and I was seeing it from the "status and winner's" perspective.[10]

Male competitiveness also extends to our support of our favorite sports teams. We're tremendously loyal, and we enjoy watching "our team" win. "My team is playing tonight on TV. I can't let my team down"—that's the way a man can reason.

This can lead to a situation where a wife says something like, "Honey, could you pick up Sandy at school after her practice tonight?"

"No," the husband answers, "my game is coming on early, and I want to watch it with the guys."

"She really needs to spend time with you," the wife says. "You've been so busy lately." (She senses he needs to be in "community" with his daughter, and she's probably right.)

"Honey," he says, "I want to watch the game. Let her walk. She needs the exercise anyway. If she gets healthier, it will reduce our medical bills." (That's logical, isn't it?)

"You're impossible!" she says.

"I'm not impossible," he insists. "You're manipulative! I can see what you're doing!"

What's going on here? Two things for the man: (1) Loyalty to his team is important to him; and (2) He wants to win the argument with his wife. He's in competition even during the discussion. If he thinks it's necessary to win, he might even start getting harsh, knowing his wife will probably give in. He realizes intuitively that she's cooperative and helpful and more concerned about the state of their connection than she is about winning an argument. But while he wins the battle, he's not really winning anything, because he's not paying attention to what's going on in the overall relationship. When most men take the time to really think about it, they know the relationship is far more important than the football game or even "winning" the discussion. But in the heat of the argument, the desire to win may dominate.

A wife can be confused when her husband reacts negatively to her attempts at helping him care for their children. Subconsciously, we men think we can do as good a job of rearing them as you women, even though common observation shows that you generally have an edge in knowing how to nurture kids. Your natural advantage can actually annoy us because we reason, *Who does she think she is, anyway?* The fact is, men can learn to be great parents. But we can also get our competitive fires turned up by a mother trying to help us become "a better parent."

Here's a perfect opportunity to offer praise to the mother of our children. Why not just say to her, "Thank God for moms! You sure do a great job with the kids, and thanks for helping me to remember more of what our children need." That will raise her energy level by several notches.

Driving is still another area we men see as a contest. This is also an area where women like to "connect" with us by being verbal. "Aren't you following the car ahead a little too closely?" a wife might say. But we men know that if we back off a bit, some other driver will cut in on us, and then we would be "losing" to that driver!

I remember a winter day recently when, for some reason, Norma and I had switched cars with our good friends Jim and Suzette. Norma and I were driving their van, and they were just ahead of us in our car. There was a bit of ice on the road, and I can enjoy a little ice, though nothing dangerous. But Norma hates any amount of ice.

As we made a left turn, I was thinking about how, if you punch the gas just a hair, you can skid a little and have some fun! I wasn't going to do it much because I know Norma gets nervous (and I made sure there were no cars coming the other way). So I stepped on the gas just a bit, and guess what: We ended up spinning a whole 360 degrees into the other lane!

Norma closed her eyes and screamed, "I can't believe this!"

In the car ahead, Jim and Suzette saw what has happening, and Suzette said, "I can't watch!"

But Jim, getting more into the spirit of the thing, said, "Way to go, Gary! I give you an 8.5 for that spin!"

Likewise, my reaction was "Yes! That was a good one! If you're going to spin, you've got to make it a winner!"

My point is simply that we men are in competition all the time. The encouraging thing about this is that more and more, all over the country, I see men taking up the challenge to be better lovers of their wives and children. It's like being in competition: Who can be the most supportive husband and father? (And wives can jump into this by praising our efforts to "win" at being a better mate and parent.) But it's a friendly competition as I've seen a nation-wide movement of men coming together by the hundreds of thousands in major events to say, "Let's help one another learn how to love our families better. We're going to do whatever it takes." This kind of competition is excit-ing to me and extremely beneficial to our country's welfare and stability. Wives, this is something that's worth supporting. You can say to your hus-band, "I really appreciate your competitive spirit. I love that, because I see everything you're willing to do to make our family better."

And husbands, we can praise our wives and give them that energy lift by saying, "Honey, I'm so glad I married you, because I see your interest in the whole area of staying lovingly connected, and I know I need that con-stantly with you and the kids."

Difference 5:
Men Tend to Be Controlling—Women Tend to Remain Agreeable

This gender difference is closely connected to difference 4—competi-tion/cooperation. You see, most men think that a "boss" of anything is a winner; a wife challenging a husband can be a threat to a man's need to feel like a winner. But I refer separately to this controlling/agreeable difference, as it hits right at the heart of a man's deepest need—feeling significant.

Men usually like to be in control. Research has shown, for example, that when men and women talk, the conversation "follows *the style of the men alone*. . . . When women and men talk to each other, both make adjustments, but the women make more."[11] As we've seen, women desire verbal communication—to create intimacy—and many will let the man lead—to preserve the connection and keep conversation going.

Why do men value being in control? The whys of these differences are impossible to ferret out. We generally equate having control with being highly esteemed. But think about it: When a controlling person—male or female—lightens up his or her attempts to control someone else, isn't that "controller" then perceived to be more "loving"?

When testosterone is flowing, there's one particular thing we men wish we could control about our wives—sex whenever we want it! But as we'll see in chapter 14, that's not how good sex works. Sex is a reflection of the overall state of the relationship. A lot of wives just aren't as interested in this area as their men are. According to my good friend Dr. Kevin Leman, a nationwide Gallup poll discovered that the average woman says sex is only number 14 on her list of favorite things to do with her husband. Number 13 is gardening.[12]

In some circles the word *submission* in the context of marriage is a real hot button. But I've found that it's only an issue when one partner—usually the husband—wants to control and even dominate the relationship, which is not a lasting, giving type of love. When both people love each other in a genuine, honoring way, however, that word *submission* doesn't seem to be a problem. (The word basically means "agreeable.") In my own informal research, I've asked many women, some of them avowed feminists, "How would you respond to the word *submission* if your husband were really loving and sensitive and caring and treated you like a very valuable person?"

Most women say, "I wouldn't have any problem with it at all. I could respond to a man like that." (Some also ask, "Do such men exist?") In fact, I haven't had one woman get after me yet for asking that question. So submission isn't really an issue when our focus is on trying to outlove each other.

One of the best solutions to a "battle of the sexes" is to just understand that it exists. It's a maturing man and woman who can comprehend our basic natures and look seriously at why the male wants to run things and why the female wants to not make waves. As we both see these tendencies and accept them as natural, we can then start to adjust our relationship to what works best for us. This calls for temperance, tolerance, and conflict resolution along the lines discussed in chapter 13.

Drawing Closer, Not Apart

Clearly, there are a lot of potential differences between a husband and wife, and we tend to be attracted to our counterpart. Some of those differences are general in nature; others are male-female distinctions that usually hold true (though "any randomly chosen woman might do better at a 'male' skill than a man, and vice versa"[13]). Men and women can be critical of one another because of these differences, or we can learn to praise the other for his or her unique and complementary characteristics. In doing so, we can energize the other and strengthen our marriage.

Men, when is the last time you looked your wife in the eyes and said, "I appreciate so much your emphasis on relationships and all you do to build ours up. The things you do to make our house into a home and the time you give to the kids—you're terrific"?

Women, when is the last time you looked your husband in the eyes and said, "I really appreciate the way you're always doing your best for our family. Your dedication and hard work mean a lot to me"?

I suggest this exercise. Sit down and ask yourself this question: *How can my mate's differences help me in every area of my life, and especially in our marriage?* Just stop and think about some of the areas that your mate has helped to enrich. If mostly negative things come to mind at first, keep trying this exercise, or refer back to chapter 4 and try counting the pearls your mate has given you. Here are just a few of the advantages my wife has brought to me:

Help with my job. Norma has kept me out of more conflicts with coworkers than I care to think about. She has also helped me restore relationships that were broken. When we were first married, she "tutored" me when I was trying to learn how to talk with and relate to other adults in my first job. With her woman's intuition, she has also helped me understand coworkers and evaluate potential employees for our business, and I'm constantly amazed at how accurate her perceptions are. So I praise her for all these things.

Help with self-confidence. Norma has continually told me, "Yes, you can do it!" When I was stuck in an unfulfilling job, she encouraged me, "You're not using your talents. Just look what you could do!" She has also used her personality, her introvert tendencies, and her energy to help make my dreams come true and boost my confidence that I can reach my goals. Over and over I've tried to get her to pursue dreams of her own, and her reply is "Helping you and the others in our company to be successful is my dream!" For these things I praise her as well.

Help with personal finances. I have a friend who is president of a large chain of banks. He told me that he sees men as being primarily responsible for couples falling into deep financial trouble. Men tend to buy the big things, he says, and women tend to buy the things that keep the families running smoothly. NBC's *Today Show* recently ran a series on marriage. In a segment about the first year of marriage, two young lawyers explained their expectations and adjustments. A key tussle had concerned the husband's wanting to buy a new sports car while the wife wanted a house. (The wife had prevailed and the husband acknowledged they'd done the right thing.) Many women won't buy personal items if their husbands and children are in need. My wife has always been the one to keep us "down to earth" with money. She questions everything I do if it has any potential for weakening the family or threatening our security. Before we met with a financial adviser, she told me, "I'll go, but I'm going to 'sniff him out' and hear what he has to say before I'll go along with his idea." Again, that's one of her strengths, and I also praise her for that.

You can do the same type of thing with your spouse. Think of the many ways your mate enriches various areas of your life. Then praise him or her for each one.

As you get ready to pass into dreamland each night, ask yourself, *How many times have I praised my mate today? How many times have I praised my kids?* We don't often think about it, but I guarantee that every person in your life would love to be praised more and criticized less.

Praise is such a great gift, and it's so easy to give! So look at the things that make your spouse and others unique, and develop the habit of praising them for those very things. It will bring out the best in them. It will energize them instantly—and you too! And that's what makes love last.

Though the next chapter seems to be addressed to "us men," "you women" might want to peruse the pages for some specific positive ways you can "read your own marriage manual" in a way men will enjoy hearing it; it's just one more way to make your love last forever.

Forever-Love Principles

Our list of forever-love principles continues from the previous chapter:

73. Forever-love chooses to appreciate the qualities that make each person different from the other.

74. Forever-love is doubly blessed by the contributions of two unique personalities. It values variety.

75. Forever-love looks for attributes and actions to praise.

76. Forever-love steers clear of manipulative, subtle criticism.

77. Forever-love expresses energizing praise—anytime, anywhere.

78. Forever-love resists the temptation to psychologize or make blanket assumptions about a truelove's motives or reasons for behavior.

79. Forever-love asks, "How can our differences draw us together?"

80. Forever-love thinks in terms of teamwork, accentuating the strengths of both partners that can "cover" the weaknesses of either.

81. Forever-love doesn't jump to the conclusion that a truelove is intentionally trying to exasperate.

82. Forever-love knows the power of the gift of praise.

12

How to Read a Woman's Built-in Marriage Manual

Because of their age-long training in human relations—for that is what feminine intuition really is—women have a special contribution to make to any group enterprise, and I feel it is up to them to contribute the kinds of awareness that relatively few men . . . have incorporated.

—Margaret Mead[1]

We've just spent a chapter seeing how men and women are different from each other. We've discussed how a man's fact-oriented, independent, competitive spirit may serve him well in the work-world, as a provider for his family. On some levels, these characteristics may make the work-world go 'round. But those traditionally masculine qualities may not make for a happy marriage. They may not engender community and cooperation and intimate knowing of another's feelings—all keys to a good marriage. From the beginning of part 2, I've said that control and distance were symptoms of an unhealthy relationship.

What does this mean? It means if we're concerned about nurturing a love that lasts forever, we men may need to take a deep breath and humbly admit how very important our wives' intuitive natures can be to our relationships. C'mon, men, stay with me on this.

I've found that every marriage would be much better off if both partners would learn to read the wife's God-given marriage manual. What do I mean by a woman's natural marriage manual? I mean that every woman has an inborn, intuitive sense of what she needs, what the relationship needs, and what, if anything, is wrong with the marriage. The more in touch with her manual both husband and wife are, the more clearly they can see what they should do to have a satisfying marriage and the sooner they can take appropriate steps.

In this chapter we'll see how both a husband and wife can learn to get in touch with or read that manual. Act on what you read, and you're further on your way to marital delight.

I speak with confidence about this natural phenomenon, because in more than thirty years I've never found a woman who didn't have such a manual. I've had the privilege of interviewing and polling more than fifty thousand women in all sorts of situations and from around the world. And not one has failed to pinpoint what quality of relationship she has with her husband and what two or three things could be done to improve their marriage. This has impressed me as much as anything I've observed as a relationship researcher.

For the average husband, this manual is usually more accessible when the wife's overall anger level is as low as possible. Nothing does more to cloud his ability to read her manual—and block her ability to access the manual within herself—than long-lasting and unresolved anger. On rare occasions when the man does have a better feel for the state of the relationship and how it could be improved, the wife is usually hindered by anger. This is another reason it's so important to drain out as much compressed anger as possible. And remember that anger is a secondary emotion, often caused by fear. So the safer a woman feels in her marriage—safe to think, to feel, to talk, and so on—the more in tune she tends to be with her marriage manual.

How Wives Can Access Their Manuals

Wives might be wondering how to get more in touch with their manuals. Assuming you're in the emotionally and psychologically "normal" range, I'll help you get into it with these few spurring questions:

- What would it take to improve your marriage?

- What's one thing that brings you the most happiness or energy when your husband does it? How could he do it even better?

- If you could wave a wand over your marriage, what would you want your husband to change or improve, knowing it would change (and knowing he would not be upset with you for "waving the wand")?

Now, some husbands reading this section may be feeling very uneasy. I would have, too, in the early years of my marriage. I used to think that Norma had too many ideas about how our marriage should improve. I reasoned that many of her thoughts about us were purely selfish ideas designed to benefit her and certainly not me. But now that I've been married more than thirty years and been in contact with thousand of wives, I'm very relaxed about asking these questions of my wife or any other woman. I can't count the number of times a wife has said to me, "If my husband only knew how much I would do for him if he would just help me to feel secure and valued in our relationship!" When wives feel like queens, they usually relax and overdo themselves in finding ways to make their men feel fulfilled. But, again, they won't do this as well if there's too much anger in their hearts toward their husbands or others.

How Husbands Can Draw Out Their Wives' Manuals

With that background in mind, let's look at eleven possible ways to draw out a wife's built-in marriage manual.

1. Use Three Tried and Tested Questions

For years I've asked the following three questions in my marriage counseling and seminars. They do a good job of drawing out valuable parts of a woman's marriage manual. They bring up and work toward reconciling issues we dealt with in part 1 of this book: expectations versus reality.

A. On a scale from zero (terrible) to ten (perfection), what kind of relationship do we both want?

Maybe the two of you would be satisfied with being at seven or eight most of the time. It's important for both the husband and wife to respond to this first question, which sharpens the print in her manual.

B. On the same scale (0-10), where are we today in our marriage relationship, on the average and with everything thrown in?

This second question opens the cover to her "book." Nearly every woman has a more accurate answer to this question than her husband, with the man usually rating the marriage a few points higher than does the woman.

C. What would it take to move our relationship from where it is now (question B) closer to where we want it to be (question A)?

This last question is where the words jump out. Almost always, answers involve the kinds of things we're looking at in this book—more security, more affection, less anger, and so on. But one statement from wives surfaces more than any other: "If we could just improve our communication skills!" Many of them say that's all they want for the rest of their marriage; if they got it, they'd be satisfied. The second statement I often hear is, "If my husband could just be more affectionate and tender with me, not lecturing me when I need his emotional support. Gently touching me when I'm down and just listening to me without comment or solutions. And best of all, not getting mad at me when I need him emotionally."

These three questions have continually allowed couples to shorten the time it takes to improve their relationship. As a man and husband, it took me some time to get used to the idea that my wife had a better ability to read our marriage status. Frankly, it used to intimidate me. And at times it irritated me. But today, I've stopped fighting reality. It amazes me how accurate wives are at seeing the condition of their marriages. Instead of resisting this idea, I've found it tremendously helpful to husbands who take the time to listen and understand what women have to say about improving relationships.

I'm not saying that all women are perfect or that any are 100 percent right all the time. I'm saying that they seem to be right *most* of the time. They may appear at times to be selfish, whining, nagging, overbearing, or demanding, but I've discovered that almost always, they're expressing a need within the relationship that's not being adequately met. This need can be with the kids, with themselves, or just in the overall relationship. But, in some ways, wives are like building inspectors; they see things that, if left unnoticed, could damage the building in the future. A husband does himself a real favor in overall health and emotional well-being if he listens to what his wife has to say concerning their marriage. Married men who are satisfied in their spousal relationship tend to take better care of themselves and do better in their jobs.

2. *Make Sure She Feels As Safe As Possible*

This point was made above, but it needs to be emphasized over and over. If a woman feels safe, secure, loved, and honored in her marriage, she will find it far easier to get in touch with her needs and her intuitive sense of how things are going.

3. Simply Ask How the Relationship Can Be Improved

Sometimes a straightforward question is the best approach: "What can we do better?" or "What do you think makes for a great marriage?"

Once the question is asked, the husband needs to listen carefully and respectfully. According to Dr. Howard Markman of Denver University, who studied many couples over a long period, the main factor in shutting down a relationship is a husband clamming up—closing himself off and distancing himself emotionally from his wife.[2] But asking, "How can we improve things between us?" goes in the opposite, healthful direction, strengthening the connection and allowing the wife to access her marriage manual.

4. Don't Argue When She Starts to Read Out of Her Manual

And notice that I said the man has to listen *respectfully*. As one woman put it to me, "It's very important, while my husband is listening to me, that he not react or think I'm being critical."

Her comment points to a double "pain" in which many women find themselves. On the one hand, she wants her man to be concerned about the health of the relationship and work with her to make it better. If he's not interested, she feels the hurt. On the other hand, if she says anything about how things can be improved, he may take it as personal criticism and get defensive, and things can easily grow worse rather than advancing. If this happens repeatedly, a woman can close her manual because she no longer feels safe enough to keep it open.

Unfortunately, I sometimes spring this trap on my own wife without even being aware of it. I'll ask, "What would it take to improve our relationship?" When she responds, I'll say, "Wait a minute. That's being too picky."

"Don't ask my opinion if you're going to be critical of my answer," she'll say.

What I can do then is explain that I'm just trying to get a better understanding of what she's saying and ask her not to close her manual. But better still is just to listen and strive to understand her without reacting or arguing.

If you're a husband with an overbearing personality, your aggressiveness or demanding approach can be intimidating, making your wife hesitant to read even a sentence out of her marriage manual. Think of that manual as having a latch with a lock on it. If she doesn't feel safe, she may take only the first step of unlocking it but still may not unlatch it. She may be very sensitive about this, so how much she reveals depends a lot on how safe you make her feel. And most of the time, arguing with her to open it and read it on demand will double-lock it.

If you're a wife, you may be saying, "I could never share my marriage manual with my husband because he would blast me. I could suffer for months, even years, if I suggested anything about wanting our relationship to improve." If you're living with a man who has a strong personality, and especially if he has some perfectionistic tendencies as well, the only way you might be able to get his attention in reading your manual is by hitting him alongside his head with a big stick (figuratively speaking, of course).

I haven't yet had to recommend that a couple divorce, but I do some-times recommend a brief period of separation in the case of an overly domi-nant male—to get his attention and force him to deal with the issues. If it's possible for you to do it, taking a few days away from him and telling him the reason, lovingly and firmly, can sometimes be that "stick." Before taking this approach, however, and because this approach can be explosive, it might be well for you to double-check your situation with a trained counselor or pos-sibly with a respected minister who has training in marriage counseling.

Beware, however, of going to the extreme of becoming a nag—of con-tinually reading out of your manual without a request from your husband. I'll say more about this under statement 11.

5. Get the Support of a Loving Team

When you're in a loving, supportive group of three or four other couples, you may feel safer in revealing your marriage manual. It's like going to a counselor, where you feel safe expressing your feelings and opinions. You may even get to see some of the fine print.

A small support group is so important to a marriage that in my video series I have called small-group participation one of four "musts" of a great marriage. (The others? Things we're covering in this book: (1) Honor; (2) Daily resolution of anger; and (3) The monitoring of the wife's marriage manual.) Because of the critical role of support groups to a great marriage, I will return to this subject as I wind up this chapter.

6. Allow Her to Read from Her Manual at the Time When She Feels Most Able to Share

A wife may, for example, feel safer or more in the mood when the two of you are out on a dinner date. Men, ask her when and where is best for her.

I learned the importance of this the hard way. When I discovered that Norma had this built-in marriage manual, I used to demand that she read it to me whenever I wanted so I could grow and we could have an improved marriage. That was not only heavy irony, but it also shut her down from time to time and made her close her book completely.

Just four years into our marriage, Norma and I decided to spend a weekend in a hotel room and concentrate on how we could improve our relationship— my ideas, her ideas, back and forth. We also agreed that over that "retreat" weekend, we would try something new that had been recommended to us by a marriage expert. We would not eat for a day and drink just water so we could spend all our time and energy focusing on our marriage. It sounded like a good idea to both of us at the time. But by Saturday night, a major problem had arisen: Norma was starving! She was desperate to go eat.

I, on the other hand, am so goal oriented that I wanted to stay in the room and stick with our plan. Soon we were in the middle of a serious disagreement and not speaking to each other. So there we were in the coffee shop; she was enjoying scrambled eggs, and I was just staring at her and not speaking. Some love retreat! We had to learn, starting early in the relationship, that because we're both unique individuals, we're going to be different in our approaches to her manual. And we both had to adjust to our differences in order for her to feel safe in reading from it.

7. Discover New Communication Resources

For some couples, having the wife write out some sections of her manual is very helpful; it also serves to give a lasting record of what's going on inside her. Try out the various methods described in the chapter on communication, and then regularly use those that work best for you and your spouse. Learn to use and reuse the method called "drive-through communication." Take extra time to understand it and try it, because the couples I've worked with find that method to be at the top of the list.

Maybe your best method will be using word pictures, such as, "Read me the fine print under the section on improving our sexual relationship." Word pictures are an effective and powerful way to get a point across; you can get your mate to understand you and feel your feelings instantly.[3]

8. Ask Other Women to Share Their Marriage Manuals with You

This might be your mother or grandmother, your sister, your wife's sister, or maybe even a female friend of your family. I've done this myself for years, asking women in groups or individually what they think makes for a great marriage. Some women will feel safer articulating their manuals to someone who is not their spouse. After all, we have few reasons, if any, to criticize what they say, because they're not talking specifically about us. And if one or more of these women knows your wife well, it's amazing what you can learn. When I take the time to explain to a wife that I'm trying to improve my marriage, most have not only tried to help me, but they usually get excited about seeing a man doing something specific to enrich his relationship.

If your wife doesn't feel good about your reading some other woman's manual, her concern is usually filed under the "security" section in her manual. Whenever I find a wife who is somewhat jealous of her husband becoming too friendly with another woman, especially talking about improving their marriage, it usually has something to do with how secure she feels in her husband's love and value for her. If a conflict should come from your friendliness with other women, use the conflict to find out what it would take for her to feel more secure and loved. Listen to her, and look at your own motives. This can be a great opportunity to reestablish your lifelong commitment by assuring her of your love and devotion "till death do us part."

Also, once again, if your wife has too much unresolved anger stored in her heart, then no matter what you say or do, she probably will not become more secure in your love. Her anger needs to drain somewhat before your relationship can improve.

9. Use Reverse Role-Playing

The psychiatrist who wrote the best-selling book *Passive Men, Wild Women* said reverse role-playing is the best method he has ever found to help husbands make lasting changes for the better.[4] This reminds me of the forever-love principle that says:

> **Forever-love tries to view a situation**
> **through the eyes of a truelove.**

This is something you can do by yourself in your living room or office. Picture your wife in the room with you, sitting in one of the empty chairs, and ask her what it would take to improve your relationship. Then, if you can, even though you might feel silly, go over and sit in the empty chair where you pictured her, and talk back to yourself as you think she would.

Next, move back to where you started and see yourself listening and responding. If you "get inside her mind" and start saying the things you imagine she would say, you'll be amazed at the insights that come.

10. Ask Her What You Do for Her That Gives Her Energy and What Takes Energy Away

What discourages her, and what gives her hope? This is another way to pull out the fine print in a woman's marriage manual. (We'll discuss this point at greater length in later chapters.)

11. Analyze the Main Points of Criticism You've Heard from Your Wife over the Years

These may have to do with you, the house, the kids, her job or yours, the general state of her life, or whatever. Think of two or three that have persisted for some time, write them down, and look at what they actually reflect.

Norma has criticized some of my manners for most of our married life. What does that tell me about her marriage manual? Well, most women easily and tightly connect to their husbands and become a part of them. The way we look and act can become a reflection on them. So when we bite our nails in public or make loud body noises at home, it can subtly disconnect them from us. It makes them feel, for that moment at least, that they are not a part of us. They can even feel devalued.

Then, too, women are very concerned with their husbands' reputations. They usually want their men to be respected and successful. So when we do something embarrassing in public, they're afraid we're going to be humiliated—and they along with us. This kind of analysis of a wife's criticisms can add a lot to a husband's understanding of her marriage manual.

We've covered eleven ways to draw out a wife's intuitive sense of what's best and enriching for your relationship. Husbands, take what you hear and "go for" a better marriage. Take specific steps to act on your wife's intuitive knowledge of the hairline cracks that could eventually "bring down the house."

A Word of Caution to Wives

Women need to remember that too much of anything can sour the whole process. My grandson Michael, for instance, loves the *Spot* book series, and he's always asking his mother—and me when I go over there—"Read me Spot." That's fine for the first time or two, but after the third or fourth reading of the same book, this grandpa starts to get bored and lose interest in Spot and his adventures.

In the same way, women who read their marriage manuals to their husbands too often—who are constantly reciting them without a request—can become tiresome. They're like a dripping faucet; like a desert sun that beats down on you all day long; or like being trapped in a locked room with someone who just won't quit jabbering. That's the way their husbands can perceive them.

Holding the readings to once a week, once a month, maybe even once a year for some manual chapters is sometimes enough to have a great impact on your marriage. An interesting manual is something your man wants to read. But if he's *forced* to read it (listen to it), then no matter how good it is, he's going to get tired of it, stop listening, and move on to something else.

Wives, how can you tell if you're overdoing it? Well, when you say something that may help improve your relationship but that could be perceived as critical, do your husband's eyes get that "vacant-house" look (you can tell some lights are on but no one's home)? Does he know everything you're going to say as soon as you get the first three words out? While you're talking, does he play raisin and shrivel up before your eyes? In a typical day, how many times are you critical, and how many times do you praise him? Keep track for a few days, and if the ratio isn't seven praises or more for every negative comment, you're being too critical and maybe reading too often. (The same holds true for your husband. If he overdoes it with criticism, you may stop reading your manual to him altogether.)

Wives, appreciate and praise any and all steps he takes in the right direction. In six months or a year, if you get discouraged, think back and consider how far you've come. Occasionally remind yourself that your husband is not your all-sufficient, perfect god (or parent). And remember that your ultimate happiness comes from finding peace based on your internal well-being not on outward circumstances.

A Further Word about Vital Small-Group Support

When we veer off course from time to time, as all couples do, a small group can make the difference between marital life or death. It is critical to making love last forever.

My favorite story is of a couple—Bill and Nancy—whose relationship was in such deep trouble that Bill had decided to walk out and divorce Nancy. But, they didn't divorce; they even turned their crisis into a deeper relationship. Unfortunately, at about the same time, another couple—friends of theirs—headed in the same direction. But this second couple went through with their divorce, it seems because they did not have the advantages Bill and Nancy had; they failed because they tried to fix their marriage on their own. If you're in serious trouble, most often it's just too difficult to make it on your own.

You see, before Bill and Nancy went through their crisis, they had been involved for some time in a weekly meeting with three other couples close to their age. These couples met primarily for friendship and mutual encouragement. Committed to learning what it would take to stay in love, the couples agreed to read various marriage books or watch relationship videos. Then each week, at one of their homes, they would discuss the subject and encourage each other in their separate journeys. They grew to trust each other and eventually felt safe in receiving advice from one another.

They had been meeting for about a year when Bill announced his intention to divorce Nancy. He had been holding his true feelings inside and had been afraid to share his hurt with the group or with Nancy. So when he shocked her with the news, she immediately called those other friends in the group. It was like calling 911. Literally within minutes, one of the other couples was at their house. The wife began to comfort Nancy while the husband took Bill on a jog around the block to talk things over.

As they jogged Bill expressed his frustrations and reasons for wanting to leave. The husband listened attentively, but he also tried to help Bill see things in a fresh light, and he pledged to stand with Bill and Nancy for support as long as it would take to work things out. By the end of their second circuit around the block, Bill was willing and energized to give the relationship another chance. This loving commitment was so overpowering to Bill that he held his face in his hands and cried tears of hope. He wasn't sure things could work out, but he knew others were there for them, no matter what happened.

Bill and Nancy stayed in the group but couldn't make any real promises that things would get better. What Bill discovered, however, was the key to their renewed life together. They received added strength from the other couples to keep working on their marriage. In a sense, the group was like a spare battery. They didn't let them get the divorce. The group members stayed with them, at times into the late evenings, listening and comforting them.

Bill and Nancy worked hard on rebuilding their marriage. And I'm happy to report that today, a number of years later, their marriage is stronger than ever—one of the best I know.

Most of this chapter has dealt with being willing to read a wife's marriage manual. That takes humility. But I propose that joining a small group can be a more humbling challenge for men. Remember, our gender likes the world to think we're in control, on top of it, independent, and self-sufficient. Being part of a support group acknowledges the need for interdependence and calls for a level of vulnerability. It can be scary for some men.

What is so powerful about being in a small, loving support group? I believe there's a dynamic similar to what anyone can find in a healthy family setting, an AA group, a church-family meeting week after week, or the support of a well-trained counselor. I have been amazed at the staying power a small group of friends or couples can give anyone who wants to stay in love in a marriage or build better relationships in a family or friendship.

Let me take a moment to make clear what I'm not saying about small groups. I'm not urging you to pick just any two or three couples to make up your support team. These couples should be friends, people in your local clubs or church, possibly other parents in your children's school. You need to find couples with whom you can feel safe and with whom you would enjoy meeting week after week. On the other hand, after you've been in one or two groups, you may also realize that you can pair up with other couples of different ages and interests. Because our struggles in marriage are relatively common, Norma and I have found it possible to form a group with total strangers. We found common ground and shared a high degree of commitment to seeing our marriages improve. The main problem arises in a group when one or two members are not really interested in growing and maturing or when one person wants too much control.

I witnessed firsthand just how effective support systems can be in strengthening even an entire nation. When I spoke in Ghana, West Africa, I saw thousands of extremely well-behaved young people (elementary and junior-high age) gather at a mass meeting in a field. In fact, they so impressed me that I asked about it. And what I learned is that in Ghana and other parts of Africa, the extended family is very close and is involved daily in raising the children. Grandparents, in-laws, cousins, aunts and uncles, and friends and neighbors, too—all watch over and help emotionally support these children and hold the kids accountable for their actions. If a young child is seen doing something questionable, the entire village gets involved to correct the child. Everyone seems to look out for each other. In other words, families support each other and hold each other accountable.

Here in the United States, where extended family members often live hundreds or thousands of miles away, small support groups fill a real void. One of the best reasons to start or stay in a group is to gain a sense of loving accountability, which we all require if we're to keep growing toward an increasingly mature love. It's amazing how much easier it is to stay on track if you know someone is going to ask, "How has it been going this past week?" Or if, after you report a minor conflict, someone asks, "How would you two do it differently next week?" Because we want to be able to give a good report to the other couples, we're more motivated—energized—during the week to do the things we know we should.

This whole idea of joining a small support group may seem scary, but I've found that the small groups Norma and I have belonged to have all resulted in solid growth for us as a couple, and we've also developed lasting friendships. There's a lot of laughter, too, because we're all so much alike.

Just getting together regularly, encouraging each other and being reminded that you're not alone in your efforts to make a better marriage can be tremendously energizing. In the small groups my wife and I were a part of in one particular city, we didn't lose a single couple to divorce over a three-year period. All together there were more than sixty couples, and many were strained out almost to the point of divorce when we started the groups. Norma and I saw couple after couple getting stronger each week. This was my first exposure to support groups, and it made me a true believer!

Need yet another reason to join a small group? I've discovered that in this context men seem to learn what forever-love means—by watching other men love their wives. Week after week, men get the opportunity to see how it's done. Men are often more receptive to learning what makes a good relationship from other men than from their own wives. The biggest and most lasting changes I've seen in husbands have come through involvement with small support groups.

One of my organizations, a nonprofit corporation called Today's Family, provides a number of helpful materials for couples who want to start or join an existing support group in their area. Write or call for more information.[5]

I've never met a couple doing really well that hasn't had help from others in some way—from extended family, friends, good marriage books, or a qualified marriage counselor. We all need such help to make it through the many barricades that block our attempts to stay together and in love.

There are many other ways of gaining support for your marriage. At least once every few years, it's refreshing to attend a marriage conference. Then, for a good "tune-up" from time to time, I recommend seeing a counselor together. This can give you new insights for improving your relationship, and it can also offer all the same benefits of being in a support group. If couples would spend just a small fraction of their incomes on a counseling session every two or three years, they would be repaid many times over.

If you want to find a marriage counselor, get lots of recommendations from satisfied clients. Don't just pick someone out of the phone book. And look for one who would see you for just a few sessions. What I'm suggesting here is some fine-tuning for a marriage that's not in crisis.

If going to see a counselor makes you too uneasy, you might consider investing in a few additional marriage and family books.[6] One particular book I recommend is *The Good Marriage* by Judith Wallerstein and Sandra Blakeslee.[7]

Summary

In this chapter we've taken a hard look at what can be learned from a woman's intuitive sense. And we've seen that going it alone is not the best route for a couple going for a lifelong love.

The next chapter may well be one you've been waiting for. You may be wishing we'd get down to the brass tacks of how to approach and resolve the inevitable conflicts that can too quickly turn positive emotion—"I love you"—to a negative "I hate you." Dr. Howard Markman says that the divorce rate could be cut in half if couples learned this one set of skills: conflict resolution.[8]

Forever-Love Principles

Our list of forever-love principles continues from the previous chapter:

83. Forever-love stays in touch with a woman's intuitive sense of what the marriage needs.

84. Forever-love is courageous enough to ask, "What would make this relationship better?"

85. Forever-love does not tune out or get defensive in the face of constructive suggestions for improving the relationship.

86. Forever-love is not so goal oriented that it loses sight of relationship and connection.

87. Forever-love analyzes longstanding complaints to find a core of truth.

88. Forever-love steps out and makes adjustments to "go for" a better relationship.

89. Forever-love measures its criticism—giving seven or more praises for every one fault-finding suggestion.

90. Forever-love doesn't make impossible demands, and it accepts the reality that a truelove is not an all-sufficient god or parent.

91. Forever-love stays in tune as it seeks out several other couples for support and encouragement through good days and hard times.

92. Forever-love doesn't go it alone but welcomes the fresh insight of other perspectives.

93. Forever-love maintains energy as it is challenged through loving, supportive accountability.

94. Forever-love welcomes a periodic checkup with a marriage counselor.

13

Conflicts:
The Doorway to Intimacy

*The idea that conflict is healthy may sound like a cruel joke if you're feeling over-
whelmed by the negativity in your relationship. But in a sense, a marriage lives
and dies by what you might loosely call its arguments, by how well disagreements
and grievances are aired. They key is how you argue—whether your style esca-
lates tension or leads to a feeling of resolution.*

—John Gottman[1]

Dr. Howard Markman claims that resolving conflicts is the key area for
staying in love and staying married. His twenty years of research indicates
that if couples learned to work out their conflicts, the overall divorce rate
could be cut by more than 50 percent.[2] Just think of it! For years the
divorce rate has been hovering at about one out of two marriages. That sad
statistic could be reduced to one out of four—if only couples would learn
effective methods of conflict resolution. And one of those saved marriages
could be yours![3]

Most of us dislike and try to avoid conflicts, especially with our spouses.
For peace lovers, this chapter has both bad news and good. The bad news is
that we're always going to have conflicts. Our valued individuality—including our personality and gender differences—make them inevitable. But the
good news is that we can not only reduce our conflicts, we can also use them
to move into deeper intimacy in any relationship.

To illustrate how conflicts can lead to deeper intimacy, let me relate (with their permission) a story about our daughter, Kari, and her husband, Roger. It was very typical of young married couples. Roger heard that his mom and dad were coming to visit. He was pretty excited about that visit, because he loves to eat. He especially loves a big breakfast, and his mom used to cook him one every day. She's that kind of loving mother, and he was the baby of the family. I know how that goes, since I was the baby of my family. But then I got married and found out that wives don't always wait on you the way your mother did. Well, Roger has learned the same lesson. And also like me, he sometimes says things that have the opposite effect of what he intended.

So, thinking as a male can, when he heard his folks were coming, Roger said, "Finally, I can have one of those big breakfasts again!" He will admit that this comment was in praise of his mother but that it also was meant as an editorial comment about Kari's not cooking him breakfasts. Maybe she'd take the hint. That made sense to him, but it didn't sit well with Kari. Instantly—*wham!*—conflict. Kari went silent.

Fortunately Roger is a sensitive and loving husband. He doesn't want to offend Kari. He wants to make sure everything is going great. This happened before their first child, our grandson Michael Thomas, was born, and already Roger was concerned about providing a healthy family atmosphere. So he opened the door offered by that conflict and asked, "Kari, how did my comment make you feel?" That was level 4 of intimate communication, which we discussed in an earlier chapter.

Now, as I've already mentioned, word pictures are great for expressing feelings. Roger and Kari have developed their own word-picture method that conveys instantly how they're feeling. Their method uses fruit imagery, and it goes like this: If something happens but it's not a big deal, she'll say, "You just hit me with a raisin." If it's a little bigger deal, she'll say he hit her with an orange. If it's bigger still, she'll say it was a cantaloupe. But this time she said, "You just hit me with a twenty-five-pound watermelon—*wham!*—and drove me right into the ground." And he instantly entered into her feelings.

Seeing his desire to work things out, she went on to explain that his comment had made her feel inadequate, not as good as his mom. She thought, *What about all the great dinners I make? How come he isn't saying, "Wow, your dinners are just wonderful! Your dinners blow my mom's dinners away"?*

Roger had a different view. He wasn't saying he had a problem with her dinners. He was saying, "I'm not getting breakfast."

Back to Kari's perspective: It's pretty hard to make a big breakfast when you're a teacher and getting up at six (before he gets up) just to be ready for work on time. And what he said, thinking it was going to motivate her to want to make his breakfast, was not the way to get things done. (I think she had even mentioned to him before they married, "I don't do breakfast," but I guess that's the kind of thing you overlook at the time when you're just starting to grow in love.)

What came out of this conflict? He knew how she felt, he reinforced how much he loved her, and he found out one important way to avoid conflict in the future. I'll add more to their story in a few pages.

That's an example of using conflict as a doorway to intimacy, of getting past opinions to feelings. When conflict is used this way, we don't need to be afraid of it; it actually becomes a good thing that moves the relationship forward.

We actually *need* to have disagreements. That doesn't mean we go looking for fights. Should we keep fighting just so we can enjoy the deeper intimacy of making up? By no means.

But when conflicts do occur, they can bring benefits (produce pearls) if we use them in the right way. With that hope in mind, let's take a closer look at the anatomy of a conflict, beginning with why they happen in the first place.

Why Most Conflicts Occur

Conflicts—disagreements that can escalate into fights—occur for a number of reasons. Part of the following list of primary causes comes from Dr. Carol Rubin, a clinical instructor at Harvard Medical School, and her coauthor, Dr. Jeffrey Rubin, a professor of psychology at Tufts University.[4]

Power and Control

Conflicts happen because there are power and control problems in the home. Who is going to make the decisions? Who's the boss? When there is vying for authority—*boom!* Conflict. It happens when we least expect it.

When one person tries to smother the other with too much control or doesn't let the other think or feel independently, conflict smolders or erupts.

Insecurity

Someone's feeling insecure or unsafe in a relationship causes arguments. If you think your mate is drifting and creating distance, for instance, you're likely to feel insecure, and conflict is a natural result.

Some personalities hold things in for a long time, and then they explode. It might be because they don't feel safe to bring up those things when they first are perceived as a problem. In time the unresolved anger explodes "out of the blue."

Differences in Values

Conflicts arise out of differences in values. He thinks it's okay to drink alcohol at every meal, and she can't stand it. She thinks it's fine to tell people someone's not home when a call comes in, and he thinks that's lying. He wants to attend church every Sunday, and she likes to go only at Christmas and Easter.

It's important to remember here that not all differences can be eliminated. In such cases, it's healthy to say to each other, "We'll never agree on this issue, but I still love you, and I hope we can learn more about each other's feelings and needs through this conflict."

Competition

Conflict can grow out of competition. Some people can't stand to lose at anything, even in a casual game of checkers. Or perhaps the husband is bothered by the fact that his wife earns more than he does, and he's determined to outdo her in that area.

Personal Differences

Couples fight over normal male-female differences and normal personality differences. We can count on those two areas to bring a continual flow of conflicts. That's why I've taken two chapters (10 and 11) to expand on those subjects and show how to understand each other and then use that understanding to make love last rather than to tear the relationship apart.

Misunderstood Feelings and Unmet Needs

I believe this is the major reason for conflict—when one, or more likely both, spouses have unmet needs. Dr. Stephen Covey says this in a different way. He claims that all conflicts are caused by unfulfilled expectations in "roles and goals."[5] One spouse may think, *That's not what you're supposed to do in our relationship. I fix the car, and you fix the meals.* Or one may say to the other, "I've always wanted to go on in my education. You knew that. We'll just have to go without that new couch until I finish." We expect others to know our needs and feelings, in fact, even if we haven't mentioned them.

It's been extremely helpful to me to understand that whenever I'm in conflict with someone, one or two things are occurring: Someone's feelings aren't being valued and understood or someone's needs are not being valued and met.

Knowing and meeting your mate's (and children's) needs is a basic part of intimacy, and it's also important that your needs are understood and that you're reasonably sure they'll be met. (That's why the first part of this book is so vital; it gives us a plan for handling our feelings and needs, including those that cannot possibly be met by a mate.) But needs unnecessarily go unmet when we get too busy—when the spouse and kids aren't getting enough time with us or there's just not enough conversation.

The Circle of Conflict

Growing out of one or more of those causes, conflict tends to go in a circle. Let me show you what I mean with a typical example. A wife with a "perfectionist" personality needs a certain measure of neatness and order in her home, but her "carefree" husband couldn't care less. So the woman might say something like, "I am so frustrated around this house! Look at this mess! Nobody ever picks up anything!"

But the husband, who may be clueless, placing less value in or having less need for neatness, may say, "Yeah, you know what? If you would just get better organized around here, you wouldn't be so frustrated." Or he may ask, "You need more energy? Are you still taking those vitamins we spent all that money for?" "Are you getting your rest?" Or simply, "What's the big deal?" Mr. Fix-it offers solutions and opinions but finds it hard to get down to discussing feelings or needs.

As a pattern, this couple may easily exchange clichés and facts, but when they get to opinions—*wham!*—tension flares, based on disagreement. If they're like a lot of couples (maybe most), they may go silent for a while or escalate to a hotter conflict. They don't enjoy conflict. One spouse may not feel safe enough to get to the deeper levels—expressing feelings or needs. One may have little hope that expressing feelings will make any change. One may express needs inappropriately, in a rage. One, again, may be clueless that feelings and unmet needs have anything to do with the problem.

For any number of reasons, the couple moves back to clichés, because that's real safe. Then they share some facts, followed by opinions again, and *boom!*—back to conflict. They just circle in those three areas and never go to the deep levels of communication where disagreements can lead to a closer, more intimate bond—deeper intimacy.

We're not doomed to an endless cycle of unresolved conflict. But if you're stuck on a merry-go-round, you'll need to take the risk of stepping out of old patterns.

What Doesn't Work in Resolving Conflicts

For a marriage to grow as a result of conflict—for healing to occur after conflict—we need to learn to move toward resolution. But some patterns just don't do the job as well as we'd like.

What doesn't work for healing resolution? For starters, *withdrawing into yourself.* I used to do this because it's what I often saw my father doing. If you withdraw, however, you don't get your needs met, your spouse's needs don't get met, and your relationship suffers. So withdrawing is not the solution. In fact, Dr. Scott Stanley says that the worst thing for a marriage is when the husband clams up and distances himself from the family.[6]

Yielding—giving in—isn't a satisfactory pattern either. While one person wins and therefore peace prevails for a season, the other person loses, and ultimately, the relationship also loses. If both partners don't win, the relationship is weakened.

A third pattern? You could be the winner—the opposite of yielding. But again, one of you ends up a loser, so the relationship loses.

How about *compromise?* Isn't that healthy? Sometimes you just don't have time to resolve the issue right then, so you each settle for half a loaf. But remember that compromise is only a temporary solution because it's still a win-lose situation for both of you and for your relationship. Postponing is okay, but if you don't get back to the dispute, you lose a doorway to a deeper intimacy that we'll discuss in a minute.

Everybody Wins

Let's work through another pattern in which everybody wins—both parties and the relationship. Here you *keep working on the conflict until you both feel good about the solution.* The issue is resolved. You both know your feelings are being understood. And you both feel your needs are being met. It may take some deep conversation over a couple of days or longer, but your attitude and approach are always saying, *Let's work to resolve this issue, where we both feel like winners.*

A few years ago, Norma and I found ourselves embroiled in a dispute. We had taken our youngest son, Michael, to college for his freshman year and had been with him for three or four days. Now we were getting ready to leave, and Norma was sitting on the hotel bed, misty-eyed. We had to get to the airport soon, and I was eager to be on our way. "What's wrong?" I asked.

"I don't know," she said. "It's just real hard for me. This is our baby, and I just hope everything turns out okay here for him."

Oh, brother! I thought. To say I was insensitive to her feelings at that moment would be a major understatement. So I said something like, "We have got to get going. Come on."

But she said, "I'm just sitting here thinking about the empty nest, the trauma a mom goes through in losing all her kids."

I was thinking it might be a fun time for us with the kids all gone, so I wasn't empathizing too well. I replied, "Well, we have to let him go, you know. Let's get moving."

Norma looked across the room into my eyes and said, "You know, what I need right now is what you teach!"

Obviously, we had a conflict of feelings and priorities. Now, at that point I could have become sarcastic or defensive. I could have said, "I can't believe I have to perform all the time! Do I have to go up on the stage now?" Or I could have said, "Which of the twenty areas I teach do you need?" I (or she) could have withdrawn—walked into the bathroom and shut the door to avoid any further tension. One of us could have quickly (or not so quickly) yielded; for me that might have meant saying, "Okay, what do you want?" all the while resenting her condemnation of my behavior. She, on the other hand, could have said, "Okay, let's get going," all the while resenting my unwillingness to listen and understand. As for compromise, if we had been really late for the plane, we could have said, "Let's continue this on the plane or when we get home."

Fortunately, we had a little time to spare, and we had progressed a little beyond the other unhealthy tactics. Swallowing some pride and opening the doorway to intimacy, I walked across the room to Norma, and she scooted over on the bed to make space for me. I sat down next to her, put my arm around her, hugged her, and asked, "If you were the weather right now, what would be happening to you?"

"It's a real drizzle—rainy, cold, and foggy," she said.

"And if you were a flower?" I asked.

"Right now I've lost all my petals," she said, "and they've fallen on the floor. You stepped on them when you walked over here." (*She is so quick!*)

When I asked what she needed, she mentioned some things I might do with Michael that I hadn't even thought of. I listened and made mental notes. She felt better immediately, and we headed home much more at peace with each other and in deeper intimacy.

As I held Norma that day and listened, I felt the tension between us turn to peace. I knew we were working things out. I felt I had won something—new ideas for how I could stay in contact with my son. I'd learned something new about Norma and her fears of the empty nest. I know she felt she was winning, too, because even though I'm still capable of being irritated by the discovery that I'm doing something wrong, she knows she is generally safe in bringing up any issues that are between us. She knew I had heard her out, and she knows I want to resolve any conflicts we have.

It's not always possible to come to a resolution where you both feel good about the outcome. But it is possible to restate your commitment to each other at any point. You can say things like, "I still love you and always will. We can't seem to agree on this issue, but I'm committed to you for life, and I'll never stop loving you over any disagreement." Such commitment and lasting love has a way of softening the dispute.

Reaching Resolution: Developing Personal Keys to Intimacy

If a conflict is ultimately going to draw a couple closer together, they need a set of "fighting rules." That list becomes the key to what I call the doorway to intimacy. If you don't have such boundaries on how you fight, you may say or do any number of things that shut down communication— that slam the door on intimacy.

Even in the best of circumstances, a couple usually walks through the doorway to intimacy after the tension of the conflict is starting to cool down. Most couples I work with can't enter intimacy in the midst of a heated conflict. Nor can Norma and I. It's afterward, when we can think about each other's feelings and needs, that we move closer to each other.

Door Slammers

A few modes of operation predictably shut and lock the doorway to intimacy. One of the most common is the use of accusatory "you statements": "*You* always do this." "*You* never remember that." "As far as I'm concerned, *you'll* never change." These statements immediately put the other person on the defensive. If you want to draw closer, the key is to use "I statements." If the husband is late for dinner, for instance, the wife might say, "*I* feel uneasy, or uncomfortable, when that happens, because *I* don't know where you are. *I'm* concerned about you when you don't call . . . " That's a lot more effective than "*You're* always late. I can't believe it. Why do you do this? *You* never change." Such an approach will only make a person want to run away or fight back.

Sarcasm, disrespect, and screaming are all door slammers too. Denying the conflict isn't the solution, but neither is a temper tantrum. David and Vera Mace report that:

> Studies of the family by Murray Straus have shown that individuals who vent their anger tend, over time, to produce more and more anger and to vent it more and more vigorously until they finally resort to physical violence. . . . Venting anger almost invariably gets the other person angry too, and then you are going to need more and more anger to continue the fight.[7]

Kindness, respect, and calmness, on the other hand, are keys that open the door. Exactly what works best for you and your spouse is something you can work out on your own. Such keys will improve all your conversations, but they'll be especially valuable during times of conflict.

Key Lists

My son Greg and I have developed a set of keys to the doorway of intimacy in connection with his doctoral studies in psychology. I'll show you our list of fourteen suggestions that have worked for us and many others. Then I'll give you a similar list by Dr. Harriet Lerner, who is one of the leaders in the field of conflict resolution. From these two lists, you and your spouse can make your own list of rules in the space provided on page 232. If *rules* seems too harsh a word, think in terms of *keys to intimacy*.

The Smalley "Fighting Rules"

1. First clarify what the actual conflict is. Make sure that you understand your partner as clearly as you can before proceeding to a

resolution. Listening is vital here! Endeavor to work for understanding in two key areas: your mate's *feelings*, and then, *needs*.

2. Stick to the issue at hand. Don't dredge up past hurts or problems, whether real or perceived. But if you tend to veer off the issue, you might want to see if there is any other key factor in this conflict, such as fatigue, low estrogen levels, low blood sugar, stress, work problems, or spiritual or emotional issues.

3. Maintain as much tender physical contact as possible. Hold hands.

4. Avoid sarcasm.

5. Avoid "you" statements. Use the words "I feel" or "I think." No past or future predictions ("You always . . ." "You won't ever . . .").

6. Don't use "hysterical" statements or exaggerations. ("This will never work out." "You're just like your father.")

7. Resolve any hurt feelings before continuing the conflict discussion. ("I shouldn't have said that. Will you forgive me?")

8. Don't resort to name-calling. Don't allow the conflict to escalate your tempers. If this happens, agree to continue the discussion later.

9. Avoid power statements and actions. For example: "I quit!" "You sleep on the couch tonight!" "You're killing me!" "I hate you!"

10. Don't use the silent treatment.

11. Keep your arguments as private as possible to avoid embarrassment.

12. Use the "drive-through" method of communication when arguing. (Repeat back what you think the other person is saying.)

13. Resolve your conflicts with win-win solutions; both parties agree with the solution or outcome of the argument. Work on resolution only after both understand feelings and needs.

14. Above all, strive to reflect honor in all your words and actions during the resolution of your conflicts.

Dr. Harriet Lerner's Key Rules

1. Do speak up when an issue is important to you.

2. Don't strike while the iron is hot. (Watch your timing.)

3. Do take time to think about the problem and to clarify your position.

4. Don't use "below-the-belt" tactics.

5. Do speak in "I" language.

6. Don't make vague requests.

7. Do try to appreciate the fact that people are different.

8. Don't participate in intellectual arguments that go nowhere.

9. Do recognize that each person is responsible for his or her own behavior.

10. Don't tell another person what he or she thinks or feels or "should" think or feel.

11. Do try to avoid speaking through a third party (someone speaking for you and you're not there to clarify).

12. Don't expect change to come from hit-and-run confrontations.[8]

The Master Key

When it comes to conflict resolution, everything I say here is based on an underlying rule for a long, happy marriage: Keep anger levels low every day!

Doing that calls for communication—primarily at the deepest level, where one talks about feelings and needs. It calls for openness and for forgiveness—a desire for the relationship to be the best it can be.

The ancient Scriptures are full of amazing insight and wisdom. You may be familiar with the passage about anger: "'In your anger, do not sin': Do not let the sun go down while you are still angry."[9] That is a commentary of sorts on an even older line of poetry:

> In your anger do not sin;
> > when you are on your beds,
> > search your hearts and be silent [be at peace].[10]

If anger and its symptoms of distance and control are an underlying theme of your marriage, I suggest you "search your hearts" and go back and reread the issues I addressed in part 1. If marital conflicts ever resort to violence, see a marriage counselor to work through these issues.

Pearls from Conflict

The disputes—disagreements—in your marriage will never vanish. But there are pearls to be found in those disputes. That's one word picture. Another picture is the one I used above: Conflicts can be doorways to intimacy. Here's how. (I give special thanks to Dr. Gary Oliver for his insights and research in this area.)

Conflicts Reveal Feelings and Needs

Conflict is a doorway into intimacy because it's a way to discover who a person is. As soon as we hit the wall and are in conflict, we have to open a door so we can walk through it to find out what the other person feels and needs. Instead of reverting to silence or clichés, we can adopt an attitude that says, *I'm kind of glad we're having this conflict because it'll result in both of us knowing more about each other and loving each other more.*

Norma and I were recently locked in a prolonged argument about my travel schedule. I still speak a great deal across the country, and we don't live near a major airport. So I wanted to investigate the possibility of leasing a company plane to use on speaking trips. But Norma has been against the idea of small planes for quite some time.

As we went back and forth on this issue, it was increasingly clear that we weren't going to agree. So we stepped back to ask, "What are our deepest feelings about renting a plane?"

I found out that she fears the smaller planes because of all the publicity that comes when one crashes. She feels they're unsafe, so she believes riding in them is taking an unnecessary risk. I also learned that she wants me to value her uneasiness about the plane and to respect her expression of her true feelings.

From me, she found out that flying in a private aircraft would allow me much more time at home and create less stress for me at the airports. I felt the convenience of having our own schedule (as opposed to having to follow the airlines' schedules) would add a lot more pleasure to my job. She listened and did understand, but it didn't resolve the situation.

So we used our "911" group of friends to help us out. A "911" group is two or three very close friends who love us and whom we love in return. On rare occasions we call these friends and ask for their input in some conflicts. We met with our friends, and they helped us sort through the problem. I agreed to drop the discussion for three months while I gathered all the facts about how much a plane rental would cost, how safe it is, and what the actual time savings and convenience would be. Norma agreed that we would bring up the subject again at the end of that time so we could come to a conclusion on the matter.

For me, the meeting provided new insight. I hadn't understood that Norma had been feeling as though I was badgering her over the issue. She felt smothered by my strong interest in renting a plane and also by my lack of awareness of her feelings. She was right—I hadn't seen our talks as smothering to her. But with the help of our loving friends, we were able to be more objective and put the conflict on hold. And we both felt more understood and safer in revealing our feelings because of the dispute.

A few months later, we met again with our support group, and I explained that it's my nature always to be looking for a better way to do things. When I said how tired I was of having to drive an hour just to get to the nearest commercial airport, one member of the group replied that lots of people have to commute an hour each way to their jobs. "You're just a big baby!" she said as we all laughed. But in the end, Norma agreed that if certain safety concerns were met, such as having two pilots in the cockpit, she probably wouldn't be too nervous and could relax with the small-plane idea.

Conflict is one of the best ways to take us beyond our feelings all the way to discussing our needs. In the above scenario, Norma needed assurance that I—her family—was safe, not taking unnecessary, life-threatening risks. I needed to reassure her that I understood her concerns and took them seriously. I needed Norma to understand my desire for greater efficiency and less wasted time spent commuting to and waiting in airports for scheduled airline flights.

Remember the breakfast story from the beginning of this chapter? After Roger asked Kari how she felt and she told him, he then asked what she needed. *What can I do to show you I love you?* She replied, "I need for you to praise me for the things I do and the things I get excited about doing." In other words, she needed him to do more than just avoid insulting her; she needed to hear words of appreciation for the things she does. And since then, he has made an effort to give her that praise. He's become the kind of husband dads hope their daughters will find. (My special thanks to the Gibsons, his parents.)

One of the best ways I know of to meet another person's needs is by developing your own love language. This only works if your relationship is fairly healthy to begin with; if it's not, you might not be willing to give this a try. But if things are going reasonably well, this can be great.

As I've already mentioned, normal conflicts can reveal that my feelings or my needs are not being understood or valued. As we work through a conflict—discovering deep feelings and needs—we can develop a love language based on the alphabet of that new knowledge.

Or think again in terms of pearls: Over years of marriage, this love language becomes like a necklace, made from the pearls hunted and found after conflicts, in answer to the question "What can I do to show you I love you?"

As a result of conflict, over time, you can create a love language. Here's how. You and your spouse should each list five or ten practical and specific things you would like to have the other person do for you—things you believe will really meet your needs. You agree: "This makes me feel as if you love me. I have a need, and when you do this, it meets that need." Your mate's doing one of these for you (or vice versa) expresses love and honor.

Write out this list and post it someplace where it will serve as a daily reminder. It might be in your closet if you don't want everybody in the world to see it. Or you can put it on your refrigerator. But put it in a place where you can be reminded every day.

I've asked seminar participants to write items that would be in their love language. One woman told me she would love to have her husband learn to pick up on her hints better. For instance, if she says "I'm really tired" at the end of the day, she would love for him to pick up on that and respond, "Let's go out to dinner so we don't have to cook tonight." A love-language list is much more effective, however, than hoping your mate will pick up on your hints.

Another woman said she would put this on her love-language list: "On my husband's days off, a lot of times he gets involved with the boys and in doing stuff out in the garage. And when I come home from my really hectic day, I need for him to stop what he's doing for just a few minutes and say, 'I'm so glad to see you. It's great to have you home.'"

A professional woman said, "I need my husband to respect my need to be engaged in activities that he doesn't find fun. For example, I love to just go play in my front- and backyard 'sandbox'—to plant flowers and make our place beautiful. But he has ways of belittling me that are funny to him but hurtful to me. He calls me his little Polish farmer, or he'll tell me I've got a rednecked farmer tan. It would be wonderful if he would praise me for how the yard looks or even join me in the garden."

These comments describe simple yet significant needs. Developing your own love language is a great way to find out what your spouse needs and also to get your own needs met. Conflicts are often an open door to a discussion and an awareness of such needs.

I'll give more specific examples of what might be on your love-language list in chapter 15, where we discuss the energizing concept of "marital banking."

Before I go on, I pause one more time to address any skeptical reader. *Wait*, you say, *you don't know my husband. He knows how I feel, he knows what I need, and he just doesn't give a rip about anything but himself.*

Whoa! If that's your view of life, I make several reminders and suggestions. First, consider this question: Are you sure? Have you really talked about underlying priorities? Have you listened to your mate's feelings and needs? Have you clearly expressed yours? Can you see baby steps of progress you can praise?

On the other hand, start back at the beginning of this book: Your own contentment with life doesn't rely on what your spouse will or won't do. You have the ability to set boundaries and ask that they be maintained. I once more recommend Harriet Lerner's excellent book *The Dance of Anger*, which is subtitled *A Woman's Guide to Changing the Patterns of Intimate Relationships*. If you and your spouse are in an unsatisfying dance, it takes just one of you to change the record. And the new tune could save your marriage. See the endnotes of this book for other helpful resources. At the beginning of this chapter I mentioned a husband and wife who disagreed about how neat the house should be. One recent book even gives principles for living beyond the conflicts presented by those aggravating housekeeping differences.[11]

Conflicts Provide Opportunities to Express Affection

Conflicts can open a doorway to intimacy by surfacing feelings and needs. But conflicts also provide an opportunity to express physical and emotional affection. We all need to be hugged. We all need to be loved on.

To illustrate this point, let me give an example of how *not* to do it. A young husband told me about a conflict he and his wife had before they married. She had invited him to dinner at her place, where she had baked him lasagna. He got to the dinner table, and she served the lasagna—which turned out to be as hard as a brick. So he said, trying to inject a little levity into the situation, "Do you serve chain saws with this?"

As you might imagine, she immediately got up and ran down the hall, crying. He called after her, "And another thing, enough of this sensitivity stuff!"

Believe it or not, he proposed to her later that same night, and she said yes. (Was she blind or what?) But at the moment, this was a big conflict that instantly brought her feelings and needs to the surface.

What could the young man have done at that point to help the situation? He could have put his arm around her, held her, and said, "I can't believe I say things like that. I don't know how I learned to be so sarcastic, but I don't want to hurt you. Will you forgive me?" Now she might need some time to warm up (or cool down). But his contrite spirit and gentle touch would have started the healing and resolving process.

Sorting Out the Big Issues: A Practical Approach to Reaching Resolution

Norma and I use this practical step-by-step method for conflict resolution every time we get into a big disagreement over some major issue, such as where to live, borrowing for a new car, or changing churches. Our approach involves making two lists. Let me explain.

Suppose our disagreement is about how to parent our children, which was often the case in years gone by. I was a tolerant father in the sense of not having a lot of rules, because that's the way I was raised. Norma, on the other hand, wanted a little more order in the home. As the kids grew older, I would also start pushing them to get out and do various activities. But Norma would say, "I don't think they're old enough. They're not ready yet."

I remember the time she expressed her concern with a great word picture. "You know how this makes me feel?" she said. "I feel like I'm the mother bird in a nest up in the tree. We've got these three little birds in here. And papa bird flies in now and then and says, 'Hey, why don't you guys get out and do some things? It would be boring to me to be in a nest all the time. You've got to jump out and enjoy yourself.' But I know how immature their feathers and bones are. I know where all the cats in the neighborhood are. And if you push our chicks out now, they're going to hit the ground and get hurt or gobbled up in a hurry."

Well, whenever we got into a big conflict like that, we would pull out a blank sheet of paper and draw a line down the middle, dividing it in half. At the top, on one side of the line, we would write, "All the Reasons We

Should Do This." At the top on the other side, we would write, "All the Reasons We Shouldn't Do This."

In listing reasons, we would start by gathering all the facts. Then we would go deeper and find the feelings involved. Each of us would say, "Well, I feel this about that idea." Finally, we'd get to the level of needs: "I have a need, and if we do that, it will mess with my need."

Before long, we would have eighteen to twenty reasons on one side of the paper and maybe fifteen to eighteen on the other. Having it all down on paper—both the pros and the cons—and knowing that we were both heard and valued usually helped us resolve our conflict. We didn't have to win or lose. Maybe it was Norma's idea we went with, or maybe it was mine. But I never felt I was compromising or giving in. I always felt it was the right thing to do. Usually as soon as all the facts were on one piece of paper, it was pretty obvious what ought to happen. The facts won or lost, not us. This method objectified the conflict and took it further out of the emotional range.

Sometimes, however, if we were still deadlocked on an important issue, or if the kids didn't like the outcome, we would need to take this method one step further. We would then rank each statement on both sides of the line. We would ask the question of each statement, "Is that a factor that will have long-lasting effects?" If we believed it would affect us for more than ten years, we'd put an L beside the statement. If we believed there was only a temporary effect, we'd put a T beside the statement. When we were finished marking each item, pro and con, we'd add up the L's and T's and see which side won. This analysis seemed to resolve the issue every time, even with the kids involved.

Sometimes when people come to me for counseling, I'll listen for a while, and then all of a sudden they'll say, "Okay, what shall we do?" If I don't know what to tell them at that point, it's probably because I don't have enough facts yet. The more facts I get, the more pieces of the puzzle I have and the more clearly I can see what the whole picture is and present it to them. And when they see the factual picture, they generally know what to do. I don't have to solve the problem for them. So part of being a counselor is just gathering the facts and laying them out clearly for a person or couple to see. Then I say, "Here it is. What do you think?"

This fact-gathering method has solved so many conflicts through the years for Norma and me. It has a way of calming us down and making us feel safe and highly valued, which is a major factor in resolving conflicts.

Summary

Remember the bad news at the beginning of the chapter? Conflicts are inevitable in any relationship. But the good news overrides the bad: I challenge you to see any disagreements with your spouse as a doorway to intimacy. Let conflicts be that doorway into a better understanding of how you both feel and what you each need.

In the last of his Chronicles of Narnia series (*The Last Battle*), C. S. Lewis describes his characters facing a battle to end all battles. But at a strategic point they walked through a doorway into a stable; some people claimed the stable held a life-threatening creature. But once through that doorway, they discovered "in reality they stood on grass, the deep blue sky was overhead, and the air which blew gently on their faces was that of a day in early summer."[12] Walking through that door had taken them to a heavenly kingdom. And once there, they could continue to go "further up and further in,"[13] making increasingly awesome—wonderful—new discoveries that they couldn't have fathomed before they had walked through that seemingly threatening door.

That's how it can be in a marriage; conflicts have the potential for drawing you and your spouse closer and closer to each other. There's not a monster behind your conflicts. It's a matter of opening the door to intimacy—not closing it, slamming it, or locking it.

Open the door. Walk through—and you learn more about the delights of marriage, including intercourse, than you ever dreamed possible. Intimacy isn't just talking; you know it's much more. When's the last time you both really enjoyed your sexual relationship? Is sex mostly physical? In the next chapter we'll show how good sex is a combination of four important ingredients. Have fun!

But before we move on use the space on page 232 for notes that will begin your own set of "fighting rules." If you are in or starting a small support group with other couples, consider getting input from others as you finalize your rules.

Forever-Love Principles

Our list of forever-love principles continues from the previous chapter:

95. Forever-love knows that marital conflict is inevitable.

96. Forever-love sees conflict as a doorway to greater intimacy and knowledge. "Through this disagreement, what new insights can we gain about us as a couple? How can this eventually draw us closer?"

97. Forever-love doesn't go looking for a fight just to find the joy of making up.

98. Forever-love finds courage to break out of longstanding, circular fight patterns.

99. Forever-love doesn't clam up in the face of verbal conflict.

100. Forever-love doesn't feel compelled to give in and maintain peace at any price.

101. Forever-love doesn't gloat, "I win. You lose."

102. Forever-love approaches conflict saying, "Let's work to resolve this issue so that your needs and mine are met."

103. Forever-love says, "I love you," even when a resolution isn't reached.

104. Forever-love sets down fighting rules—boundaries that aren't to be crossed.

105. Forever-love knows how to say "I'm sorry" and "I forgive you."

106. Forever-love looks beyond disagreement and conflict to identify what needs are begging to be met.

107. Forever-love resolves today's conflicts today—not tomorrow.

108. Forever-love forms a private love language. Both partners develop a list: "These actions make me feel loved and honored." Forever-love reaches out and energizes a truelove by suggesting a love-language activity.

109. Forever-love considers the long-term effects of decisions when conflict is otherwise deadlocked.

Our Fighting Rules

14

Was That As Good for You As It Was for Me?

You must not isolate that [sexual] pleasure and try to get it by itself, any more than you ought to try to get the pleasures of taste without swallowing and digesting, by chewing things and spitting them out again.

—C. S. Lewis[1]

Before Dennis and Lois even sat down in my counseling office, I knew what we were going to be talking about. There's a certain hesitation, a betraying look of sheepishness, that clearly signals when a couple needs to discuss one of the most difficult and embarrassing topics in marriage. Dennis and Lois had problems in their sexual relationship, a situation that isn't uncommon, even in couples that look as if they have it all together. That was Dennis and Lois—one handsome, intense couple. I guessed them to be in their early thirties. Lois was attractive in her jeans and oversized sweater. Dennis was in khakis and a gold shirt from an exclusive country club.

"Where should we begin?" I asked, watching them squirm on the couch as they tried a hundred different ways to get comfortable.

"I'll start," Dennis volunteered. He took a deep breath then said, "I haven't had sex in so long, I forget how it goes!"

Lois burst into tears. After half a minute or so, she regained her composure enough to say, "That's not true. Dennis tends to exaggerate when he's angry."

"Or horny," he muttered.

"Actually, it *is* our sex life that brings us here today," Lois continued. "It has become a real problem in our marriage."

"Tell me about it," I said.

"We've been married for eleven years," she said, "and sex was really good for both of us in the beginning."

"Would you agree, Dennis?" I asked.

"Yeah," he replied, "and that's part of the problem. I know how good it can be, but it's just not that way anymore."

"Go on, Lois," I said.

"Well, I guess our problem is typical stuff. We started having kids, so there were lots of late nights with colicky babies. Then Dennis got promoted, so he started putting in long hours and coming home pretty late. I gained weight while I was pregnant with our second child, too, and I just couldn't lose it after he was born."

"How did all this affect your sexual relationship?" I asked.

"I guess the best way to put it is that we began to feel two very different levels of need for sex," Lois said sadly, looking at the floor. "I was always tired, fighting depression, feeling like a fat, old cow. And Dennis, even with his long hours at the office, still seemed to want sex a lot—or at least a lot more than I did. For a while I tried to keep up with him, but I found I was getting angry at his attitude. I felt he was being demanding and extremely selfish about the whole thing.

"The more we fought about it, the more we distanced ourselves from each other. Even now, when we do have sex, it's not very satisfying for either one of us, but it's particularly unsatisfying for me. I'm just lying there, letting him have his fun."

Silence hung in the air for a few moments before I asked Dennis for his view of their dilemma.

"She's got it pretty straight," Dennis agreed. "I guess I sound like a big heel when I hear how she tells the story. But you know how a man gets . . . We go so long without sex, and I feel like I'm gonna burst!"

He paused, staring blankly at the far wall. "I know Lois has had some hard times, but I think she's overreacting. Take her weight, for instance. I don't think she's overweight, but she's convinced she's fat."

"Do you tell her she looks good to you?" I interrupted.

Lois was shaking her head in the background while Dennis stammered, "Well . . . I guess not as much as I could, but she knows how I feel. What's the big deal?"

"The big deal is that I feel ugly!" Lois snapped. "I don't want to make love to you if I'm feeling all gross-looking!" She was leaning forward on the front edge of the sofa now.

"You just seem to go from one crisis to another," Dennis said unsympathetically. "And it's always our sex life that has to pay the price."

His anger had taken him as far from Lois as he could get. In a matter of moments, this husband and wife who had sat down together were at the opposite ends of my couch.

Dennis and Lois were going through experiences common to a couple married eleven years. Things change. People change. Dennis and Lois had changed. The more they could understand those changes, the better their chances of improving their life together, including their sexual relationship. I used much of the material in this chapter in counseling sessions with Dennis and Lois. We spent several sessions together, and their sexual relationship started to improve before we ever talked directly about that aspect of their marriage.

Nothing in marriage is more misunderstood than the sexual union. It's more than the physical act that sexually unites a couple. And probably the most important thing Dennis and Lois learned is that a sexual relationship is a mirror of an entire marital relationship. They weren't struggling with a sexual problem as much as they were with relational issues that were diminishing their sexual enjoyment. They needed to see sex in the larger context of their whole marriage. There are actually four areas of the sexual relationship that need to be developed in concert with one another if a couple is to achieve maximum satisfaction. As Dennis and Lois concentrated on other areas of their relationship first, their sexual life improved.

Before we look at these four areas, however, a few more words are necessary about differences. Men and women tend to see sex very differently, as they do most other issues.

Male-Female Differences

In an ongoing study I've conducted with hundreds of couples over the years, I ask men and women privately and in groups how they would feel if they knew they would never again have sex with their mates. Almost all the women say, "It's really no big deal if I never have sex again with my husband." But they add quickly that it would be a big deal if they were never touched or kissed or romanced again.

When I ask men the same question, they're almost always incredulous. "Give up sex?" they say. "No way!" To ask a man to give up sex is to ask him to give up eating.

Why this huge difference between the views of men and women? It's not easy for some women to understand what testosterone does to a man. The hormone fires up a man sexually. (I know the image of the male driven by testosterone is a stereotype, but in this case it's an accurate one.) The level of testosterone drops in most men around the age of forty, but many men have been shown to have significant amounts far into their eighties!

To give wives a better idea, imagine you've just been informed by mail that you've won the grand prize in a national contest. You and your husband will be whisked off to a tropical island for ten days of first-class service at a four-star resort. You'll also be given fifteen hundred dollars a day in spending money, unlimited luxury limousine service—in other words, the works! Naturally, you can't wait for your husband to walk in the door so you can tell him the good news.

Now imagine that when he does come home, you greet him by saying you have some wonderful news. But he responds, "Not now, dear. I'm really tired, so I think I'm going to take a nap." As he walks to the bedroom, he adds, "Don't tell anyone else the news. I want to be the first to hear it."

When I ask the women in a seminar audience how they would feel in this situation, most say they would be highly frustrated.

A man's testosterone level makes him feel as if he has won the grand prize . . . almost every day! He can't wait to "tell" you about it. But a disinterested wife responds, "Let's talk about it tomorrow." Imagine the way that makes him feel. Some husbands are so highly testosterone-loaded that they're literally trembling on the other side of the bed while you're drifting off to sleep. Perhaps that will help you understand why he gets frustrated when you put off his physical advances.

Four Areas of Intimacy That Are Vital to Sexual Satisfaction

Sex is more than a physical act. Good sex is the reflection of a good relationship. It's the icing on top of what's right in a marriage. Satisfying sex is admiring a trophy fish after all the skills went into catching it. I've learned that fulfilling sex has at least four separate aspects that work together—they must work together if we are to catch the "biggest ones."

Four aspects of intercourse contribute to good sex. As Denver psychologist Gary Oliver once said to me in terms of marriage, "All of life is foreplay."

Intercourse literally means "to get to know someone intimately." In our culture, we have reduced the word to refer only to the act of sex. Conversely, we've nearly forgotten a traditional meaning of the verb *to know*—which was "to have sexual intercourse." Biblical history starts the whole human lineage with this line: "And Adam knew Eve his wife; and she conceived. . . ."[2] The two words *intercourse* and *knowledge* are closely aligned.

For now, let's return to a simpler day when the word *intercourse* had a broader meaning. A conservative, small town in the middle of Pennsylvania Amish country is named Intercourse—and it's not referring to sex.

Verbal Intercourse

In earlier times, people used the word *intercourse* when speaking of an intimate conversation. Obviously, we have to be sensitive to our current culture, so it's not advisable to have a discussion with your next-door neighbor and then yell over the fence, "It sure was good having intercourse with you earlier today!"

But verbal intercourse is vital to a healthy sex life. It involves getting to know your mate through conversation and spending time together. This is especially significant to most women, who are amazed that men can have sex at almost any time without regard to the quality of the relationship. The women usually want to connect with their partners through verbal intimacy before they can enjoy the physical act. Knowing this, years ago I decided I'd do everything right . . .

The first time Norma and I visited Hawaii, I envisioned a vacation filled with sexual passion. I knew that Norma loved to sightsee, so on one of our first days there, I invited her to drive around the island of Maui. She was thrilled.

We drove from the southern part of Maui, where our hotel was, all the way to the northern beaches. We talked, laughed, saw whales, and discovered roads and little villages that weren't even on the maps! It was a wonderful time of verbal intimacy. And as a male, I knew this might lead to some wonderful sexual intimacy later on.

As we started making our way back to our hotel, however, I discovered that the gas gauge in our rental car was on E. I did my best to keep this information from Norma, not wanting to ruin the moment or jeopardize the rest of the day!

She began to get suspicious, however, when I started coasting down as many hills as I could. "Why are you taking the car out of gear?" she asked.

"Oh, no reason," I countered. "Just another way to have some fun!"

But the farther we drove with no gas station in sight, the more nervous I got. Then I suddenly felt as if we were completely out of gas. I went to put the car in neutral again, but thanks to my nervousness, I forgot that this was a rental car, an automatic, not the stick-shift I was used to. Full-force, I hit what I thought was the clutch. Unfortunately it was the brake. The car screeched to a halt in the middle of the road, throwing Norma's head right into the dashboard. (This was before the days of seat-belt laws.)

She wasn't injured, but she screamed, "Gary, what are you doing?"

I didn't have the courage to say what I was thinking, which was, *I'm ruining any chance I had for sex tonight!* Rather, I confessed the gas-tank problem, and we just sat back and laughed together. And I didn't ruin the day or night after all.

What makes a vacation like that so special? For many couples, it's the only time during the year that they carve out interrupted time to talk and listen to each other. Far away from phones, faxes, secretaries, and appointments, it's a rare opportunity for relaxation and getting reacquainted.

What's good for vacations is also good for life. As a couple, work at giving each other the time you need to relax, talk, and listen to each other. Thinking back to the opening story, Dennis and Lois discovered through counseling that they had allowed the busyness of their lives to sabotage their verbal intimacy. As a result, they made talk times a priority, and their relationship showed immediate improvement.

We already discussed communication techniques in chapter 9, but the issue is so important I'd like to summarize here some ways that busy couples can make time for verbal intercourse.

Twelve Ways to Find Time to Talk to Your Spouse

1. You're both home from work at the end of the day? Set aside a fifteen-minute period at some point to discuss—reflect on—your respective day's activities.

2. Make a rule that the TV is off during dinner, encouraging conversation. For that hour, let the answering machine take all phone calls except emergencies.

3. Write a monthly date night into your schedule that *cannot be broken.*

4. If your schedule permits, get together for lunch once a week—even if you're just brown-bagging it in the park.

5. As a couple, attend one of your children's sports games or other performances. It's amazing how conversation can develop while you sit and watch your child or on the way to and from the game.

6. Take a walk together after dinner. It's a good time to talk, and it's also good for you physically.

7. If you are allowed some flexibility in your work schedule, go in late one day—after the kids have all gone off to school. Enjoy the hour with your spouse.

8. Read a magazine article or book together that you both feel will stimulate a discussion.

9. Don't be afraid to use baby-sitters just to give you time alone to talk.

10. Write each other little notes that begin, "I have something really amazing to talk with you about the next time we're together."

11. Once or twice a year, plan a weekend getaway for just the two of you.

12. Ask your best friend to hold you accountable to meet with your mate at least once a week for a meaningful conversation.

(Remember that a certain sex killer is to combine a serious discussion about some conflictive issue while on a fun date, during an intimate talk, or just before or right after the sexual experience. Plan your conflict discussions during the week at a specific time and day and use the ideas presented in Chapter 13 to resolve your arguments.)

For more ideas, ask people whom you respect how they find the time to talk as a couple. You may be surprised at their unique suggestions.

Emotional Intercourse

Sharing deep feelings with each other is emotional intercourse, and it's vital to sexual satisfaction. It's that sense of connectedness that occurs when you're both tracking on the same emotional level. This involves conversations that deal with more than facts alone. Any conversation might start with facts. Then any fact in a relationship can be connected to emotions with the question: "How does that set of facts make you feel?" This is especially significant to women. They are often most responsive to sexual intercourse when the entire relationship is open and loving—when they feel that their husband understands and values their feelings.

Another couple, Dave and Vicki, were struggling with this issue when Dave first came to see me. "I'll shoot straight with you, Gary," he said. "I'm not getting any sex from my wife, and I'm very frustrated."

As I listened to him explain his situation, I suggested he go back to his wife and seek to communicate his feelings through the use of an emotional word picture. "The analogy will get out on the table the deep feelings you have about this issue," I told him.

So that's exactly what he did. And then she responded with a powerful word picture of her own.

"Honey, we have a problem," he told her that night. "I want you to hear how I describe it."

"All right," Vicki agreed.

"When I'm away from you at work, I feel like I'm out in the middle of the desert. It's steaming hot, and I'm slowly baking. But when I get home, I feel like I've entered an oasis."

Vicki smiled and said, "Well, that's good."

"Not really," Dave went on. "You see, when I come home, you look so good to me that I want to enjoy our relationship completely."

"Meaning what?" she asked.

"Sex," Dave answered. "We just don't have sex anymore, so I feel that instead of being in an oasis, part of the oasis is a mirage. The beauty of the oasis doesn't all seem to exist."

He sat there for a moment in silence. As tenderly as he could, he asked her, "How can I make the mirage back into the real oasis we once had?"

Vicki had been listening, and they were connecting on an emotional level. After a minute she responded, "I'll tell you how to return to the oasis. I'll even do for you what you just did for me. I'll paint an emotional word picture to make it clear.

"I feel as if I'm one of your prized rare antique books from the nineteenth century," she began. "Early in our marriage, you would pick me up and admire me, make sure I was free from dust, polish the gold-leaf edges, and just take good care of me overall."

Dave smiled at her knowingly.

"But something has happened to that rare book," she continued. "You don't care for it the way you used to. It has become dusty sitting on the shelf. The gold leaf is covered with a tarnish that could be removed if it just had a little attention. Now I'm just one of many rare books."

She was getting through to him for the first time in a long while, because he responded, "How can I give this book more of the attention it deserves?"

Vicki was able to tell him what was important to her—things like saying "I love you," and even things that Dave considered unrelated, like spending time with the kids. She also remembered fondly the days when Dave used to send her flowers and cards.

The more the two of them talked on a deep emotional level, the more they were able to help each other. This communication at the deep levels of feelings and needs changed Dave and Vicki's sexual relationship into a richer, fuller, and mutually satisfying one. It's still not perfect, but then I've never met a couple for which it was.

Physical Intercourse

Now we get to the real thing, right? Slow down. What we tend to zero in on is actually a small part of the physical relationship. When thinking of physical intercourse, think more in terms of touching, caressing, hugging, kissing, and romancing.

From my interviews and counseling with women, I've concluded that most women need eight to twelve meaningful touches a day to keep their energy level high and experience a sense of connectedness with their mate— a hug, a squeeze of the hand, a pat on the shoulder, a gentle kiss. There are approximately five million touch receptors in the human body—more than two million in the hands alone. The right kind of touch releases a pleasing and healing flow of chemicals in the bodies of both the toucher and the touched. Studies have shown that people get healthier even as a result of tender attention and touch of animals—dogs and cats. Everybody wins when we touch each other in a proper way.[3]

To emphasize just how important good touching is, let me describe some of the research that's been done with people as well as animals. In college, I studied under a professor who was an expert on the sex life of rats. A great specialty, right? But we students learned a lot from him, and in one of our experiments (which would probably not be allowed today), we would take a litter of lab rats and divide the newborns into two groups. Group A was hugged and petted regularly by the students. Group B was never touched. Otherwise, the two groups were fed and watered the same. Then, when they were still small, we put them one at a time on a platform six feet above a cement floor and pushed them off. (The more sensitive students hated this research.)

When the little rats from Group A hit the floor, they were able to get up quickly and scamper away. But Group B's rats all died. The only difference? Loving touch seemed to have made the Group A rats healthier and stronger.

A neurosurgeon friend of mine did his own study on the effects of touch. When he made his daily hospital rounds, he would stand the same distance from all his patients and spend the exact same amount of time with each of them. However, he also touched half his patients on the hand, arm, or face. The other half he didn't touch at all. That touch or lack of touch was the only variable in all the visits.

As the patients were released from the hospital, he had the nurses ask patients how often the doctor had visited them during their stay and how much time he had spent with them. The findings were amazing. Those patients who had been physically touched by the doctor perceived that he had visited them twice as often as those who had not been touched. And the "touched" group perceived the visits to have lasted twice as long as did the other group. Because of studies like this, some medical schools are now teaching the importance of touch.

At Purdue University, a study was conducted with librarians. Half were asked to touch those who came in to check out or return books or ask for information. The other half were to conduct business as usual, with no touching. And the study concluded that those who were touched had higher regard for the librarians and the books in the library, and they followed the rules more willingly.[4]

All of these studies help to make the same point: God has made each of us (even, apparently, lab rats!) to need and appreciate tender touch. And I would add that nowhere is that more important than in the marital relationship.

I know it's difficult for some couples to talk about sexual intimacies. Some marriage experts have reported that the two hardest things for couples to talk about are death and sex. On the lighter side, that explains the shyness of a young minister who always wanted to be invited to speak outside his church. His opportunity came when a women's organization in town asked him to address their luncheon. He was eager to please. "What do you want me to talk on?" he asked.

"We would like to have you talk on sex," they said, and he said okay.

He was home working on his talk when his wife came into his study. "What are you doing?" she asked.

"I've been invited to speak to a women's group," he told her.

"Oh, what are you speaking on?" she wanted to know.

He was too embarrassed to tell the truth, so he said, "Uh . . . I'm speaking on, uh, sailing. I'm going to talk to them about sailing."

She got a puzzled look on her face, but she just said, "Oh, that's good," and walked away.

The next week, after the minister had given his speech, his wife ran into one of the meeting's organizers in the grocery store. The woman came up to the wife and said, "Your husband! Wonderful speaker! He knows so much about that subject!"

"Really?" the wife said. "He's only done it twice. The first time he fell off, and the second time he got sick!"

It's not just difficult for ministers to discuss this topic; it's hard for all of us. But regardless of how tough it is to talk about sex, the whole relationship will be much better if we give each other a lot of tender physical touch throughout the day.

Spiritual Intercourse

Some people sincerely wonder about an old motto: The family that prays together, stays together. But a few years ago as I mentioned earlier, Dr. Nick Stinnett conducted a highly publicized study at the University of Nebraska. After looking carefully at hundreds of families that considered themselves healthy, his research concluded that healthy families possess six common characteristics. And one of those characteristics is "a shared personal faith in God."[5] And surveys taken by sociologist Andrew Greeley indicate that "frequent sex coupled with frequent prayer make for the most satisfying marriages."[6]

Spiritual intercourse may be the highest level of intimacy. A husband and wife can know each other as they both turn to and know God—heart to heart. Scripture writers repeatedly used a marriage metaphor to refer to the relationship God wants to have with those who turn to him. And the Spirit of God has an otherworldly ability to draw two people into harmony, being "one" in spirit.

Consider this saying: "A cord of three strands is not quickly broken."[7] Some writers have seen that truth as a picture of marriage: Man-woman-God bound together in a strong union.

A man and wife can grow spiritually intimate as they pray together, worship God together, attend study groups or retreats together, or simply discuss spiritual lessons and insights. Spiritual intercourse involves knowing one another in the context of a shared faith. And through that faith a couple sees value and meaning to things that would otherwise be meaningless.

Dennis and Lois, our case study at the beginning of this chapter, had always been of the opinion that people—even married couples—shouldn't discuss religion or politics. But after they learned about spiritual intercourse, they had one of their liveliest conversations ever. Then they visited local churches, finally finding one where they felt comfortable. This was a whole new arena for them but a vital link to their marital health and happiness—their union.

In a chapter titled "Praying Together: Guardian of Intimacy," in their book *If Two Shall Agree: Praying Together As a Couple*, Carey and Pam Rosewell Moore quote one couple's strong statement:

> The most important goal of prayer together is that it keeps our relationship as a couple intimate and close, and it keeps our hearts open before the Lord as a couple. There is a lot of unspoken accountability in our walk with the Lord and with each other.[8]

The Moores go on to say,

> Daily prayer can serve as the guardian of the marriage, for the husband and wife who pray together do not pray alone. God Himself is present. . . . He will . . . encourage the formation of an ever-closer bond and He will lend His strength to that bond.[9]

Getting to Know You

Dennis and Lois continued to go through a rigorous examination of their married life to improve each of the four areas of intercourse. As previously mentioned, Dennis had allowed himself to become too busy to talk with and listen to Lois. Purposely cutting back his work schedule was not easy for such a career-minded man, yet he was willing to pay that price, and his decision provided the two of them with some much-needed sharing times.

Through those discussions, they both came to understand the deep hurts they had inflicted on each other unintentionally. Lois was extremely sensitive about her weight, a pain Dennis had virtually ignored. Once he realized the extent of her pain, he was much more supportive. He made a point, for example, of telling her how much he loved her and how very attractive he still found her. Lois, for her part, better understood Dennis's feelings of rejection because of their sporadic sex life, and she made an effort to be more available to him. All these hurts took some time to heal, but it happened.

One problem was Lois felt that Dennis touched her only when he was trying to initiate sex. Dennis admitted that to be true. So I gave them some assignments to touch each other but not allow it to end in consummation. This was particularly helpful to them as they learned to support each other emotionally and express affection.

The blending of these four aspects of intercourse provides the complete context for a healthier sexual relationship. They're like the four sides of a building . . . all are essential for a sound and lasting structure.

Improving Sexual Intimacy

Once you're establishing the verbal, emotional, physical, and spiritual connections, you can follow some additional steps to improve the sexual dimension of your marriage. First I'll give five general suggestions that either a wife or a husband can try to enhance the physical act of sex. Then I'll offer some suggestions that are specific to each of the partners.

Both Partners

Take the initiative sexually. This is generally appreciated by your partner, especially if it's not your usual mode of operation. The change of pace will energize your experience.

Take care with your appearance. Your spouse will value the effort you make to look attractive. I'll say more about this in the specific advice below.

Take more time to enjoy the sexual experience. Routinized sex—relegated to ten minutes after the TV late news on Saturday night—is the kiss of death to a vibrant sex life. Don't be in a hurry. Think in terms of the four areas of intercourse we've discussed, and then take an unhurried walk through all of them. It can make a sexual evening very special.

Pay attention to the atmosphere in which you'll make love. Beyond candlelight, soft music, and a fire's glow (which are all great ideas), don't overlook some basics like a locked door. Visitors aren't welcome, even if they're members of the family. This is a time for husband and wife, and no unpleasant surprises are appreciated.

Express your desire. Many couples feel that the sexual act expresses how much they are attracted to each other, and they use sex in place of verbalizing the desire to be together. But words such as "I love you," "I need you," "I'm crazy about you," "You look great," and "I'd marry you all over again" have an encouraging and stimulating power all their own. So tell your mate often how much you enjoy being with him or her.

For Men

What would your wife say if she were asked how you could improve your sex life? My research shows that women often answer along these lines:

Be romantic. Women love to feel connection with their spouses, and nothing accomplishes this better than romance. By becoming a student of your wife, you can learn the best way to produce romantic feelings within her. For some it is flowers, cards, or a small gift. For others, it's sharing in work around the house and lightening her load. Still others look to a night out on the town, a concert, or dinner in a nice restaurant.

Men can be a little rougher than their spouses in sex. But women love tenderness in a man. They always have, too—this is not just some "sensitive nineties man" fad. Women respond to romance, and most desire more of it.

Take time with foreplay. You cannot lose by spending extra time touching, hugging, and cuddling your wife. These acts are like giving her an injection of pure energy. Ask your wife where and how she likes to be touched, and be responsive to her needs. Conversely, if something you desire makes her uncomfortable, respect her wishes.

Remember also to freely touch your wife with caresses that won't necessarily lead to sex. Praise her, tell her how desirable she is, and give her spontaneous hugs.

Make yourself sexy. Stan is a typical guy. He loves his wife, Andrea, and is always ready to make love at a moment's notice. Andrea is consistently amazed by this attribute. She was recently surprised when he came in the back door after gardening in the muddy dirt for four hours. Sweaty, dirty, smelly, and unkempt as he was, when he saw her bending over in the kitchen, he let out a low wolf whistle and offered her an invitation for some immediate fun.

Andrea, like most women, finds her husband attractive, but that isn't always enough. Did he really expect her to be interested in a sexual encounter after he had just finished four hours in the mud? No way!

At first Stan was hurt by her cool response. He prided himself on keeping in shape and looking good. So Andrea had to explain that she wasn't rejecting him. She just felt more inclined toward making love if there was "a total package," as she put it. That included a clean and scrubbed, freshly shaven ("I hate stubble," she says), cologne-wearing Stan; clean sheets on the bed; soft light; and a classical CD playing softly in the background.

Andrea's reaction had nothing to do with Stan's fear that he was overweight or soft in areas that were once muscular. It was more about *atmosphere*. Stan needed to listen carefully so he could learn how to provide her idea of the perfect evening. It's only fair that he learn from her, because, another time, he'll want her to try his idea of romance (in some room other than the bedroom when the kids are away at their grandparents' house).

For Women

Many wives wish they could find the key to unlock the sexual aspect of their husband's life. So here are some ideas specifically for women.

Understand his tremendous sexual needs. As discussed earlier, the two of you probably view sex from different perspectives. More than likely, he desires sex more often than you.

With that insight, there may be occasions when you're willing to have sex even if all four areas of intimacy are not in place for you. This should only be once in a while, however, not a regular pattern. He needs to be sensitive to your needs just as you're sensitive to his. For example, if your hormones make you wish your husband were in Siberia for several days a month, he needs to understand that and be patient.

If your husband ever struggles with impotence, which is most commonly caused by performance anxiety, refer to the book *Intended for Pleasure* by Ed and Gaye Wheat. It's not uncommon for older men to need stimulation from you to be aroused. Here in the nineties, there are a number of excellent books on the subject of "good sex."[10]

Find out what he really enjoys. A man is thrilled when his wife asks him what he likes in regard to sex and then gives it a try. This does not mean you have to violate your inner convictions or participate in a sexual activity you find offensive. But there may be many things your husband thinks of in his fantasy life that you could fulfill for him and enjoy yourself.

The sexual relationship is a place where creativity should shine. Sex was never meant to be dull, boring, or routine. Take the initiative to instigate some variety in your sex life. Few men will respond, "No, this isn't what I want. Let's go back to doing it exactly the same as we have for the last twenty years."

Make yourself sexy. Having read my account of Stan and Andrea, a woman could conclude that nothing is necessary on her part to keep the sexual fires alive. But the reality is that a balance needs to be achieved. Just as a woman appreciates the "total package" from her husband, so a man is entitled to the same consideration from his wife.

You'll want to have those magical occasions when you take a leisurely bath, slide into something sexy, spray a little perfume around, dim the lights, and turn on the station that plays the late-night love songs. Your husband will enjoy that atmosphere just like you do. It's another way to contribute to the variety that's so helpful to a healthy sexual relationship.

Juicy Fruit

Fortunately, Dennis and Lois were able to bring back some of the passion in their marriage. But it wasn't easy or quick.

Many couples have a hard time discussing sexual matters with each other, so the thought of raising the issues with a third-party counselor is even more stressful. But many qualified counselors can provide confidential assistance in improving this area of your relationship. Add to that the plethora of good books, tapes, and study courses available, and it's exciting to see that so much help is accessible to you and your mate.

"I'll admit," Dennis told me much later in our counseling, "I was angry and embarrassed that our sex life had deteriorated to the point that we had to enlist the help of a counselor. That can be a bitter pill for any person to swallow—especially a man. But it really was one of the smartest moves I ever made. There was so much about Lois that I didn't understand, along with a bunch of stuff I never even knew about her. These discoveries wouldn't have occurred without our reaching out for help."

As Lois summarized in one of our final sessions, "I now see the importance of putting sex in its complete context. Now Dennis and I think, feel, talk, and connect with each other. We're enjoying the fruit of a healthy relationship."

That was a good choice of words on her part, because a couple's sex life can be compared to an apple tree. If we nurture the tree and keep it healthy, we're going to have fruit on it. But if we neglect it and don't nurture it, it's not likely to bear much fruit. If we get impatient for fruit in the springtime, remembering the delicious taste of apples and complaining that we haven't had fruit lately, we might start picking the blossoms off. But they don't taste like fruit, and once you pick them off, you'll never get apples.

A healthy tree needs water, sunlight, air, and fertilized soil—it takes all four ingredients. Likewise, when we nurture a marriage verbally, emotionally, physically, and spiritually, we can watch the love and intimacy and knowledge grow. And as they develop, the marital tree will provide a steady supply of fruit. Then any time we want, basically, we can pick off the fruit and eat it, and it's delicious! Why? Because we've nurtured the sex tree—the relationship. Then we can have cinnamon apple butter from time to time; French apple pie; apple dumplings with caramel sauce; and apple cobbler with ice cream. But we can't have any of those goodies unless we first have the apples.

Don't settle for anything but the best. Don't let your sexual relationship deteriorate into just the physical act. Enrich your life together in all four areas of intimacy and watch your sexual love relationship become forever-alive.

Every engaged couple I've ever talked with has an excited anticipation about married life. They look forward to being together, sharing every aspect of life together—talking, sleeping, hugging, and sexual intimacy. But every married couple knows how reality can change one's hopes and dreams.

The purpose of the next chapter is to help you keep your dreams alive—pulling the threads of the second part of this book into a method that can divorce-proof your marriage.

Forever-Love Principles

Our list of forever-love principles continues from the previous chapter:

110. Forever-love knows that good sex is a reflection of a good relationship.

111. Forever-love makes—even schedules—time for talk. "Tell me about your world. I'll tell you about mine."

112. Forever-love freely expresses feelings in mutual, nonthreatened self-disclosure.

113. Forever-love is renewed and energized by tender touch.

114. Forever-love is bonded by a shared personal faith in God.

115. Forever-love "goes for connection" on four levels: verbal, emotional, physical, and spiritual.

116. Forever-love remembers to romance.

117. Forever-love takes time for play. Foreplay.

118. Forever-love sex thrives on variety within monogamy.

15

Divorce-Proofing Your Marriage

Cast your bread upon the waters,
for after many days you will find it again.
—Ecclesiastes 11:1

I've learned a practical, simple principle that can work wonders in reviving love and keeping a couple together happily. In some ways it underlines most of the principles we've already discussed at length. It's a good method to use—or a mind-set to have—all the time. And it can produce immediate results when a marriage is in crisis.

A story from the early years of my own marriage will introduce the images I use to describe this great tool:

When Norma and I were first married, I was not very responsible financially. Growing up, I had never learned how or even that it mattered. I didn't know anything about keeping a checkbook register or spending wisely. Norma, on the other hand, was a detail-oriented person who worked in a bank. So it was obvious that she should keep the family books and pay the bills, which she was happy to do.

But problems arose right at the start and lasted five years. Each of us had a checkbook and wrote checks on one joint account. (Can you see the conflict brewing?)

I had my own system: I wrote checks as long as I had them in my book—until I ran out of checks; I hoped—or assumed—there was enough in the bank to cover them.

But too often Norma would confront me: "We're overdrawn again."

"We can't be," I'd answer with a grin. "I still have checks in my book. It's impossible."

Sometimes she would be in tears. "I can't keep track of this. It's driving me crazy."

We also had a secondary conflict. We disagreed about when to pay bills. Norma preferred to pay them as soon as they came. But I wanted to hold on to our money as long as possible, paying our bills at the end of the month, just before payday. I liked the idea of having money, because you never know when an emergency might come up. With my check-writing habits, however, there wasn't always enough left at the end of the month to pay all the bills, let alone saving for emergencies.

"We have two late notices on this one bill," Norma would say, exasperated.

"Don't worry about it," I'd respond, which was not what she wanted to hear. My philosophy was that you don't have to do anything until you get the fourth or fifth notice. You just keep shuffling late notices to the bottom of the pile until they appear at the top again and can't be ignored any longer.

Then the day came when Norma had taken all she could. She tearfully approached me once more and laid all the bills, her checkbook, and the budget in my lap. "I've had it!" she declared. "I can't take it anymore. From now on, this area is all yours. It's up to you whether we sink or swim." Years later, she admitted her despair that day: She figured she was really giving away our home, our car, and the rest of our financial life, because there was no way I would be able to handle it properly.

Fortunately, with the pressure on, I decided to learn how to be responsible. I got some help, grew to respect a budget, and worked my way out of the mess I had created. For the next fifteen years, I kept the books and paid the bills. And as I started to do all this, I learned a crucial but simple principle: You've got to have more money in the bank than you spend every month. Income has to exceed outgo. That's about as basic as family finance gets.

Now let me make the application to how you can divorce-proof your marriage. The principle is simple, yet the impact is powerful. My hope is that this idea will become a part of your life, just like pearl-counting and the other principles I've learned to live by and have presented in this book. The principle is this: To divorce-proof your marriage, make sure you are making more "deposits" to your spouse than "withdrawals."

Basics of Marital Banking

Before we discuss what I call marital banking, we need to define a few terms.

A *deposit* is anything positive, security-producing—anything that gives your mate energy. It's a gentle touch, a listening ear, a verbalized "I love you," a fun, shared experience; the list could go on and on. Temperament, gender, and birth order influence one's personal definition of a deposit. Going for long walks in the woods with a spouse may energize an introvert in the same way a houseful of holiday company (entertaining) energizes an extrovert.

A withdrawal is anything sad or negative—anything that drains energy from your mate. It's a harsh word, an unkempt promise, being ignored, being hurt, being controlled; the list could be long. Some withdrawals differ from temperament to temperament; something perceived as a withdrawal for one person might be a deposit for another person. But too much control or being absent too much, physically or emotionally, are always major withdrawals, and as I mentioned in chapter 8, these are the two biggest factors in unhealthy relationships.

The more you keep a positive balance in your relationship account, with "giving" deposits exceeding "draining" withdrawals, the more secure that relationship will be. There's something very basic about the saying, "If you're happy, I'm happy." *If you're energized, I'm energized.* Enthusiasm—for life, for romance, for "us"—is contagious.

And if your marriage is in rough shape because you've been making a lot more withdrawals than deposits, beginning now with a concerted effort to make deposits can help you turn things around faster than anything else I've seen. By the way, once again, this will work in any relationship—with your friends, your children, your parents, and your coworkers, as well as with your mate.

I've been promoting this idea of marital "banking" for years, and I'm glad to see other authors offering variations on this same idea.[1]

Now let's look in more detail at how this principle works.

Your Personal Banking History

You and your spouse both have a personal-relationship banking history. As in real banking, your current account balance is the direct influence of past deposits and withdrawals.

The first step in making personal-banking principles work for—not against—your marriage is for you to record and learn to understand your own personal-relationship banking history. Start by thinking through and writing down various withdrawals and deposits you remember from your younger years.

What Are Withdrawals to You?

In one of the TV commercials for my video series, you may have seen a couple, Kevin and Julie. They tell just a little of their story there in the commercial. I'd like to tell you the rest of it here, because Kevin's experience illustrates the impact of childhood events.

Once married, Kevin made all kinds of withdrawals from Julie. For years he was controlling, harsh, critical, arrogant, angry, and abusive. That's when he was home. (He frequently wasn't.) Finally, Julie thought she couldn't take it anymore and got a court order to keep him away. She also had the locks changed on the house. When he arrived home that night and couldn't get in, he was, well, upset.

Kevin went home with a friend who had some of my marriage-help videos. A sobered Kevin watched a few, including the one about marital banking. Acting on the advice to record the withdrawals made in childhood, he started writing phrases—actions, words, and attitudes—that had caused him pain or drained him of energy as a young boy and teen.

When the withdrawals were on paper for him to contemplate, he saw that the withdrawals made from him looked amazingly like the actions, words, and attitudes that Julie complained about. He was passing on to others the abuses that had been done to him,. He determined that he was going to do his best to stop the negative withdrawals and replace them with deposits. (More about that in a minute.)

In my own life, a big withdrawal drained me any time someone—usually my father, later a boss—would exert excess control over me. I mentioned this earlier: I vividly recall my father and I going fishing together. If I started catching fish in one particular place, he would come over, literally shove me out of the way, and say, "Fish somewhere else."

Sadly but not surprisingly, that withdrawal from me became a pattern for how I related to others. In time I became a controlling person with my wife, and I also got in the habit of making the exact same withdrawals from my kids. This was very evident one day when we were fishing in a Colorado stream—and I was reeling them in. When all three of my kids approached with their fishing poles, I said, "No, no!"

Greg knew what I was thinking. Finally he screamed, "Dad, we are not trying to fish here! Kari broke her leg!"

With that news, for a brief second I thought, *Ohhh, I'm going to have to leave this great fishing place!* I handed Greg my pole and said, "You fish here for a while so I don't miss anything." Then I took care of Kari. Even when we're aware of the reality—the record—of our childhood withdrawals, we can still not really understand how influential they are in terms of our current practice.

So jot down some of the withdrawals drained from your emotional-relational account as you were growing up. This exercise can be useful to you in two ways:

1. It can help you, as it did Kevin, identify potential ways you are making withdrawals from your spouse's account. If a parent drained energy from you by doing x, y, and z, are you similarly draining energy from your spouse?

2. It can help you as you think through some of the things that are relational withdrawals from you today. What does your mate do that drains energy from you? Are some of these withdrawals directly connected to—triggered by—things that happened in your childhood?

As opportunities arise, share your childhood and current relational withdrawals with your mate (using "I feel" statements or word pictures, not accusations).

What Are Deposits for You?

What energized you as a child? As a young adult? While withdrawals frequently are caused by elements beyond our control (an emotionally healthy person doesn't seek out draining withdrawals), deposits tend to be things we initiate or search out. And while withdrawals are often seen as being "done to" us, relational deposits are often things "done with" or "done for" us.

As for deposits in my own background, one of the biggest was singing with other people. Starting when I was in third grade, my sister taught me every popular song of the day, and I would harmonize with her. I got so much energy from that! Then I started singing with three or four friends. Rather than dating a lot as teens, we would go for long drives, singing on wheels. I enjoy close harmony so much that sometimes I wonder if I should have been a singer instead of a speaker! (Then I listen to myself sing in the shower, and I know why I'm only *speaking* in public.)

Think through your own childhood and up through the early years of your marriage. Then write down what some of the major relational deposits have been. Again, this exercise can be useful to you as you consider how you tend to make deposits to your spouse's account. Do you "make deposits" that are more suitable to your own needs than to your spouse's? It can also help you as you think through your current-day relational deposits. What does your mate do that energizes you? Are some of these deposits directly connected to things that happened in your childhood?

As opportunity arises, discuss your deposit history and current balance with your mate.

Banking with Your Spouse

The second step in using this principle involves discovering what constitutes a deposit or a withdrawal for your mate.

What Are Withdrawals for Your Mate?

As you might guess from my descriptions of the first years of our marriage . . . when I eventually asked Norma to look back and reflect on those days, she was hard-pressed to think of deposits I had made. Unfortunately she had no problem remembering plenty of withdrawals. She may have been charmed with me in our courting days, but living with me was no energizing venture.

For example, because I was so much into control, her stomach would turn every time I called a family meeting. She would say with her eyes and sometimes with her words, "I hate your meetings." For the longest time, I never understood why. Then I came to learn that too much control or too much distance in relationships drains people of their energy.

Another big withdrawal for her has to do with my driving habits. She's helped me understand the seed of this negative reaction to what I perceive as perfectly passable driving skills. When Norma was in high school, she was in a major car crash with some friends. The car went over a cliff, and two of her friends were killed. Norma suffered a broken neck and was in a cast for a long time. It's perfectly reasonable that she has a healthy fear of a car going out of control. If I'm driving and get distracted and veer a bit too much toward the edge of the road, she'll say, "Oohh, you're over too far." That's a withdrawal. And if I make light of her concern and tension, that's a serious withdrawal. On the other hand, if I make a point of driving carefully, that's a big deposit.

My snoring is another major withdrawal for Norma—keeping her from getting sleep and draining energy from her. This withdrawal doesn't fit the pattern I've previously presented—where something in childhood affects the present. Nor does it involve something I "do to" Norma. But it is something I do—or utter—that affects her negatively. And it is something one can make efforts to stop.

Of course she had to convince me of the reality of this annoying pattern. She once recorded the sounds and played the tape back to me so I couldn't claim my "innocence." Can you imagine sleeping next to a rumbling diesel engine all those years? I've been kicked and told to roll over on my side many times, but nothing has worked so far. I've looked into new approaches to knocking out the noise. And I've just been fitted for a breathing device that completely stops my snoring, and, by the way, I have twice the energy each day.[2]

Think back over your experience with your mate. Write down actions, attitudes, or words (or noises!) you are sure she or he perceives to be withdrawals. But then—to increase the intimacy of your conversation and to confirm your assumptions—ask your spouse whether your memories and perceptions are accurate.

When couples attending my seminars talk to each other about this, common withdrawals for women include "being treated like I don't exist"; "he's never on time," and "he travels too much in his job." Common withdrawals for husbands include "she's always on my case" and "she doesn't initiate sex."

What can you do to reduce the number of withdrawals you make to your spouse's account?

What Makes a Deposit to Your Mate?

Previously I noted that making a deposit in someone's account often involves doing something "with" or "for" someone. I've learned that for Norma, a huge deposit has to do with shopping—especially Christmas shopping. She likes to start shopping for presents in January. Now, I'm not big on shopping in the first place, and I hate to buy a present and then hide it somewhere; I want to give it to the person right away. So for the first several years of our marriage, I frustrated Norma and made big withdrawals by waiting until December 24 to do my shopping.

As we talked and I learned in this area, I came to understand that I could turn things around and make huge deposits just by changing my attitude toward shopping. So now, even though I still don't care to shop by myself, I make an effort to be enthusiastic when I'm doing it with her, whether she's buying presents or looking for a dress for herself. I try not to be like the guy who found out his wife's credit cards had been stolen, yet a year later he still hadn't reported it because the thief spent less than his wife had!

Now, for me, fishing is my shopping. If she suggests taking a picnic on the boat, I know she's saying, "I love you." She doesn't actually go fishing with me. She would rather bring a book along and read. That's okay—I just like to be with her on or near the water.

In chapter 13, on conflicts, I suggested a couple have a love language—actions you both know the secret meaning of: *I love you.* That love language is closely connected with this idea of marital banking. The energizing love language is based on an alphabet of deposits.

Today, Norma and I are best friends. We love finding out new things that make deposits into our accounts with each other. We go out of our way to make sure we're making more deposits than withdrawals.

When I ask seminar attendees for things they consider to be deposits, common responses include "him chatting with me when he gets home from work," "daily verbal expressions of love," "it's a big deposit when she initiates sex," and "I love it when he plays with our kids." That last one is a prime example of something a man might never identify as a deposit unless he asks for feedback. My wife, too, has told me that it's a big deposit for her when I praise and encourage our kids—and especially the grandkids.

Dr. John Gottman has actually figured out through his research the ratio of deposits vs. withdrawals for long-lasting, loving marriages: It's an average of *five positive deposits* for *each negative withdrawal.* In other words, at the end of a week, month, or year, the deposits should outweigh the withdrawals five to one.

Don't Rely on Guess Work

What's the best way to find out what your spouse "receives" as a withdrawal or deposit? Ask! If you're both familiar with this concept, you might say straight out as you do something with honoring intent: "I'm hoping this is a deposit with you. Does it work?" The response you get will tell you if you missed the mark or hit the bullseye.

I've touched on this before, but it bears repeating: In the best of marriages, one spouse may think he or she is making a deposit, but it turns into a big withdrawal. Considering this problem on the lighter side, perhaps you've heard of the couple who decided that a big deposit for them would be learning how to do something together—like duck-hunting. They asked an expert what equipment of "outfit" they needed. He answered, "Well, if you're going to be successful, you've got to have a really good hunting dog."

So they bought a champion dog and then set out on their first hunting expedition. They started before sunrise and stayed with it all day, into the evening, but with no ducks to show for all their time and effort. Finally, exhausted, the man said to his wife, "I don't know. Maybe we're doing it wrong. I think we're not throwing this dog high enough into the air."

Have you tried to make a deposit and it turned out somewhat like the "duck hunt"? You felt as if your "check" bounced?

What really matters to most spouses is that the mate tried to do the right thing. But if you find that your mate is reacting negatively to your well-intentioned deposit attempts, I suggest you allow some time to pass and feelings to cool. Then, by explaining the situation, you can redeposit the "check" in a different way.

Norma has another need that I've had a hard time understanding over the years, and we've been using drive-through talking to help me get it straight. I finally came to realize that she wanted my praise for the great job she does as the manager of our business. But what she had said initially was, "Would you ask me things like, 'Could I do something for you today to help with your job?'"

Now, I wasn't going to ask that kind of question very often, naturally. I've got enough stuff to do of my own. And at first I didn't understand how her question related to her need for praise, either. So I asked, "What exactly are you saying?"

"I don't actually want you to do parts of my job for me," she said. (I wouldn't know how to do them anyway, and I could foul things up in a hurry.) "I want you to notice what I do and praise me for it. And when you ask, 'Is there anything I can do to help?' it gives us an opportunity to talk about what I do." That recognition is a big need to her. But the way she expressed her need needed to be clarified before I could "get it."

When it comes to deposits and withdrawals, *don't guess. Express.* I trust that by talking with your spouse, you'll find out what causes withdrawals and do those things less often. You'll also find out what makes deposits and do those things more often. You'll both be energized in the process.

Thank-You! Thank-You!

Ask your mate to praise you when you intentionally or unintentionally make a deposit into his or her relational account. This will reinforce your positive behavior. Who doesn't thrive on praise? That recognition will energize you, so your energy as a couple spirals upward. A deposit and then a thank-you in return earns a couple *mucho* interest. Let's call it a joint high-interest savings account.

Of course this works two ways. Praise your spouse for deposits—and everybody wins double interest.

Deposits Have the Power to Save a Marriage

Let me give you an update on Kevin and Julie's marriage: Kevin took this marital banking principle very seriously. With his new understanding, he worked hard to reduce his withdrawals from and increase his deposits to Julie's account. Gradually, this tremendous, sustained change in Kevin got through to Julie.

She later told me, "I could tell he wasn't really excited about saying 'I love you,' listening to me, and touching me gently. I could see he was forc-ing it. As he would listen to something I was saying, he would quickly get preoccupied, but he was trying. When I saw his effort right in front of me, it was a major deposit, and he warmed my heart. That's why it was so easy to say, 'Let's keep going. I think we can make it together.'"

They did keep going, and Kevin did keep trying. If you saw them today, you'd be impressed with how sensitive he is and how responsive she is, and you'd never guess they had been on the brink of divorce just a few years ago.

This simple banking principle can save a marriage—even return that marriage to days of joy.

I once got a call from an irate husband. His wife was divorcing him, and he growled out, "I can't believe it! How can she do this after twenty-five years? I haven't been that bad!"

As I talked further with him and then with his wife, I found that he was a very controlling, belligerent person. Even in talking with me, he exhibited these characteristics. At one point in a phone conversation, as I've done several times now, I interrupted him to say, "I hate to tell you this, but if I were your wife, I don't think I could stay with you either!"

I learned that the wife didn't have any other man in her life, and she actually wanted to get back together with her husband—if only he could understand what he had done to drive her away; if only she could see evidence of change in him. She just couldn't live with him anymore the way he was. Her attitude gave me hope that things could eventually be worked out.

The wife pleaded with me to help them, but she was too fearful to stop the divorce proceedings. I had a gut feeling that there could be a good outcome to this one. Deep down, both wanted reconciliation. This was the best scenario for reuniting a couple. And the husband was motivated. "I don't want a divorce," the husband told me. "Tell me what I need to do."

As I said, there seemed no stopping the divorce, but I could see hope for eventual reconciliation. "There's really nothing you can do to stop the divorce," I told him. "Your wife has a lawyer, and the court date is set. But I'll go with you and support you through the whole process." And I assured him I'd work with him to do what we could to renew the relationship.

We went to the courthouse on the appointed day, and I waited on a bench outside the hearing room. After a while he came flying, furious, out of the settlement room. "That's it!" he shouted. "She wants too much from me, and I won't do it!" He was as angry and controlling as he had ever been.

I admit I got a little upset myself—at him. "What?" I said. "We're talking about trying to get the two of you back together. Give her more than she asked for. Do it! Just remember you're going to get back together, so what difference does it make?"

He thought about that for a minute, and then he went back in and gave her much more than she had requested, which did confuse her. Unfortunately, at that point the divorce went through.

The good news, however, is that his wife agreed to see him—with some small hope that things might still work out. So I started teaching him how to treat her—how to make more deposits than withdrawals. "What does she really like?" I asked.

"She loves for me to be tender and listen to her," he said.

"You can practice doing that," I said. And so we worked on it, and he applied it on their "dates."

This went on for about six months after the divorce. He would do well for a while, making a lot of deposits. Then he would get upset about something and blow his stack, making massive withdrawals. Along the way, he gave me regular reports on how things were going.

At the end of that period, he called one day and said, "Well, I totally blew it last night. I withdrew everything I've deposited since the divorce. It's ridiculous. She'll never want to remarry me now. I'll be surprised if she even wants to talk to me again."

He went on to give me the details of what had happened, and finally I said, "Look, just keep at it. Don't give up. When you see her tomorrow, open up. Admit you were wrong and that you wish you could get all this stuff down quicker. Then you might tell her something like you're sorry she has to go through your stumbling times. Tell her you understand what you did, and explain it to her so she can see you're becoming more sensitive and aware of your behavior."

"All right," he said with resignation. "It's just so humiliating to admit what a jerk I am almost every other day."

"Hey, I have to do it!" I said with a smile in my voice. "If I have to do it, you can. We're in this together. Okay?"

The next day, after meeting with his ex-wife, he called me. "Guess what?" he said. "I went over, admitted I was wrong, and asked if she would forgive me again. I knew she never would, but she did. And then—would you believe it?—she touched me and asked, 'What are you doing this afternoon?'

"'Nothing,' I said.

"And she said, 'How would you like to go back to the same judge who presided over our divorce and ask if he would marry us?'

"'Are you serious?' I asked.

"She said, 'Yes, I think it's time. Don't you?'

"I shouted yes and threw my arms around her."

They did remarry shortly after that, and had twelve more years together—happy years. He had retired and had a lot of time available to make up for the former hurt. In their last two years together, she developed a serious illness. He lovingly cared for her before she passed away. He told me later that she was so tender during their twelve-year "second marriage" that it was worth twice what the first twenty-five years had been. He went on to say, "Those were the greatest years of my life. I can't even imagine being happier. I've lost a great friend, but what treasured memories I'll always have!"

What did he do in those six months of courtship? Deposits, deposits, deposits! And what did he do in those last twelve wonderful years? Deposits and more deposits. Of course he also made some withdrawals, but he would admit them and ask for her forgiveness right away. As a result, they had an incredible marriage, even through days of pain.

What's Your Balance?

What does your marital bank account look like? If you were to ask your spouse today, "What's my balance?" what would the response be?

Whatever the answer, you can start improving your balance instantly by making deposits and by practicing self-restraint—refraining from making costly withdrawals. Do this regularly for a month or two. Then ask the question again. And watch your balance soar.

Another ancient saying summarizes the principle of relational banking: "Cast your bread upon the waters, for after many days you will find it again."[3] Give love and you will receive love back. This concept gives new meaning to the phrase "no deposit, no return." If you make no deposit, you'll get no return. Make deposits and you not only energize your spouse, you energize your marriage and your own life.

Think of this as responsible relationship banking. Practice it and reap the bountiful rewards: the pleasure of seeing your love grow stronger with every passing year—as you and your spouse walk together into the forever.

The type of love that makes the greatest deposits and lasts the longest is featured in the final chapter. We want love to last, but I've found only one kind that can't fail!

Forever-Love Principles

Our list of forever-love principles continues from the previous chapter:

119. Forever-love "deposits" more than it "withdraws."

120. Forever-love seeks to understand its own personal history. "In the past, what actions have consistently drained energy from me?"

121. Forever-love seeks to understand its own personal history and use that insight to energize the marriage.

122. Forever-love asks for feedback. "What energizes or drains energy from you?"

123. Forever-love goes for clarity. Don't guess. Express.

124. Forever-love says, "Thanks. I needed that."

125. Forever-love is energized as one person takes a step to renew the other and the relationship.

16

A Love That Lasts Forever

Greater love has no one than this, that he lay down his life for his friends.
—John 15:13

For years I've been urging the thousands of people who read my books, watch my videos, and attend my seminars to see how much we need to help each other develop the "greatest" love. I call it heroic love—a love that sacrifices itself for the enrichment of the other, that doesn't seek its own good but chooses to satisfy the desires of the beloved.

But don't get the impression that heroic love is all self-sacrifice. From looking at my own marriage and hundreds of others, I've come to understand that enriching the life of another is often more satisfying than doing something for ourselves. As we reach out to another, our own needs for fulfillment and love are met.

I've seen that the most satisfied, joyous couples are those that have learned heroic love and practice it daily. When a husband and wife both want their partner to receive life's best before they do, you have a marriage that's going to exceed every wedding-day dream. Their love not only lasts; it continually grows.

That's the kind of relationship Charlie and Lucy Wedemeyer enjoy. If our world could raise its vision of love to the level of this couple . . . I can hardly imagine what it would be like to live on this planet.

More than fifteen years ago, doctors diagnosed thirty-year-old Charlie Wedemeyer as having progressively debilitating and paralyzing ALS—

commonly called Lou Gehrig's disease. They gave the California high-school football coach one year to live. But Charlie proved them wrong. Despite the relentless, progressive nature of his illness, he continued coaching for seven more years.

When Charlie could no longer walk, Lucy drove him up and down the sidelines in a golf cart. When he could no longer talk, she read his lips and relayed his instructions to the players. And in his dramatic last season as a coach, after he had gone on twenty-four-hour-a-day life support, his team won a state championship!

Lucy Wedemeyer is a heroic lover. She says that from the very beginning of Charlie's illness, they've focused on what they have together rather than on what they're missing. She admits it hasn't been easy, but she says in her book,

> I think we communicate and understand each other better today than we ever did. While I've learned to read Charlie's lips, I find I often don't have to. His eyes almost always tell me exactly how he feels, and his eye-brows punctuate those feelings as they bounce up and down or I watch his forehead furrow into a wrinkle. And if you don't think someone in diffi-cult circumstances can find happiness and contentment, if you doubt the contagious quality of joy, well, you've never seen Charlie smile.[1]

When the ALS struck, the Wedemeyers had two young children and mountains of dreams they would never realize. One week after they were told of his impending death, while watching snow drift by the window of a borrowed mountain cabin, Lucy looked into Charlie's eyes and recognized the same raw emotions she felt churning inside herself. She had never felt more love for Charlie, or more loved by him, than she did that special evening. And yet, she says,

> I'd never in my life felt such pain. Such anguish. Tears filled our eyes. Neither of us dared speak for fear the floodgates would open. So we just sat silently, holding hands across the table, basking in the bittersweet warmth of that moment, wishing the romantic spell could somehow make time stand still. All the while wondering how much time we had left together.[2]

When I first met the Wedemeyers at one of my seminars, I couldn't help but see the radiant joy on Lucy's face and the contentment in Charlie's eyes.

They're the type of heroes I would love to be like someday. No matter what I go through with Norma, we both hope to have people look into our eyes and see a similar enduring fire of love—for life and for each other.

Lucy prays daily for continued strength, because Charlie needs constant care. Some realities of her life are harsh and ever-present, and still she says, "I wouldn't trade my life for anyone else's. It's been so rewarding."[3] How can she mean that? That's the beauty of heroic love. It can move mountains, cross rivers, and overcome any obstacle and for the joy set before it. No one's life is laughing-happy every day, but people like Lucy have such a deep sense of satisfaction and love that, no matter what occurs, they rest on an underlying assurance that everything is still okay.

Every marriage will have its better and worse times, its springs and summers and falls and winters. Forever-love allows that full range of seasons. Enjoy the bright colors and warmth of good days. Accept the dark, rainy days, the cold of winter, and the hot summer winds of disagreement and of waiting for someone to say, "I'm sorry. I was wrong. I love you. Will you forgive me?"

With our society driven more and more by instant everything, many of us are losing the awareness that some of the best things in life take longer and aren't enjoyed until, like ripe fruit, they're ready to be picked. Charlotte, for example, came close to giving up many times with her husband, Mike. But if she had, it would have been too soon.

Mike, like me, didn't know how to love his wife in a way that made her feel loved. He and I struggled through many seasons—many ups and downs—together as we learned the things I teach in this book. And as he grew in his own happiness and in his sensitivity to her needs, she found herself in the kind of relationship she had dreamed about before they married.

Not long ago I got a letter from Charlotte. "I never thought the day would come," she said, "when my life with Mike would be so wonderful. As you know, we've had our 'down times.' But this last year has been worth all we went through. Whatever we didn't have before has long since been forgotten because of what we have today."

Unfortunately, many couples don't wait for that exciting season that wipes out the memory of the difficult times. That good season is like picking delicious fruit after a hard winter, wet spring, and hot summer. The juicy apples need all three seasons to taste delightfully good.

But many other couples have come to realize that it's perfectly normal for a marriage to go through different seasons—of drought, worry, sadness, anger and also times of plenty, happiness, and overwhelming joy and laughter.

I close this book with my personal warranty: No matter what struggle you may have right now that tempts you to leave your marriage, there's a workable solution for you! Start by applying the principles in this book. Get professional counseling if you need it. Through the research and counseling expertise of many people, there's no shortage of excellent help for couples today.

Perhaps this book will give you all the help you need; at the very least, it will give you a big headstart. If you'll work at applying the lessons of this book, and if you'll seek out whatever other assistance you may need, you, too, can one day bask in the delights of forever-love.

Don't give up until you find it.

Appendix

Three Character Qualities:
Prerequisites to Dating for the Smalley Children

Before our children could date, they had to demonstrate that they understood three character qualities: honor, responsibility, and resistance to peer pressure. We watched and constantly assessed them to determine when they understood the concept of honor and when they fully realized *they* were responsible for their actions and the way they handled their emotions. We also wanted to make sure they were able to stand up to peer pressure if they needed to and that they understood the consequences of premarital sex. In this appendix, I'll share with you how we presented those requirements.

1. Honor: The "I'm Third" Perspective

We told our children that honor was to be given in three ways: to God, to others, and to oneself. The "I'm third" perspective involved learning the primary importance of one's spiritual journey. God was to receive the highest honor, a 10 on a scale of 1 (none) to 10 (highest). Other people were to receive high honor, let's say 9.2 to 9.9. Then self should receive a 9.1 rating. You can see we never led our children to think they were unimportant: 9.1 is way up there. It's just that God is worth our worship; the highest commandment in life is to love God with our whole hearts.

We expected our children to respect their church attendance and pay attention to what was taught. They weren't to use degrading names for others, and they were to show regard for people in general as well as the environment/creation. They seemed to have a healthy respect for themselves, which we constantly tried to reinforce.

We tried to watch for growth in this area; as they kept asking if they were ready to date, we would evaluate their progress.

2. Responsibility: For One's Actions and Emotions

We wanted our children to understand that their emotion of anger, springing from fear, hurt, and frustration, was their responsibility. By example, we showed them that it's not what happens to us that determines our emotions; it's how we *respond* to what happens.

We knew they would be hurt and frustrated in the course of the dating process, and learning to take responsibility for their actions and emotions gave them an edge in their teen years.

This is one way I taught them to understand and control their anger: I encouraged them to respectfully ask me a difficult question when I got angry with them (sometimes blaming my frustration or hurt on them). The question? "Dad, are we making you angry, or are we revealing something about you?" This forced me to be honest. Sometimes I had to say, "Yes, you're showing me just how self-centered I am." (And I didn't like seeing this in myself.) Through our example, our children learned little by little how to assume full responsibility for their emotions.

3. Self-Control and Understanding the Consequences of Premarital Sex

We waited to see when our teens would be able to stand up and say no to their peers if they needed to. The stronger their personal convictions, the easier it would be for them to state their beliefs and respectfully stand against peer pressure. Considering the temptations that come with dating, we wanted them not to dishonor someone, especially sexually.

As a family we outlined several consequences of premarital sex. Our kids were very familiar with these, adding to their being ready to date. Here are a few of those consequences:

1. It dulls our soul toward God and God's ways.[1]

2. It reinforces our self-centeredness, our sensual focus, and keeps us away from our loving focus on God and others.[2]

3. It hinders our awareness of the needs of others, especially our future mate or good friends; it tends to make us less sensitive to the needs of others and more concerned about our own sensual needs. When we are preoccupied with our own stimulation, we are more capable

of saying hurtful things and missing opportunities for love. (We have ears and eyes but can't hear or see others.)

4. It makes us susceptible to sexual diseases.

5. It increases our need for greater stimulation in sexual contact, which then can increase the potential for sensual conflict in marriage.

6. It can reduce our satisfaction in the marital sexual relationship, which cannot compete with the backseat of a car. Sexual encounter flashbacks can further hinder our concentration on our mate's needs.

7. Research has found that couples who have had premarital sex have a greater chance of marital dissatisfaction and divorce.

8. It increases one's chances of sexual addiction.

9. It reinforces the notion that sex is an act when sex should be seen as a reflection of a loving relationship. Meaningful sex is a relationship. If this notion is not understood, treating sex as an act can erode a loving marriage.

10. If sex is primarily thought of as a separate physical "act," either the man or the woman can feel like an object instead of the valuable person he or she is in reality and in God's sight.

11. Premarital sex increases the possibility of guilt and resentment building between the two people involved. Either can feel used and after the encounter, discarded.

12. As guilt and resentment build, they can result in a whole host of additional negative consequences. (See chapter 2.)

13. Premarital sex can be a form of medication for lack of love and acceptance from parents. The need for approval or acceptance can be so great that especially a girl can reach out for love as one would for food or vitamins. We must learn how to forgive our parents and past offenders to ensure God's help as we say no to our strong sexual urges.

14. Pregnancy outside of marriage and/or abortion can affect anyone negatively. What's more, it usually hurts parents and friends. Abortion can reduce one's chances of having a normal pregnancy.

The two basic motivations in life are desire for gain and fear of loss. But fear of loss is usually a slightly stronger motivation. Finding more reasons why you should abstain from sex before marriage greatly inhibits becoming sexually active.

Notes

Chapter 1. Love's Best-Kept Secret

1. Clifford Notarius and Howard Markman, *We Can Work It Out* (New York: Putnam, 1993), 29.

2. I credit a number of authors, including M. Scott Peck, Stephen Covey, Michele Weiner-Davis, Howard Markman, and Harriet Lerner, for laying out a "map" that leads to the "buried treasure" of a fulfilling life apart from what others or our circumstances bring us. They've opened our eyes to the truth that we can choose the way we approach life.

3. Stephen R. Covey, *The Seven Habits of Highly Effective People* (New York: Simon & Schuster, 1989), 71.

4. Harriet G. Lerner, *The Dance of Anger* (New York: Harper & Row, 1985), 122–53.

5. Ibid., 64.

6. See Irene Goldenberg and Herbert Goldenberg, *Family Therapy: An Overview* (Pacific Grove, Calif.: Brooks/Cole, 1980, 1985).

7. Howard Markman, Scott Stanley, and Susan Blumberg, *Fighting for Your Marriage* (San Francisco: Jossey-Bass, 1994), 22.

Chapter 2. The Number One Enemy of Love: Unresolved Anger

1. William Stafford, *Disordered Loves* (Boston: Cowley, 1994), 86.

2. Notarius and Markman, *We Can Work It Out*, 237–56.

3. Charles Bass, *Banishing Fear from Your Life* (Garden City, N.Y.: Doubleday, 1986), 18–19.

4. Markman, Stanley, and Blumberg, *Fighting for Your Marriage*, 22.

5. Personal interview with Dr. Scott Stanley.

6. See 1 John 2:9ff.

7. Debbie Barr, *Children of Divorce* (Grand Rapids: Zondervan, 1992), 48.

8. Earl D. Wilson, *Counseling and Guilt* (Dallas: Word, 1987), 42.

9. M. Scott Peck, *Further Along the Road Less Traveled* (New York: Simon & Schuster, 1993), 39.

10. See Richard C. Meyer, "Making Anger Work for Us," *Faith at Work* (Summer 1995), 3.

11. Redford Williams and Virginia Williams, *Anger Kills* (New York: Times Books, 1993).

12. "Anger Can Trigger Heart Attacks, Study Shows," *The American Heart Association Newsletter* 85, no. 23 (11 April 1994): 33.

Chapter 3. Seven Ways to Unload Unresolved Anger

1. John Powell, quoted in Phyllis Hobe, *Coping* (New York: Guideposts, 1983), 127.

2. Peck, *Further Along the Road Less Traveled*, 63.

3. Covey, *The Seven Habits of Highly Effective People*, 29–31.

4. See Proverbs 9:7.

Chapter 4. You Can Turn Your "Sand Storms" into Pearls

1. Scott M. Peck, *The Road Less Traveled* (New York: Simon & Schuster, 1978), 15; *How to Stubbornly Refuse to Make Yourself Miserable about Anything—Yes, Anything!* (Secaucus, N.J.: Lyle Stuart, 1988).

2. LynNell Hancock et al., "Breaking Point," *Newsweek*, 6 March 1995, 59.

3. Geoffrey Cowley, "Dialing the Stress-Meter Down," *Newsweek*, 6 March 1995, 62.

4. For more information about Fresh Start, call 610-644-6464.

5. Charles Colson, "Simple Sand," in *A Dance with Deception* (Dallas: Word, 1993), 123.

6. See Andy Andrews, *Storms of Perfection*, vols. 1 and 2 (Charlotte, N.C.: Internet, 1992, 1994).

7. For more help with pearl-counting, see Gary Smalley, *Joy That Lasts* (Grand Rapids: Zondervan, 1986, 1988).

Chapter 5. How to Balance Expectations and Reality

1. I'm grateful to Dr. Dan Trathen of Denver for helping me work through the lessons in the following preventive plan.

2. Irene Goldenberg and Herbert Goldenberg, *Family Therapy: An Overview*, 152–59.

Chapter 6. Avoiding Hurt Is My Responsibility

1. Winston Churchill, as quoted in John Bartlett, *Familiar Quotations*, 15th ed. (Boston: Little, Brown, 1980), 743.
2. See Henry Cloud and John Townsend, *Boundaries* (Grand Rapids: Zondervan, 1992).
3. See Cloud and Townsend, *Boundaries*. For more direct help, I recommend your nearest Rapha Counseling Center or Minirth Meier New Life Clinic.
4. Matt. 19:19.

Chapter 7. Finding the Power to Keep Loving

1. Frederick Buechner, *Wishful Thinking* (San Francisco: Harper & Row, 1973), 40–41.
2. Howard Markman, Scott Stanley, and Susan Blumberg, *Fighting for Your Marriage*, 285.
3. Nick Stinnett and John DeFrain, *Secrets of Strong Families* (New York: Berkley, 1986).
4. Rom. 15:13.
5. See James 4:8.
6. See 1 John 2:9–10.
7. Smalley, *Joy That Lasts* (Grand Rapids: Zondervan, 1986, 1988).
8. See Deut. 6:5, Lev. 19:18, and Luke 10:27.
9. Phil. 4:19.
10. Matt. 6:21.
11. See Heb. 11:6.

Chapter 8. Five Vital Signs of a Healthy Marriage

1. Erich Fromm, *The Art of Loving*, quoted in *Visions of Faith* (Basingstoke, England: Marshall Pickering, 1986), 315.
2. Irene Goldenberg and Herbert Goldenberg, *Family Therapy: An Overview*, 28–54.
3. Ibid., 55–85.
4. Pam Smith, *The Food Trap* (Altamonte Springs, Fla.: Creation House, 1990), 23.
5. William F. Arndt and R. Wilbur Gingrich, eds., *A Greek-English Lexicon of the New Testament and Other Early Christian Literature* (Chicago: University of Chicago Press, 1957), 119–20.
6. See Matt. 6:21.
7. Markman, Stanley, and Blumberg, *Fighting for Your Marriage*.

Chapter 9. The Number One Request: Better Communication

1.   Paul Tournier, *The Meaning of Persons* (New York: Harper, 1957), 143.

2.   Based on a personal interview with Dr. Gary Oliver, Southwest Counseling Associates, Littleton, Colorado. See David Mace, *Love and Anger in Marriage* (Grand Rapids: Zondervan, 1982).

3.   Markman, Stanley, and Blumberg, *Fighting for Your Marriage*.

4.   For additional examples of what a family constitution might look like, see Gary Smalley and John Trent, *The Hidden Value of a Man* (Colorado Springs: Focus on the Family, 1992, 1994), 182–84.

5.   For the three-hundred word pictures, see Gary Smalley and John Trent, *The Language of Love* (Colorado Springs: Focus on the Family, 1988, 1991).

Chapter 10. Understanding Personality Types: A Key to Lovability

1.   See Tim LaHaye, *Understanding the Male Temperament* (Grand Rapids: Zondervan, 1970), and Florence Littauer, *Personality Plus, Updated and Expanded* (Grand Rapids: Fleming Revell, 1992).

2.   For more information about Dr. Trent's seminar, contact him at Encouraging Words, 12629 N. Tatum Blvd., Suite 208, Phoenix, AZ 85032, 602-953-7610.

Chapter 11. How to Bring Out the Best in Your Maddening Mate

1.   Deborah Tannen, *You Just Don't Understand* (New York: William Morrow, 1990), 294.

2.   John Gottman, *Why Marriages Succeed or Fail* (New York: Simon & Schuster, 1994), 29.

3.   Kevin Leman, *The Birth Order Book* (Grand Rapids: Fleming Revell, 1985).

4.   Tannen is the author of *You Just Don't Understand* (New York: William Morrow, 1990).

5.   Bernie Zilbergeld is the author of *The New Male Sexuality* (New York: Bantam, 1992).

6.   John Gray, *Men Are from Mars, Women Are from Venus* (New York: HarperCollins, 1992).

7.   Sharon Begley, "Gray Matters," *Newsweek*, 27 March 1995, 50.

8.   Tannen, *You Just Don't Understand*, 43.

9.   Zilbergeld, *The New Male Sexuality*.

10. Tannen, *You Just Don't Understand*, 43–47.

11. Ibid., 236–37.

12. Kevin Leman, *Sex Begins in the Kitchen: The Art of Staying in Love*. Video available from Dr. Kevin Leman, 4585 E. Speedway, Suite 110, Tucson, Arizona 85712.

13. Begley, "Gray Matters," 54.

Chapter 12. How to Read a Woman's Built-in Marriage Manual

1. Margaret Mead, *Blackberry Winter*, as quoted in John Bartlett, *Familiar Quotations*, 15th ed. (Boston: Little, Brown, 1980), 853.

2. Markman, Stanley, and Blumberg, *Fighting for Your Marriage*, 22.

3. For three hundred sample word pictures, see Gary Smalley and John Trent, *The Language of Love* (Colorado Springs: Focus on the Family, 1988, 1991).

4. Pierre Mornell, M.D., *Passive Men, Wild Women* (New York: Simon & Schuster, 1979).

5. Contact Today's Family at 1483 Lakeshore Dr., Branson, Missouri 65616; 800-84-TODAY.

6. See Markman, Stanley, and Blumberg, *Fighting for Your Marriage*; Henry Cloud and John Townsend, *Boundaries*; Gary Smalley and John Trent, *The Language of Love*; Gary Smalley, *If Only He Knew* (Grand Rapids: Zondervan, 1982); and Michele Weiner-Davis, *Fire Your Shrink* (New York: Simon & Schuster, 1995).

7. Judith Wallerstein and Sandra Blakeslee, *The Good Marriage* (Boston: Houghton Mifflin, 1995).

8. Markman, Stanley, and Blumberg, *Fighting for Your Marriage*, 38ff.

Chapter 13. Conflicts: The Doorway to Intimacy

1. John Gottman, *Why Marriages Succeed or Fail*, 173.

2. Markman, Stanley, and Blumberg, *Fighting for Your Marriage*, 38ff.

3. I have long wanted to write a book about the importance of staying together in marriage. I've never written it because other authors have already done it; among them are: Markman, Stanley, and Blumberg, *Fighting for Your Marriage*; Wallerstein and Blakeslee, *The Good Marriage*; Judith Wallerstein and Sandra Blakeslee, *Second Chances* (New York: Ticknor and Fields, 1990); Gottman, *Why Marriages Succeed or Fail*; Michele Weiner-Davis, *Divorce Busting* (New York: Summit, 1992); and Diane Medved, *The Case against Divorce* (New York: Donald Fine, 1989). If you want to be encouraged about your own marriage, let these authors open your eyes wider to the wonderful possibilities (even if you're in a second or third marriage).

4. See Carol Rubin and Jeffrey Rubin, *When Families Fight: How to Handle Conflict with Those You Love* (New York: Ballantine, 1989), 39–60.

5.   Stephen R. Covey, *The Seven Habits of Highly Effective People*, audio version (New York: Simon & Schuster Sound Ideas, 1989).

6.   Markman, Stanley, and Blumberg, *Fighting for Your Marriage*.

7.   David and Vera Mace, *How to Have a Happy Marriage* (Nashville: Abingdon, 1977), 112.

8.   Harriet G. Lerner, *The Dance of Anger*, 199–201.

9.   Eph. 4:26.

10.   Ps. 4:4.

11.   Sandra Felton, *When You Live with a Messie* (Grand Rapids: Fleming Revell, 1994).

12.   C. S. Lewis, *The Last Battle* (New York: Macmillan, Collier, 1956; 1970), 136.

13.   Ibid., 161.

Chapter 14. Was That as Good for You as It Was for Me?

1.   C. S. Lewis, *Mere Christianity* (New York: Macmillan Paperbacks, 1952), 96.

2.   Gen. 4:1.

3.   F. B. Dresslar, "The Psychology of Touch," *American Journal of Psychology* 6 (1984): 316.

4.   Helen Colton, *The Gift of Touch* (New York: Seaview/Putnam, 1983), 102.

5.   See Stinnett and DeFrain, *Secrets of Strong Families*.

6.   "Talking to God," *Newsweek*, 6 January 1992, 42.

7.   Eccles. 4:12.

8.   Carey Moore and Pamela Rosewell Moore, *If Two Shall Agree: Praying Together As a Couple* (Grand Rapids: Chosen Books, 1992), 200.

9.   Ibid., 201.

10.   See Ed and Gaye Wheat, *Intended for Pleasure* (New York: Bantam, 1992); Clifford and Joyce Penner, *Restoring the Pleasure* (Dallas: Word, 1993) and *The Gift of Sex* (Dallas: Word, 1981); and Bernie Zilbergeld, *The New Male Sexuality*.

Chapter 15. Divorce-Proofing Your Marriage

1.   Some of my favorite writers give a different perspective on this concept, including Willard F. Harley Jr., *His Needs, Her Needs* (Grand Rapids: Fleming Revell, 1986); as well as Covey, *Seven Habits of Highly Effective People*; Weiner-Davis, *Divorce Busting*; Peck, *The Road Less Traveled*; and Henry Cloud and John Townsend, *Boundaries*.

2.   I was checked at a sleep-disorder clinic in a hospital. It's been a miracle.

3.   Eccles. 11:1.

NOTES **279**

Chapter 16. A Love That Lasts Forever

1. Charlie and Lucy Wedemeyer, *Charlie's Victory* (Grand Rapids: Zondervan, 1993), 20.
2. Ibid., 60.
3. Personal interview.

Appendix: Three Character Qualities: Prerequisites to Dating for the Smalley Children

1. Eph. 4:17–20.
2. Phil. 2:3ff.

For information on Gary Smalley's speaking schedule,
a catalog of videotapes, books, and cassettes, or a free issue of
Gary's Homes of Honor magazine call **1-800-848-6329** or write:
Today's Family, 1482 Lakeshore Dr., Branson, Missouri 65616.

OTHER RESOURCES INCLUDE:

Books

Love Is a Decision

The Key to Your Child's Heart

The Blessing

Joy That Lasts

The Hidden Value of a Man

The Two Sides of Love

The Language of Love

The Hidden Keys of a Loving and Lasting Relationship

Video Series

Love Is a Decision

Hidden Keys to Loving Relationships

Homes of Honor Small Group Series

About the Author

Gary Smalley is an internationally recognized speaker on family relationships who has sold more than 12 million copies of his books and videos. Best-selling titles include *Love Is a Decision*, *The Blessing* (with John Trent), and *For Better or for Best*. Gary has been featured on hundreds of radio and television shows, including *The Oprah Winfrey Show*. He has presented "Love is a Decision" seminars to hundreds of thousands across the U.S. He is president of Today's Family based in Branson, Missouri, where he and his wife Norma live. Gary and Norma have three children: Kari, Greg, and Michael.

You've Read the Book . . .

Now Take the Next Step

With this outstanding new small-group series by Gary Smalley and LifeWay Press, you can strengthen marriage relationships in your church family and among your friends. Now, Smalley's insights can be experienced in an interactive study based on this book.
Resources include:

Making Love Last Forever Adult Workbook
Twelve-session interactive workbook leads married couples to understand how to develop the best kind of love and how to balance your happiness with that of your mate's.
7200-87 • $12.95

Making Love Last Forever Leader Guide
Offers administrative guidance, training aids, and learning activities for conducting small-group study with several couples.
7200-88 • $5.95

Making Love Last Forever Leader Kit
Contains one adult workbook, one leader guide, and a videotape featuring 12 vignettes — one for each study. Also includes promotional introductory segment.
7700-59 • $59.95

To order, contact Lifeway Press Customer Service Center, 127 Ninth Avenue, North; Nashville, TN 37234; **1-800-458-2772.** Fax: (615) 251-5933. You can also order by Compuserve. Our address is 70423,2526

★ Priority Code: MLLWT